Educational Policy
and Educational Inequality

Educational Policy and Educational Inequality

PAUL LODGE

TESSA BLACKSTONE

Martin Robertson . Oxford

First published in 1982 by
Martin Robertson & Company Ltd.,
108 Cowley Road, Oxford OX4 1JF.

British Library Cataloguing in Publication Data

Lodge, Paul
    Educational policy and educational inequality.
    1. Educational equalization — Great Britain
    I. Title II. Blackstone, Tessa
    370'.941   LC213.3.G7

ISBN 0-85520-192-4

Typeset in 10 on 12 pt Vladimir by
Pioneer Associates, East Sussex

Printed and bound in Great Britain
by Billing and Sons Limited
Guildford, London, Oxford, Worcester

To our parents

Contents

Introduction

There is one sense in which social democracy can be said to have failed us. It is this: it has not found ways of giving all children, all young people and all adults an equal education. There are some who spend many years being educated; many of them have much money, time and attention lavished upon them. There are others whose educational experience is limited to the years of compulsory schooling and on whom less than half the resources allocated to the most educationally privileged is spent. Over the last quarter of a century these facts have become known to a growing number of informed people. How they respond to them will depend above all on their ideological beliefs about the kind of society they believe is desirable and possible. Some will regard it as an inevitable (indeed, acceptable) outcome of differences in the distribution of intelligence, of talent, of drive. They will see no contradiction in the collective provision of education on a generous scale for those already privileged in material terms, while the poorer members of the community are provided for less generously. Others believe that this division of educational spoils is unjust. Some of them also believe that it is wasteful. We share these beliefs. Our starting-point is our belief in the need for a more equal society. Extremes of wealth and poverty within industrial societies degrade them and their members. Great differences in the amount and quality of education that individuals and groups receive are debasing too. Partly because of the existence of these differences, the distribution of power continues to be so unequal that many members of these societies have little or no control over their own destinies.

A second starting-point of this book is a belief that people have it within their capacity to bring about changes that will make society more equal. The inevitability of substantial inequality is not proven. Social engineering has become a pejorative term in certain circles. It should not be. Although much of this book comes to somewhat

gloomy conclusions about the limited success of the educational
policies which have been introduced with the aim of achieving
greater equality, these conclusions should not be interpreted to
mean that nothing can be done. The problem is that so far we have
not tried hard enough. We do not accept the views of those who
cynically dismiss the possibility of social change through social
reform.

Educational experiences outside the home are, and will continue
to be, of considerable importance in shaping people's lives. While
the great importance of family background in determining life
chances must be acknowledged, these chances can be altered by
educational experiences. Where these experiences are negative in
their impact on the individual, they are likely to have long-term
effects far more serious than their immediate impact. Children,
young people and some adults spend many hours of their lives in
educational institutions, even though they spend more outside them.
The length of time they spend inside them and what happens to
them while they are there are not unimportant influences whose
effects can be wiped out by luck and other chance factors.

There is a considerable literature on education and equality, most
of it written in the last two decades. Many contemporary social
scientists have been fascinated by this relationship. Sociologists in
particular have written extensively about it, often examining it as a
facet of the study of social stratification. However, relatively few
books on the subject have been directly concerned with the
examination of contemporary policies. This book tries to look
critically at some of those policies, whose perpetrators wished to
redistribute educational resources in the interests of greater equality.
In so doing, it attempts to document in some detail the processes of
educational policy formulation in contemporary Britain.

In order to do this it first describes the institutional framework in
which educational policy is made in Britain. It identifies the key
actors and describes the constraints under which they operate.
Thus chapter 2 describes the role of the Department of Education
and Science and the local education authorities and touches on their
relationship. Chapter 3 examines the work of teachers' organizations taking the National Union of Teachers and Campaign for the
Advancement of State Education as case studies.

Each of these chapters is written from the perspective of the
pursuit of educational equality. Thus as well as including some

discussion of the respective power and influence of each of these bodies, they describe the extent to which making education more equal has been pursued by the organization concerned.

The second part of the book consists of a number of case studies of selected national policies which have been pursued in the last twenty years. They have been chosen, as implied above, because in each case they were perceived as measures which would redistribute educational resources towards the less educationally privileged, either within or between age groups. In a number of cases they had other goals too, but what they had in common was a belief shared by those who introduced them that they would make the system more equal. The cases studies are the expansion of nursery education (chapter 4), the introduction of positive discrimination, mainly in primary schools (chapter 5), the abolition of selection at the age of 11 (chapter 6), the raising of the school-leaving age (chapter 7) and policies with respect to post-school education (chapter 8).

The book begins by attempting to provide a historical background to the development of educational policy during this century and the values that have guided it. It tries to sketch, as briefly as possible, some of the conflicts between the goal of educational equality and certain other goals which have shaped the development of the educational system in contemporary Britain. Clearly, policy relates to what obtains, and what obtains is in large measure an historical legacy, the roots of which lie in the nineteenth century. Two themes central to the development of state education are touched on: namely, education as social control, and education as a means of securing national efficiency. Chapter 1 tries to convey a sense of the dominant values that, historically, have influenced educational development, and which, arguably, still comprise a substantial part of the value mix in education, including the value of equality of opportunity.

The evidence regarding inequality in education has grown each year since the 1944 Education Act, which established the principle of secondary education for all children. In the early 1950s the work on social mobility of Glass and others at LSE[1] provided well documented evidence of the strong relationships between social-class background and participation in different kinds of education. Soon after this the Early Leaving Report came out, providing empirical evidence of the high level of drop-out at the top end of secondary schools among able pupils from working-class homes.

Further confirmation of this finding was provided by the Crowther

Report (1959). At about the same time educational sociologists were beginning to demonstrate that selection for grammar schools was based not purely on academic attainment but also on social factors. This led eventually to proposals for comprehensive secondary education (see chapter 6). Further Government inquiries in the 1960s (Robbins, Newsom and Plowden) all provided more documentation of serious inequalities in the output of the educational system. Plowden, the last of these reports, suggested that the inputs, in the form of teachers buildings and other resources, should be varied to take this fact into account. This proposal and the way it was implemented is discussed at some length in chapter 5. The Plowden Report also argued, as had Margaret McMillan in the years before the First World War, that nursery education in particular should be expanded in order to extend the opportunities of young children from disadvantaged backgrounds. The chequered history of pre-school education in Britain is described in chapter 4. The response to the major differences in the proportion of young people from different social classes staying in full-time education beyond the school-leaving age was the advocacy of the extension of compulsory schooling by raising the school-leaving age. The strengths and weaknesses of this response are described in detail in chapter 7. Unfortunately, the measure was not accompanied by any coherent attempt to expand part-time education at the post-school stage. Instead, successive Governments expanded higher education for the elite, as Robbins had recommended and as we document in chapter 8.

This book is not a work of sociology, though it draws extensively on sociological studies of aspects of the educational system. It is not, for the most part, based on original research presenting new findings. Instead it is a critique of a number of recent educational policies and the way in which they have been implemented. This critique is informed by an ideological commitment to egalitarianism. It relies heavily on official sources. However, we have tried to stand back from the values and assumptions implicit in much of this material. We also refer to relevant research findings of those working outside central and local government. Hence this book is designed not as an academic study accessible only to a small minority but as a work of reference for a wider audience of laymen interested in education, as well as for students who have recently started the study of social and educational policy and administration.

The study was jointly conceived and jointly undertaken. However, some two-thirds of the book were drafted initially by Paul Lodge and one-third by Tessa Blackstone. Paul Lodge was responsible for drafting chapters 1, 2, 5, 6, 7, 8 and 9 and Tessa Blackstone for chapters 3 and 4 and the Introduction. We are grateful to the following friends and colleagues for comments on various draft chapters: Paul Wilding, John Lambert, Gregory Lodge, Alan Crispin, John Welton, Kate Jenkins, Joan Sallis and Alan Evans. We are also grateful to various past and present members of the executive of the Campaign for the Advancement of State Education and the librarians at the National Union of Teachers for help with chapter 3. Last, we should like to thank Caroline Bridges, Phyllis Thomas and Cynthia Carrel for their patience and tolerance in typing what was in parts an almost illegible manuscript, which called for cryptographic as well as secretarial skills.

We end with the words of R. H. Tawney, which are as relevant today, in a context in which public expenditure on education is being cut, as they were when he first wrote them in 1931:

As a society sows, so in the long run it reaps. If its schools are sordid, will its life be generous? Will it later unite by an appeal to economic interests those whom in nurture and education it has taken pains to put assunder? If it sacrifices its children to its social conventions and its economic convenience, is it probable that, when men, they will regard it with affection? Apart from such considerations, the mere economic loss involved in withholding from four-fifths of British children the educational opportunities required to develop their powers is extremely serious. The nation has not such a plethora of ability at its command that it can afford to leave uncultivated, or under-cultivated, the larger proportion of that which it possesses. The principle to be followed is, after all, simple. What a wise parent would desire for his own children, that a nation, in so far as it is wise, must desire for all children. Educational equality consists in securing it for them.[2]

1

The Historical Background

This chapter establishes the long-standing nature of educational inequality and conveys some sense of how inequality has persisted through time, despite the undeniable advances in state education that have brought many, if not disproportionate, benefits to working-class children. For the most part we concentrate on the social terms of major educational legislation of this century, especially the discussion leading up to the 1944 Education Act. Despite all that has transpired since the passage of that Act, it is still both the central legislative pillar of contemporary education and (supposedly) the major expression of modern, formal commitment to social justice in education. As such, it is the essential touchstone for our subsequent analysis of post-war policies. Obviously, there are serious limitations to approaching the development of education from the standpoint of legislative peaks, not the least of which is that legislation is at several removes from actual provision. But legislation is a kind of social stocktaking and formalization of goals. Precepts, assumptions, prejudices often figure in the parliamentary and extra-parliamentary preamble to legislation in a way that, in short, is tantamount to a society (or key societal figures) talking to itself (themselves) about education. By attending to the terms of that discourse, we can better understand both the continuities and the discontinuities of educational provision.

At the outset of the nineteenth century education for the working-class was regarded by some as a positive threat to the stability of the social order, by others as at best wasteful and unnecessary. By the close of the century few questioned the need for state elementary education. Yet this commitment to working-class education was bound by a rigid, narrow vision of education appropriate for an inferior social class. Elementary education was segregated from the essentially middle-class grammar and public schools as well as from the universities. Further, elementary education was cast in the

1

severely minimalist terms of general Victorian parsimony towards
welfare expenditure. For example, Forster, in moving the 1870 Act,
laid stress on 'the least possible expenditure of public money'[1] and
the need not to undermine voluntary effort and parental contributions. At this time only two-fifths of working-class children between
the ages of 6 and 10 were at government schools, and only a third
between the ages of 10 and 12. Given this, it might have been
expected that the Government would have shown a greater
commitment to funding education. In fact, Forster, on noting that
education in the New England States in the USA was free at all
levels, commented that the prospect of this provision's obtaining in
England would alarm the Chancellor of the Exchequer.[2] Not only
that: he also presented[3] elementary education in terms that invited a
sense of the compatibility of the social vision that underlay the class
legislation of the Poor Law and educational reform. This was not
simply parliamentary artifice; it marked a real affinity.

Even minimal education was not so much an act of benevolence
towards the working-class but more a means of serving the interests
of the dominant groups in society. Although the development of
state education *was* attended upon by those with humanitarian and
progressive attitudes towards working-class education — no tragedy
is complete without a chorus — this embellishment does not conceal
the fact that middle-class advocacy of reform was rooted more in
self-interest and instrumentality than in benevolence. Elements of
the urban working class were perceived as a threat to the social
apparatus of the capitalist system. Education was part of a design
to contain this threat. Kay-Shuttleworth, one of the most prominent
Victorian educational reformers, argued that by education 'can the
workman be induced to leave undisturbed the control of commercial
enterprises in the hands of capitalists'.[4] In his view the 'great
object' of working-class education was that as well as affording
security to property and social order, it should inculcate in the
children of the labouring classes the view that they were 'destined to
earn their livelihood by the sweat of their brows'.[5] The manipulative
sentiments behind such observations are obvious, even allowing for
the need for interpretative caution, given the tendency of Victorian
reformers to pander to the fears, interests and prejudices of their
largely middle-class audience.

Not only was education designed to fit the working-class child for
his pre-ordained place in the industrial order, but it was also

intended to accompany and neutralize working-class acquisition of a measure of political participation. Since it would have been undesirable to deny such participation, Victorian reformers hoped that education would secure a 'responsible' (that is, acquiescent) exercise of enfranchisement. The Benthamite radicals were among the first to advocate education as a means of ensuring that democracy was manipulated so as to achieve the incorporation of the working-class in a social order over which the middle-class held sway.[6] Lowe's view that 'it will be absolutely necessary to compel our future masters to learn their letters'[7] is unwittingly revealing. Compulsion entails subordination. This belies 'masters'. Forster presented the political desirability of education in terms of 'the good, the safe working of our constitutional system'. He continued: 'we have given them political power; we must not wait any longer to give them education.'[8] Again, this gift relationship betokens hierarchy and subordination.

But it was not simply a case of providing elementary education to keep the working-class in their industrial and political place. There were compelling economic reasons (or, rather, beliefs) for expanding working-class education. As Forster argued:

> upon the speedy provision of elementary education depends our industrial prosperity. . . . uneducated labourers are, for the most part, unskilled labourers, and if we leave our work-folk any longer unskilled . . . they will become over-matched in the competition of the world.[9]

This expansionist theme was not necessarily in fundamental conflict with the principle of social control through education. Working-class education was such that it was likely neither to engender a radical consciousness nor to obstruct the elevation of some unskilled labourers to the rank of industrial mechanics. Furthermore, such elevation would confirm the hierarchical nature of society and would deplete working-class leadership. Forster's advocacy was to echo for more than a century as often, in the name of economic growth, the state was to guide educational expansion.

Of course, reforming impulses emanated from other than middle-class sources. Increasingly, the labour movement brought forward ideas about educational reform. And some developments within the education system brought distinct benefits to working-class pupils. But such forces were both generally contained within a balance of social power unfavourable to working-class aspirations and subject, in some instances, to positive counter-policy that sought to arrest developments that threatened to blur the fundamental divide between working-class and middle-class education. The 1902 Education Act is a case in point, since ultimately it had the result of curtailing the growth of higher-grade elementary schools which, as we shall show, afforded an important opportunity to working-class pupils.

It would be a misrepresentation of the 1902 Act to suggest that its social origin was nothing more than a wish to curtail working-class educational opportunity. The Act had a breadth and complexity that belie such mono-causal explanation. As Maclure argues, 'the need for unified control of primary and secondary had become manifest, and the Counties and the County Boroughs were the obvious authorities for the job.'[10] What the Act did was to make County and County Borough Councils into Local Education Authorities (LEAs); although Borough Councils with populations of 10,000 and urban districts with populations of 20,000 became authorities for elementary education and not secondary education. Thus the Act brought to an end the locally elected School Boards that, since 1870, had developed elementary education in areas that were insufficiently served by the voluntary schools. By 1902 School Boards were responsible for a major proportion of provision, educating 2,600,000 pupils in 5700 schools, compared with voluntary provision for 3,000,000 pupils in 14,000 schools. Balfour, introducing the Act to the House of Commons, argued that the School Boards had competed with the voluntary schools in an unintended and undesirable way; that the Boards had prompted unexpected expenditure that had strained local finances; and that they had exaggerated their capacity to provide secondary education.[11] It is this last aspect of the School Boards that we wish to highlight in order to illustrate the way in which the 1902 Act was a constraining force on educational development. We do not, however, discuss the social significance of either School Boards or the 1902 Act as a whole.

In the years following the 1870 Act some School Boards developed higher-grade elementary schools which, as their title suggests, provided an advanced-level curriculum that was held by some to compete with that of the grammar schools. Indeed, a Royal Commission of 1895 expressed the view that the strength of competition from the higher-grade schools was such that the grammar schools were in danger of being swept away. This view was shared by others, not least the representatives of the grammar schools. While it would be an error to depict the higher-grade schools as a form of exclusive working-class secondary education, the fact remains that the social-class composition in these schools was markedly different from that in the grammar schools. Banks cites figures to show that in 1897 91.2 per cent of the pupils in higher-grade schools, compared with 48.9 per cent in grammar schools, had formerly attended elementary schools. In addition, 34.1 per cent of the pupils in higher-grade schools had parents who were skilled or unskilled manual workers, compared with 6.8 per cent in the grammar schools.[12] Also, the curriculum was of a less academic kind, more in keeping with working-class interests and aspirations. There is ample evidence to show that secondary education was regarded by powerful educational interests as essentially middle-class education. In Banks's view, the defence of higher-grade schools by primary school teachers was a direct challenge to the concept of education stratified on class lines.[13]

This defence proved unsuccessful. The higher-grade schools were adversely affected by the 1902 Act. There is dispute as to whether or not the object of the conservative offensive was the higher-grade schools or the School Boards. Banks claims that the conventional view of the 1901 Cockerton Judgement 'killing off' higher-grade schools, so that grammar schools dominated the field when the 1902 Act empowered LEAs to provide secondary schools, is mistaken. Cockerton was 'conceived and executed primarily as an attack on the School Boards who administered the higher-grade schools, rather than on the schools themselves'.[14] Nevertheless, Banks concedes that after 1902 most higher-grade schools became secondary schools — though she rightly stresses that pressures to approximate them to grammar schools came from parents, teachers and so on, not from the Cockerton Judgement — and that the higher-grade school tradition, though not destroyed, was subordinated to the grammar school tradition. Morant, a civil servant, was the main architect of the 1902 Act. It is difficult to speak with certainty about Morant's motivations in acting in the way that he did. To suggest that his calculated intention was to oppose working-class educational interests would be to reach far beyond the available evidence. Yet Morant's contempt for ordinary people has been attested.[15] And the indisputable outcome of the 1902 Act (whether or not the immediate object of action was the School Boards or the higher-grade schools) was to curb the development of a form of education that had been of particular value to working-class pupils, as well as to reassert the clarity of the distinction between secondary education (which was essentially middle-class) and elementary education (which was essentially working-class). This is a reasonable claim, despite the fact that Morant's concern for the survival of the traditional arts-based secondary curriculum was shared by others, alarmed as they were by the rapid growth of grant-aided science subjects. The survival of the former was ensured by the 1904 Regulations for Secondary Schools, attributed to Morant and based

> on the style and curriculum of the public schools. . . . the organization
> of secondary education was largely divisive, and its heavy emphasis
> on academic work at the expense of technical or practical activities
> influenced education throughout the century.[16]

In marked contrast to the Secondary Regulations, the Elementary Code of 1904 defined what was obviously an inferior kind of education for working-class children with limited occupational futures. There was a strong emphasis on moral training and the fostering of attitudes conducive to working-class acceptance of an inferior place in an immutable social order. For example, the Code argued that schools should 'implant in children habits of industry, self-control and courageous perseverance in the face of difficulties'.[17] These themes were strongly echoed in a Board of Education report (1906): 'Great stress was placed on "character" and "subservience".'[18] Elementary education for children between the ages of 12 and 15 was to be 'a kind of education that is likely to make them efficient members of the class to which they belong'.[19] The report supported the demand of employers that education should foster 'habits of discipline, ready obedience, self-help and pride in good work for its own sake whatever it may be'.[20] Evidence of this kind can give a revealing, if partial, view of central dimensions of the educational system, though we would stress that it would be imbalanced to portray education as an instrument by which a monolithically suppressive dominant class manipulated a uniformly suppressed working-class. There has never been unity of interest and action among those who dominate education or unity of posture among those dominated within education. For example, the working class was not regarded in an undifferentiated way. It was economically (and politically) prudent to provide a superior education for some working-class pupils. As the 1904 Elementary Code argued: 'it will be an important though subsidiary object of the school to discover individual children of exceptional capacity and to develop their special gifts . . . so they may be qualified to pass at the proper age into Secondary Schools.'[21] To this end a rigidly class-dichotomized education system was bridged by the provision of scholarships for a sponsored elite. For the vast majority of working-class children elementary education was to be of a general character-training kind that sought to ensure passive adaptability to employers' demands. Witness the 1906 report quoting with approval the view that 'a boy's career is not fixed by choice but by the accident of employment that offers itself.'[22] Thus most products of the elementary schools were without self-determination, so much factory fodder subject to the 'accidents' of the job market. This being so, technical education was undesirable, and general education was preferred: skill bases mattered less than moral training. The reality of working-class education was largely a derivative of the character of industrial labour and recruitment.

Yet the perceptions of this character were changing. As we have noted, the 1870 Act marked a shift in emphasis, in that working-class education was valued as a means of economic advance. By the turn of the century this theme is presented in strident terms by such people as the Webbs, in their advocacy of national efficiency. Writing in 1904, Sidney Webb expressed the view that

leaders of all the political parties unconsciously absorbed the idea that national efficiency depended on our making the most of the capacities of the whole population which forms, after all, as much part of the national resources as our iron and coal. . . . Public education has come to be regarded not as a matter of philanthropy undertaken for the sake of the individual children benefited but a matter of national concern undertaken in the interest of the community as a whole. It is this notion which has been embodied in the Education Acts 1902-3.[23]

But the notion of national efficiency was both elitist and

authoritarian. Webb placed stress on the need 'to carry on, by a capacity-catching scholarship system, all whose brains make it profitable for the community to equip them with advanced instruction'.[24] This, in effect, was to reject common secondary schooling and to support the idea of grammar schooling for middle-class and very able working-class pupils. National efficiency legitimated not the pursuit of social justice between social classes but the sponsorship of an elite within the context of a fundamentally class-divided education system. Both Morant and Balfour could support an elitist doctrine of this kind, since, in the ideas of the former, they regarded education as a means by which 'the impulses of the many ignorant' could be placed under 'the guidance and control of the few wise'.[25]

Some would argue that the First World War inspired a democratic impulse that compelled an advance in working-class education as a just reward for the poor, who had tolerated prescription, poured out their blood and been mulcted by inflation.[26] Fisher, in presenting the 1918 Education Bill, argued that it would lead to 'enlarged and enriched opportunities of education to the children of the poor'.[27] As a right of social citizenship, industrial workers were entitled to any form of education from which they were capable of profiting. It was taken as given that 'the principles upon which the well-to-do parents proceed in the education of their families are valid; also *mutatis mutandis* for the families of the poor.'[28] Yet this commitment to advancing working-class education by the principles of middle-class education was bounded by the curious vision that Fisher had of education for the working class.

> They do not want education only in order that they may become better technical workmen and earn higher wages. They do not want it that they may rise out of their own class, always a vulgar ambition, they want it because they know that in the treasures of the mind they can find an aid to good citizenship, a source of pure enjoyment and a refuge from the *necessary* hardships of a life spent in the midst of clanging machinery.[29]

The first thing to note about this view is that education is not seen as a means by which the working class competes for better employment. Their measure of 'profit', their rights of newly-won citizenship stop short at social class divides. Instead, industrial workers are seen as contemplative aesthetes, set bookishly amid the noise of industry, unsullied by 'vulgar ambitions' of an easier life above their station. In essence, Fisher, like many of his contemporaries, saw education as a means to 'good citizenship' — a central feature of which was putting up with the necessary hardships of industrial life. True, these hardships were subject to minor correction. In keeping with the Victorian reformist tradition of child rescue, Fisher sought to reduce the demands that industry made on the young. During the war the number of children withdrawn from school to work in industry had risen to 600,000. The 1918 Act made 14 the obligatory rather than the optional age of school leaving, thus ending part-time education.[30]

A number of motives for educational reform, other than an irresolute intention to advance working-class opportunities, can be gleaned from the 1918 Act. Fisher, mindful of industrialists' concern with the high level of strikes that preceded the war, argued that reform would 'give the industrial character of our people just that additional measure of stability that it so prominently lacks'.[31] In Fisher's view, 'a factory is like a ship, one bad hand rots the company.'[32] Clearly, parliamentary statements of this kind play to the gallery — in this instance the industrial gallery. But this is indicative of the real vested interests that educational reform must take on board, and not just in terms of parliamentary rhetoric. It might be argued that Wedgewood's contribution to the parliamentary debate of the 1918 Bill is poor evidence of the character of opposition to that measure. He argued that it was understandable that employers would favour an education scheme that turned out adjuncts to machines rather than one that turned out people with the capacity to think and act for themselves. As he put it, 'if you make the cattle think, they will become dangerous.'[33] Such anti-working-class views, while not wholly typical of the reform debate, were more stridently and effectively put than were egalitarian views. Fisher was forced to make a fundamental concession to the industrial lobby, by which continuation schools for 16- to 18-year-olds would not be introduced for seven years. In Fisher's view, had this concession not been made, the Bill would have fallen. Since Fisher described the proposal as the most novel feature of the Act,[34] it is illustrative of negative pressure exerted to impede proposed educational developments, if not a sufficient explanation of why this particular proposal failed.

The Act did not seek to bring about a fundamental change in the education system in the pursuit of social justice. Instead, in the terms of the metaphor favoured by Fisher, the Act, while not radically altering the machinery of education, sought to make it more efficient. Inefficiency was the failure to secure an optimum return on social investment by tolerating a lack of physical well-being among working-class children, who were thus unable to derive full benefit from their education. Inefficiency was the lack of 'scientific correlation between different parts of our educational machinery [in that an] important and populous centre [is] without a secondary school in any shape or form. . . . less important centre[s] have four secondary schools.'[35] This was managerial concern over what was to be known later as 'roofs over heads', over an imbalance between the supply of, and demand for, education. Maldistribution between expanding and contracting areas takes precedence over the need for redistribution between social classes. The real impulse for reform was social inefficiency, inspired by the model and rivalry of Germany (Fisher went so far as to anticipate such post-war rivalry that made educational reform imperative).[36] Of course, 'managerial' problems matter. But the point to note is that they occupy the social space of reform, while social justice is virtually excluded. It was not until 1944 that equality between social classes came to the fore in governmental legislative deliberations.

In December 1940 a letter to *The Times,* signed by the country's leading churchmen, adumbrated the primary principles on which a post-war society should be built. These included equality of educational opportunity. Indeed, in the preceding months, following the evacuation of Dunkirk, the Board of Education had been subjected to criticism in the educational press and elsewhere, which was to be expected, given the sustained retrenchment of the inter-war period. This resulted in the creation of the Committee of Senior Officials on Post-War Educational Reconstruction in November 1940. One motive for the creation of this Committee was fear on the part of senior Board of Education officials that pressure for educational reform would be such as to take control of events from their hands.[37] To counter this prospect, the Board was forced to change its stance from the inter-war one of negative containment and retrenchment in the pursuit of Treasury orthodoxy to that of leading, and controlling, a positive commitment to reform. Arguably, the Board sought to manage the terms of debate about reform, thus keeping proposals for change within the limits of the 'internal' view of desirable educational development. The senior civil servants in the Board produced, and discussed, position papers which subsequently appeared as the Green Book. The importance of the Green Book cannot be reasonably disputed. As Gosden claims, it 'charted the main features of the policy that the Ministry of Education was to follow during the twenty years following the Education Act of 1944'.[38] The official status of the Green Book was that of a discussion document. Neither the Minister nor outside parties were directly involved until the document had been compiled. However, the Minister was shown a final draft and asked to check if there were any major policy suggestions with which he disagreed. There was none.[39] The document was then to be circulated in strict confidence, and its circulation was confined largely to LEAs, teachers' unions and the voluntary sector. Members of Parliament were formally not supposed to see the document. *The Times Educational Supplement* was moved to argue: 'this country does not even favour reform by cabal in camera.'[40]

It is important to consider the extent to which the Green Book displays a concern with educational inequality. The opening paragraph states a general concern with the issue of social justice in education. The Prime Minister is quoted as having appealed for the establishment of 'a state of society where advantage and privileges, which hitherto have been enjoyed only by the few, shall be far more widely shared by the men and youth of the nation as a whole'.[41] It is then claimed that the Green Book has been informed by this ideal. The proposals have been framed so that

> the better system of education which they envisage would be equally available to all, irrespective of means. . . . the nation will expect the planning of education for the post-war world to be conceived on bold and generous lines, and will look not simply *for developments within the existing framework* of the educational system but such reconstruction of the framework itself as may be essential to progress.[42]

This is in recognition of the fact that the existing framework is a barrier to progress towards the goal of education's being 'equally available to all'. But it is far from clear what the Green Book envisages as the practical embodiment of these ringing phrases.

The Green Book goes further than the Prime Minister, who merely spoke of making advantages and privileges more widely available, an ambition which accepts the continuation of inequality. Yet there is an essential vacuity about the notion of 'availability' as a yardstick of equality. Both the inputs and outputs of the education system could remain unchanged, but it would still be possible to say that education was 'more widely available' — especially since availability is linked to the question of means. The abolition of fees in secondary education could be said to make secondary education 'more available' to children of poor parents, but it does not necessarily follow from this that the social-class differentials in access to desirable secondary education would be abolished or even significantly eroded.

At one point the Green Book seeks to define what is meant by 'equality of opportunity' in secondary education. It does not mean that all children should receive the same form of education. There should be a variety of provision to cater for 'varying requirements and capacities of the children'.[43] The provision of the same type of secondary education for all children would be the reverse of equality of opportunity, since it would not mean that all children would develop their capacities to their best advantage as individuals. 'Equality of opportunity means, therefore, acceptance of the principle that the accidents of parental circumstances or place of residence shall not preclude any child from receiving the education from which he is best capable of profiting.'[44] This definition has significance for the phrase 'secondary education for all', which is held to mean not that the same type of secondary education should be provided for all, 'but that all types of full-time education at this stage should be regarded as on a parity and should receive *equal treatment* in such matters as accommodation, staffing, size of classes etc.'[45]

This definition of equality seems to invite ready acceptance of the idea that different types of education should be provided in different types of school. Yet why this should be so is not argued. Variety in educational form could be offered within common schools, which would make it easier to attain equality of treatment as defined by the Green Book. Clearly, since it is not possible to provide schools geared to *individual* capacities, this ideal must be abandoned in favour of schools for *types* of pupils. Indeed, the Green Book's acceptance of different types of secondary schooling squares ill with the conviction that 'at the primary stage education should be the same for all',[46] and that in order to facilitate interchange at 13 (between different types of secondary schools), the content of education for 11- to 13-year-olds 'though differentiated in detail, should in general be the same in all types of Secondary School'.[47] Thus common schooling is to some extent accepted for eight out of the ten years of obligatory schooling. However, in order to provide that marginal element of two years' specialized, differentiated schooling between 13 and 15 that could not (implausibly?) be provided within common schools, a tripartite system is justified, with all the consequences that would be entailed for equality in secondary education, not the least of which is the hopeless expectation of parity of esteem for different types of schools, even given equality of treatment of the kind advocated by the Green Book. 'Different but equal' is a contradiction in terms. It is scarcely credible that the proponents of this view could have argued for it with inner conviction. If they did, they were astonishingly ignorant of the education system. In addition, 'capacity to profit' from education is determined by a pupil's experience of primary schooling and other environmental factors, which makes for an unsatisfactory basis in the allocation of secondary places. Judgements about 'capacity to benefit' are predictive, speculative and prone to self-validation, and they confirm preceding inequalities.

As we have noted, the Green Book was a document of major importance. Given this, and the argument that we advance in chapter 2 about the predominant influence of civil servants on policy-making, it should be noted that the Green Book was very much a civil servant's document. In character it scarcely passed its own test of the need to be bold and generous, going beyond mere developments within the existing system. Raising the school-leaving age to 15, continuation schools and the disappearance of the elementary schools had all been established aims well before the Second World War. True, the *sense* of priority accorded to these policies by the Green Book was novel and commendable, in that they might have secured disproportionate gains for the working class; so too was the advocacy of equal treatment in terms of accommodation, staffing and class sizes. Unfortunately, the Green Book gave virtually no indication of how this was to be secured. It amounted to exhortation rather than policy. Indeed, the Green Book marks the high point of rhetorical commitment to education reform during the war. As in other areas of social policy, with the approach of victory over Germany commitment to reform was diluted.

The 1943 White Paper *Educational Reconstruction* echoes the Green Book's concern with the poor quality of some educational provision. The document conceded that junior schools for children between 7 and 11 had tended to be the Cinderellas of education and that little new accommodation had been provided in the years preceding the war. Classes were in many cases too large, sometimes containing as many as 50 pupils: 'this is not education but mass production.'[48] As to post-11 schooling, 'there is nothing to be said in favour of a system which subjects children at the age of 11 to the strain of competitive examination on which not only their future schooling, but their future careers may depend.'[49] Hadow reorganization had proceeded slowly, so that at the outbreak of war less than 50 per cent of 11-year-olds and over were in senior schools or departments organized for children of that age. The White Paper was critical of the payment of fees in secondary schools, since parents, by paying one-third of the cost of a secondary place, could secure a place for their children to the exclusion of more able children of impecunious parents. This offended against 'the canon that the nature of a child's education should be determined by his capacity and promise and not the financial circumstances of his parents.'[50] The advance of senior (secondary modern) schools depended upon 'better buildings and amenities, and a more generous scale of staff'.[51] The White Paper argued that 'it is in the poorer parts of the large cities that nursery schools are especially necessary.'[52]

Much of the above was incontrovertible fact. Such a presentation, as a major government statement, was highly commendable. Indeed, a special feature of war might well be a greater willingness on the part of public agencies to reveal and consider inadequacies in public services.[53] Action is another matter. It is by no means clear how the Government intended to remedy educational deficiencies. Certainly, there was no obvious commitment to egalitarian or redistributive policies, despite some recognition of special working-class needs. The opening paragraph of the document notes that 'it is just as important to achieve diversity as it is to ensure equality of educational opportunity.'[54] Arguably, there may be a fundamental tension between 'diversity' and 'equality', as the White Paper recognized in a further observation that diversity must not impair social unity. 'Diversity' became a euphemism for separate development. Competitive selection, with which the White Paper was so concerned, was to give way to the classification of children at the age of 11 on the basis of school records, supplemented, if necessary, by intelligence tests, due regard being had to their parents' wishes and the careers they had in mind.[55] Even with the abolition of fees, this was a prescription for social selection.

The aspirations of the White Paper were to be advanced by the submission of LEA development plans. The Board, in approving a development plan,

> will make an education order for the area which will specify the steps which the Authority are *required* to take by way, amongst other things, of maintaining existing schools, improving existing schools and providing new schools, and will contain a timetable to which the Authority will be *required* to conform in taking these steps.[56]

This cannot be taken as a first statement of a national policy to counter educational inequality. There is no reference to the redistribution of resources or the priority to be given to working-class education. Resources are considered as part of a general policy of educational expansion, from which it might be argued that disadvantaged pupils would benefit to some extent. For example, more than half of the projected additional expenditure in the first seven post-war years was to be for 're-casting full-time education'.[57] This would include raising the school-leaving age to 15 and the completion of Hadow reorganization. Arguably, projected figures of this kind were part of the window-dressing of social reconstruction. Most certainly, they did not amount to a seriously costed programme to secure greater equality. The figures relating to young people's colleges and nursery schools have meaning only in terms of the arithmetic of unfulfilled promises.

The culmination of the debate on educational reform was the 1944 Education Act. In essence, this measure confirmed the social-class divisions in education and was rooted in a substantial degree of political expediency. Churchill had placed the Coalition under stress through the offence that he had given to his Labour partners in his cool response to the Beveridge Report. Some measure of social reform was deemed politically desirable to repair the breach with Labour and to restore the Conservatives' standing with the electorate. At the end of 1943 the Conservatives were 13 per cent behind Labour in the opinion polls. A major education measure was attractive for a number of reasons. As Butler argued, education was favoured because no other Minister had been able to bring plans to fruition, 'due to the fact that most [other] issues of post-war reconstruction impinged directly and immediately on the pocket . . . to touch the sensitive political area of economic planning and control'.[58] Butler was able to assure the Treasury that the full implementation of the Act would take a generation. Also, given the Act's hierarchical nature, it was ideologically more attractive to the Conservatives than the only other major statement of reform then under review, the Beveridge Report. The Chancellor of the Exchequer told Butler that 'he would rather give money for Education than throw it down the sink with Sir William Beveridge.'[59] The Education Bill found favour with the Government Whips, for whom, as Butler noted, 'the beauty of the Bill was that it would keep the parliamentary troops thoroughly occupied; providing endless opportunity for debate, without any fear of breaking up the government.'[60]

While it is conventionally argued that the Second World War created egalitarian forces, there is scant evidence that this was translated into educational reform in terms of marked advances in working-class education. Nor was there any action against educational privilege. Reform of the public schools is a key test of a Government's commitment to equality. As Butler noted, the Fleming inquiry into the public schools had little influence, though it had 'temporarily removed the fuse . . . Or, in a railway metaphor, the first-class carriage had been shunted on to an immense siding.'[61] The origins, as well as the outcome, of the public school issue are noteworthy. The schools themselves, rather than egalitarian reformers, pressed the suit of their ailing finances on the pre-war Government. The permanent secretary of the Board was spending the weekend with the headmaster of Winchester, who explained the plight of the schools and their need to tout for pupils. Later the permanent secretary advised on the best tactics for advancing the cause of the public schools, a service that was continued through 'planted' letters in *The Times*,[62] all of which is a piquant comment on the inner workings on the elite system and the privileged contact that representatives of the educationally advantaged have with the policy-making process. Then headmasters of 'Newsom' secondary schools had no access to the private 'weekend ear' or public '*Times* ear' of the educational establishment, nor have they since.

Perhaps the last judgement on the extent to which equality of opportunity was achieved by the 1944 Education Act ought to be left, by implication, to the political author of the Act. Butler was of the opinion that

> equality of opportunity would remain something of an empty phrase if children entered the period of compulsory schooling from conditions of family deprivation, or left it to pursue what Churchill called blind-alley occupations. Accordingly, the Act made provision, on the one hand, for a major expansion of maintained and grant-aided nursery schools and, on the other hand, for compulsory part-time education up to the age of 18.[63]

Neither transpired. Just how empty the phrase 'equality of opportunity' was became all too clear from the work of educational sociologists in later years.[64]

2

The Making of Educational Policy and Inequality

In this chapter we do not seek to give a detailed exposition of the system of educational policy-making at central and local government level or of the relationship between these two levels of policy-making. This ground has been covered in a number of texts.[1] Instead we pose this question: given that aspects of educational policy have addressed educational inequality with little apparent success, how far can this failure be located within the very nature of the policy-making process? It is clearly central to the predominant theme of this book to consider whether the policy-making process is likely to promote or to inhibit action against educational inequality. Thus we seek to establish two things: first, that officials of the Department of Education and Science (DES) are a vitally important source of influence on policy-making — indeed, in some instances the single most important source of influence; second, whether this influence is likely to inhibit action against educational inequality. It is no part of our case that the DES occupies a monolithic position in determining policy. It does not. There are many constraints and countervailing pressures that circumscribe DES action, as we shall indicate later. Also in concluding that official reactions *have* served to inhibit action against inequality, we are certainly not arguing that the DES is implacably opposed to change, especially egalitarian change. It would be an absurd caricature to portray DES officials' Canute-like, setting out to thwart the radical intentions of Labour Ministers and others. None but the intemperate would seek to blame DES officials in some fundamental sense for the persistence of educational inequality. Nevertheless, there is sufficient evidence to prompt, at the very least, a *conjectural* case that they have not done as much as they might to advance the cause of reform. The sources available are, perforce, limited. Thus conjecture is the only alternative to silence in the face of largely secret government.

The conventional view is that Ministers determine policy. Sir William Pile, then permanent secretary of the DES, in evidence to the Expenditure Committee that examined policy-making in his Department, claimed that 'objectives, priorities and decisions are settled by Ministers and not civil servants . . . Ministers expect civil servants to concentrate on means where ends have already been determined and on options where ends remain to be determined.'[2] This states very clearly that the balance of power lies with Ministers. And this view was underscored by Mulley, at that time Secretary of State for Education, in his evidence to the same Committee. Asked what his relationship was with his civil servants, he replied, 'The relationship is very simple. I am in charge of the Department and subject to the consultations that one has both with one's ministerial colleagues and with one's officials, at the end of the day I do not only have to take the decisions but to defend them.'[3] He would not accept that he was able to exert his authority over a narrow area, pointing out that he had to answer questions on all aspects of policy in the House of Commons. This is true, of course, but irrelevant to the point at issue. It does not follow from the fact that the Secretary of State answers questions in the House on all matters of policy that he determines all matters of policy.

Others have drawn a finer line between the balance of influence of Ministers and officials. Crowther-Hunt argued in evidence to the Expenditure Committee that the balance of power over a wide area tended to be with civil servants, who know more about matters than Ministers and tend to shape them in their direction.[4] Kogan's considered judgement, informed by experience as a DES official, is that 'the literature makes far too many concessions to Ministerial narcissism. The ability of even the most able Minister to create, promote and carry out policies is limited.'[5] On the other hand, Kogan would not accept that Ministers are mere pawns in the hands of civil servants. None would deny that Ministers possess ultimate authority, or that they have an important influence on policy-making. They can have a powerful and dramatic impact on the formal terms of policy, as Thatcher demonstrated in reversing Circular 10/65, which had been issued by the previous Labour Government as a means of urging LEAs to change to comprehensive schools. Thatcher did not need the agreement of officials to do this, but they could not have done it without her agreement. As Lord

Alexander noted, 'a Secretary of State who does not influence policy is not a good Secretary of State.'[6] And even though this allows for the influence of Ministers as a variable rather than as a compelling, overarching constant, 'bad' Ministers can still expect that the starting-point for civil servants in formulating policy will be 'the known political commitment of Ministers' — a phrase used by DES officials in describing the genesis of the 1972 White Paper *Education: a Framework for Expansion.*[7] Yet do civil servants respond to all such commitments with equal alacrity? Is it not likely that when there is no political indication as to the ranking of commitments (or even on occasions when there is) priority will be influenced by what might be called the 'departmental view'?

Certainly, there are good grounds for believing that officials are likely to construct a 'departmental view' of policy. The longstanding service of civil servants is a contributory factor. Kogan claims that most officials of assistant secretary rank and above have served in the DES for more than ten years and quite a few for more than twenty years, and that this continuity significantly contributes to the authority and expertise of DES officials.[8] The education officer of the Association of County Councils was asked by the expenditure committee whether a claim that the DES developed a closed mind on issues was explicable in terms of the fact that more officials entered the Department and did not leave for the rest of their working lives than was the case with other Departments. He replied 'Yes' and gave the example of a DES official who, it was believed, would have resigned rather than move to another Department.[9] Vaizey concluded a list of educational policies over which a strong departmental view had prevailed with the observation that within the Department 'there is a very good tradition. It is like joining a good ship in the Navy.'[10] Arguably, the ironside traditions of the DES sustains the departmental view against the incursions of transient politicians. Civil servants precede and post-date most Ministers, whose tenure at the DES tends to be of short duration. About two years is the average length of office. As Crosland observed, 'It takes six months to get your head properly above water, a year to get the general drift of most of the field, and two years really to master the whole field of a Department.'[11]

Of course, the existence of a 'departmental view' is one thing; whether it prevails is another. A report by the Organization for Economic Co-operation and Development (OECD) inclined to the

view that it might often do so. The OECD report went so far as to
argue:

> a permanent officialdom possessing such extreme protection and
> internal discipline becomes a power in its own right. A British
> Department composed of professional civil servants who have watched
> Ministers come and go is an entity that only an extremely foolish or
> powerful politician will persistently challenge or ignore; [the authority
> of civil servants is] often superior to that of their de jure political
> superiors.[12]

The OECD concluded that the DES was 'the most important single
force in determining the direction of tempo of educational
development.'[13]

The 'force' can be of an intensely personal kind. For example, in
the case of the binary policy, Halsey claimed that 'a very, very
important influence was exercised by one particular civil servant.'[14]
There can be little doubt that the civil servant in question was Sir
Toby Weaver. Neither is so personal an influence exceptional. Boyle
claimed that the decision in 1963 to expand teacher training was
largely attributable to a brief by William Pile, at that time the
Under-Secretary in charge of teacher supply.[15] Thus it is not difficult
to believe the DES official who claimed, 'I can honestly say that
there is not a new policy in my sector of responsibility that I have
not either started or substantially contributed to over the last
twenty years.'[16] Civil servants are well placed in the structure of
policy-making to exert such personal influence. Lord Crowther-
Hunt, writing on the basis of his experience as a Minister in the
DES, states that the

> three main policy committees were exclusively composed of high-
> ranking departmental officials. . . . Ministers were never present at
> the meetings, nor even normally saw the Minutes of the meeting. It
> was even resented by officials if, as a Minister, you tried to find out
> what they were actually discussing before they were ready to serve up
> specific recommendations.[17]

While to a degree this could be justified on the grounds of saving the
time of Ministers, Crowther-Hunt argues that some participation
from Ministers would have put them in a better position to contribute
to policy-making. Instead they were 'faced with having to make

quick decisions in the space of hours — and sometimes even minutes — on the basis of recommendations that civil servants had been chewing over for months among themselves'.[18] This must put officials in a position of advantage in relation to Ministers. It gives strength to the 'departmental view' — so much strength, in fact, that Kogan can reasonably claim that 'the Department can itself act as an interest group . . . [wielding] determinant authority and great power.'[19] Halsey has described the Department as a 'pressure group'.[20] 'Pressure group' and 'interest group' are terms that have precise and somewhat opposed social science meanings, so there is clearly room for dispute about how best to categorize the position of the DES in policy-making, though it is clear that both Halsey and Kogan wish to place the DES at — perhaps even bestriding, in some respects — the centre of influence.

All this might be held to be of less importance than we have suggested, since the power of the DES is constrained by the fact that LEAs have some autonomy and thus can act as a countervailing force. Indeed, Kogan argues that the abolition of selection demonstrates that local authorities can generate policy change.[21] However, there is disagreement about the balance of power between central and local government and the degree of LEA autonomy. The best descriptions of central-local government relationships have been held to do no more than identify ambivalences. Crosland was adamant that education was not a single organization with a managerial chain of command — 'On the other hand, I was very struck by how much influence, control, power, the Department has.'[22] Presumably Crosland had in mind such things as the fact that the DES controls capital expenditure on education and the form of examinations in secondary schools. Also, the Government is the major paymaster, providing about 60 per cent of recurrent expenditure on education. Yet these instruments of control should be considered in the context of ambivalences in the relationship between central and local government.

In evidence to the Expenditure Committee, the DES argued that although bodies other than the DES had power and autonomy, that did not mean that the education system could develop in ways that central government opposed; it did mean, however, that the DES could not secure the detailed implementation of centrally taken decisions.[23] In the inimitable terms of Lord Hailsham, at the Ministry of Education, 'You suggest rather than direct. You say to one man

"Come" and he cometh not, and to another "Go" and he stays where he is.'[24]   In fact, Pile told the Expenditure Committee that he was concerned about the discontinuity between the intentions of Government and the outcome achieved by the aggregate decisions of more than a hundred education authorities.[25] When it was suggested that the DES, in dealing with 'aberrant' LEAs, had an effective sanction at the following year's negotiation of the rate support grant, Pile denied that this was so ('We have not got any sanctions'),[26] though he conceded that the DES was pondering 'whether within the general rate support grant setting, something might be done to produce greater continuity in each sector'.[27] This lack of continuity suggests that the Department is compelled to take note of other sources of influence in the education system. It might be argued that this transpires through a process of consultation.

In Pile's view, 'there is a whole network of interfaces, confrontation and arguments conducted at the highest level of Ministers.'[28] In addition, he spoke of 'what is generally intended to be the open door in the Ministry . . . that anybody can come and tell us what they feel and think'.[29] This view was to a large extent contradicted by those groups that take part in what is considered by the DES to be a process of extensive consultation. In evidence to the Expenditure Committee, the Association of Metropolitan Authorities claimed: 'the DES traditionally consults too little, too late and with too closed a mind. It has plenty of channels open if it wished.'[30] In evidence the Association complained that consultation about the Advanced Further Education building programme had been 'totally ineffective . . . a complete lack of consultation'.[31] Other examples included the question of teachers' pay in 1970 and pensions in 1973, and the change in the grant to voluntary aided schools. The National Union of Teachers (NUT), while acknowledging that it had both formal and informal relationships with the DES that did make for a degree of consultation (even if, on occasion, this was not so much instrumental as 'something of a formality . . . with very little time allowed for proper consultation'),[32] gave the following evidence to the Expenditure Committee:

There have been a number of occasions in recent years when the Union has had cause to make strong complaint to the Secretary of State at what it considered a failure to carry out full and proper consultation with the Union and with other professional and educational interests. One thinks for example of the fact that there was no consultation prior to the decision to announce the setting-up of the Assessment of Performance Unit, and the Educational Disadvantage Unit; no consultation prior to the decision of the Secretary of State to introduce a scheme of payments for social priority schools; inadequate consultation on the question of an inquiry into discipline and behaviour in schools; virtually no consultation on developments affecting education within the EEC.[33]

These opinions are worth recording, since, as we argue in chapter 3, the NUT is the most important source of professional comment on the process of policy-making. But we are not convinced that the NUT judgement about consultation is wholly accurate. On occasions the DES may even consult too much, and in general its record on consultation is much better than those of other government Departments. Whether or not Pile's representation of consultation as an 'open door' to the DES is sound is another matter.

Certainly, in response to questioning by the Expenditure Committee, Pile presented a somewhat more circumscribed definition of consultation than his previous 'open door' model. To begin with, it was revealed that the DES tended to consult, on a formal basis, local authority associations rather than local authorities themselves. Pile conceded that consulting two or three associations was not satisfactory, but argued that he did not think a regular system for consulting 105 authorities could be maintained, 'because we should get — let us put it mildly — fifty-two and a half opinions; indeed if any two agreed I think we should be surprised'.[34] It would appear that a broad range of alternative policies is not desired by the DES, possibly because this might undermine the legitimacy of the 'departmental view'. When the DES does approach local authorities — as distinct from their associations — 'we sound out in a pragmatic way what half a dozen authorities feel or know about a subject or topic.'[35] According to the OECD report cited above, a strong feeling exists in the DES to the effect that 'informal methods, utilized by sensitive and fair-minded government servants, are superior to highly structured formal procedures which invite politically sectarian opinions and encourage demagogy, confrontation and publicity battles.'[36] Fred Mulley, then Secretary of State for Education, conveyed the distinct impression that consultation was both ritualistic and symbolic: 'I would not claim to have extra-sensory power . . . [but] you mention the group and I will tell you exactly or very largely what they would be likely to say.'[37]

There are good reasons why the DES favours informal consultation. It can mean that a genuine picture will emerge to indicate whether or not a particular policy will work. Clearly, the DES cannot consult all LEAs on all matters. But an ad hoc, pragmatic pattern of consultation means that the process can be controlled by the DES, possibly in a way that protects the 'departmental view' from orchestrated opposition. Informal consultation could make for the depoliticization of educational policy. In general, this is a bad thing, though on occasions it might enable the DES to do good by stealth by avoiding opposition from entrenched vested interests that might oppose desirable policy. It would be naive not to recognize that, as a matter of course, senior civil servants seek to avoid political conflict, and the process of consultation must be understood against this background. Sometimes consultation is genuine and well intentioned, with the DES seeking to secure a reasonable balance between formal and informal consultation. On other occasions consultation is an excuse for inaction — 'consulting into the ground' is one way of describing the process. Yet again consultation can be a matter of mere form, undertaken after decisions have been made. It is impossible for us to say how the sum of consultation breaks down into the typology we have suggested. Our guess is that it would be reasonable to assume that for the most part consultation takes the first form. We lack firm evidence to assume otherwise. That said, senior DES civil servants are none the less cautious in their stance towards influences from outside the Department. This can be illustrated by reference to the Central Advisory Council for Education (CACE) and the Advisory Committee for the Supply and Training of Teachers (ACSTT).

CACE was a means by which extra-departmental opinion could be brought to bear on policy deliberation. As such, it might have challenged the departmental view. Though CACE has a statutory basis, it has been in abeyance since 1967. Kogan noted of Plowden, the last CACE report, 'The Department didn't like it',[38] and this was long before CACE reported. Kogan at that time was a DES civil servant serving Plowden; as an insider with special knowledge, his opinion carries special weight. Raison suggests that another conceivable basis of DES objection to CACE was that it raised expectations that could not be met.[39] This is clearly a political objection.

The ACSTT was similarly neutralized by the DES. According to the NUT, the reorganization of teacher training was kept off the agenda of ACSTT by the DES. The union's objections to this 'were brushed aside': 'when we got there we found that this committee . . . was to advise the Department on how to operate the policy of reducing the supply of teachers which had already been decided. . . . it was a fiddle, a confidence trick.'[40] Crowther-Hunt argues that the DES usually managed to dominate 'outside' advisory committees, and cites the ACSTT as a good example:

> I insisted on being present [at an ACSTT meeting] because I believed my officials would otherwise introduce the question in a way which might slant the subsequent advice I received. If, on this occasion, I was trying to use this advisory committee to back me in a particular battle I was having, with my officials, it is equally true that, for the most part, officials viewed it and sought to use it as a device for reinforcing the advice that they themselves were directly and separately giving their Ministers. And if they are present much more often than Ministers, they are much more likely to succeed.[41]

Crowther-Hunt says that Ministers are not normally present, and his exceptional insistence on being present caused something of a stir. This DES stance appears to be part of a pattern. Crosland, one time Secretary of State for Education, claimed that the Department's obstructive stance towards the Council for Educational Technology was due in part to the 'intense dislike of outside councils and committees which all civil servants have'.[42]

Research findings are another potential source of external influence on DES policy-making. Yet, there again, the DES's attitude to this potential is negative. In evidence to the Expenditure Committee, Pile opined:

> I have to say, of course, that the great thing about research is that part of it is rubbish and another part (I will not be specific about the proportions) leads nowhere and is really rather indifferent; it is, I am afraid, exceptional to find a piece of research that really hits the nail on the head and tells you pretty clearly what is wrong or what is happening or what should be done.[43]

Many observers agree that research has had little impact on policy-making. Vaizey does accord a rather nebulous influence to research findings, in that the work of sociologists has influenced public opinion, and since DES officials are party to this, they too have been influenced. However, in his view, DES sponsored research has not had 'any effect on major decisions . . . though this is much more a criticism of the extremely feeble nature of educational research than it is of the DES'.[44] Of course, some research can be reasonably rejected as feeble, but Pile's view is altogether too dismissive and unconstructive, part of a consistently negative attitude to outside influences. As Maclure argues, DES scorn about the usefulness of research is 'more an automatic institutional response than the result of a rational review of the possibilities'.[45] Taylor argues that 'research is capable of producing hard data that might act as a basis for policy.'[46] Certainly, the DES was slow to use its powers under the 1944 Act to foster research. It was not until 1962, after strictures contained in the Crowther Report on the neglect of research, that these powers were used to any appreciable extent, and since then we have spent a rather small proportion of the educational budget on research — 0.16 per cent, compared with 0.6 per cent in Sweden, for example.[47] Of course, research can be a politically sensitive instrument. Research findings, insofar as they identify deficiencies, can provide political opponents with ammunition and may create demand for resources. Even research that confirms the success of policy can be problematic if it strengthens claims for more resources. Such difficulties are not pervasive or insurmountable, however. The DES could afford to take a more flexible attitude towards sources of 'outside' comment and potential extra-departmental sources of influence on policy.

Arguably, the DES pursues a strategy that is designed to contain and manage the influence of outside pressures. As the OECD put it:

> The chief features of the basis for its policy-making formation seem to be characterized by attempts to minimize the degree of controversiality in the planning process and its results; reduce possible alternatives to matters of choice of resource allocation; limit the planning process to those parts of the educational services and functions strictly controlled by the DES; exploit as fully as possible the powers, prerogatives and responsibilities given to the DES under the 1944 Education Act; understate as much as possible the role of government in the

determination of the future course of educational policy and even minimize it in the eyes of the general public.[48]

Clearly, this does not deny that others have a role in the determination of future courses of policy. In particular, LEA autonomy is a reality. Yet the formal balance of initiative and power tends to lie with the DES; there is fairly limited scope for LEAs to determine the course of central policy. Indeed, Pile told the Expenditure Committee that the Green Paper on school transport had elicited very little from the LEAs and that he doubted that they had the staff resources for serious analytical work — 'I have not seen evidence of their ability to respond.'[49] It would be foolish to generalize on the basis of the example of school transport. Nevertheless, we agree with Kogan's claim with regard to local authority associations that they are 'unashamedly reactive rather than innovative'.[50] As Kogan also notes, 'by proclaiming the liberal pluralism of a decentralized system, the DES are left free to impose their own cast on central policy choice.'[51] What is the character of this cast?

So far we have sought to establish that the DES while by no means exercising complete control, is the most concentrated source of influence in the education system. But it does not follow from this that the DES is likely to inhibit action against inequality. It might be the case that the DES uses its power to advance egalitarian measures. Indeed, Boyle referred to 'the dialectic within the office'[52] — that is to say, two traditions within the Department: the social justice tradition that supported wider opportunity, and the education for investment/education for efficiency tradition. While Boyle attests to the fact that there is no monolithic structure of values in the DES, it is unlikely that the value mix falls so neatly into two equally weighted traditions. It is true that the DES has brought forward policies to act against inequality, but their form and lack of success belies the suggestion that they derive from a half-share in the values underpinning the 'departmental view'. We would argue that action against inequality, far from being a substantial compenent in the ethos of the DES, has been a minor strand. On balance, the DES has been a conservative influence on the direction of educational policy.

Admittedly, the evidence for this contention is hard to come by, but some examples can be cited to support our case. As mentioned above, Vaizey has listed cases in which a 'departmental view' has been 'persistently enforced, regardless of the political allegiance of the political head of the Department'.[53] These were the tripartite system (1945-8), the imposition of the binary policy, and the dismantling of the colleges of education (1973-5). These examples merit attention, since they might be construed as evidence not just of DES influence on policy but also of a *conservative* influence. However, as we shall explain, there are good grounds for dissenting from this view.

There can be little doubt that civil servants had a determining influence on the shape of the 1944 Education Act (see chapter 1.) Though the Act did not prescribe a tripartite system, one subsequently developed and was central to the Civil Service view of secondary education. As Vaizey notes, 'the decision to have a tripartite system was the logical culmination of a view which had been taken in the Department over a good many years and this was not going to be easily overthrown by such wild-eyed men as R. H. Tawney.'[54] Although Vaizey argues that opinion among those who supported the Atlee Government 'was pretty strongly moving in comprehensive direction',[55] there is not much evidence for this. The stress should be certainly placed on 'moving'. It was not the case that the Board countered a strong move towards comprehensives. Then, as later, Labour was both divided on this issue and undecided. In 1965, as we argue in chapter 6, the Department was probably still pro-tripartite.[56] Stewart claims that one official 'made no secret of his hostility to comprehensive education . . . if I had stayed longer at the Department we might have come into serious collision.'[57] Stewart does add that the rest of his officials were co-operative, but that does not necessarily mean that at that stage they were pro-comprehensive.

As to the binary policy, Crosland, who was Secretary of State when the policy was announced, later claimed that his officials forced the matter on him before he had had time to consider the issue in depth. Crosland conceded that ultimately the fault was his.[58] While having little sympathy with Ministers who complain after the event that they were forced into action that they did not want to take, there is little doubt that the impetus for this policy came from officials. Kogan suggests that their pressure was a response to local authority wishes.[59] Sir Toby Weaver, a senior civil servant in the DES, is considered to have been the main architect of the binary policy. Kogan argues that the policy 'was not at all in line with the Labour Party's Taylor Committee recommendations of a few years earlier to create a large and undifferentiated system of higher education'.[60] The findings of this Committee did not command universal support within the Labour Party. Crosland himself says that he became convinced of the correctness of the policy and denied that it was anti-egalitarian.[61] He had good reasons for arguing thus. The policy was an attempt to provide more resources for part-time and vocational education for engineers and technologists in non-university institutions with a strong local base which, it was hoped, would attract more working-class students. As it happened, the attempt largely failed (see chapter 8).

At first sight, the dismantling of the colleges of education may appear to be a case of the 'departmental view' triumphing over more progressive Labour commitment. The policy was initiated by the Tories in response to a drop in the birth rate, which made a reduction in teacher supply inevitable, whichever party was in office. However, the Labour Opposition responded to Circular 7/73 (which set in train the reorganization of teacher training) by disputing the desirability of the scale of the reduction of training places. Opposition statements are often the stuff more of debating than of policy-making, so it was not altogether surprising that the next Labour Government should reduce the supply of teachers even further. To argue that this was an example of a Labour Government's going back on previous commitments under official pressure is to ignore the need to avoid massive teacher unemployment and to use scarce resources sensibly. After some delay on this question, the DES acted with speed and rigour to reduce the supply of teachers despite strong opposition, especially from the NUT. This is evidence of iron in the 'departmental view', which can readily resist extra-departmental pressure.

A final example of the role of the 'departmental view' is related to the public schools and tax relief. At various times Labour has made statements about the public schools. The 1974 Election Manifesto stated that Labour would withdraw tax relief and charitable status from the public schools. This pledge was not fulfilled. According to Crowther-Hunt, Sir William Pile played a central role in the failure of the policy. He briefed Fred Mulley, the Education Minister, on 'technical problems to which at present nobody knows the answer' and concluded that immediate responsibility for action 'lies primarily not with you but with the Home Secretary, the Chancellor of the Exchequer and the Secretary of State for the Environment. . . . I cannot think of anything that we ourselves can usefully do in the interim.'[62] Crowther-Hunt argues that the technical problems might not have been insoluble had tax and education experts outside the DES been consulted. If this was the case, the diversion of the issue on to some implausible common ground between the DES and the three Departments cited could suggest that the 'departmental view' was not entirely sympathetic to the proposal to act against the public schools.

This is consistent with the opposition that Crosland experienced when he sought to establish the Public Schools Commission in 1965.

> [Senior officials] were sceptical as to whether the government knew what it was doing. They rightly challenged me on whether there was any possible compromise solution which stood a chance of acceptance on both financial and political grounds. I insisted and got my way. I must say that much of their scepticism eventually proved justified.[63]

It is interesting to note that senior officials seemed to regard a radical solution as out of the question. Also they were presumably advising Crosland to follow a course of inaction. This was clearly diametrically opposed to the policy and social values expressed in the Labour Party's 1964 Election Manifesto.

Against Crowther-Hunt's view it could be argued that it was unlikely that the matter of tax relief and charitable status for public schools could have been resolved by the DES acting alone. It was therefore perfectly proper and reasonable to propose inter-departmental action. The explanation for failure in this area is best seen in terms of the lack of collective political will rather than the lack of technical knowledge about how to overcome the problems involved. Inadequate evidence prevents conclusive judgement. Our conjecture is that the Labour Party lacked the political will to take action against the public schools, and that senior civil servants in the DES were, in the main, against such action and used 'technical' difficulties as an obstructive device.

What, in sum, can be made of these examples? They *are* limited, amounting to no more than speculation about, sometimes glimpses of, policy-making. They could be construed as some evidence in support of our first proposition; namely, the force of DES officials in influencing policy. But the examples are not conclusive proof of our second proposition, that in these instances senior civil servants could be said to be acting in a way that was obstructive of greater equality, and still less of the hypothesis that in general the DES so acts. We doubt, however, that further analysis would show that over the years officials in the DES have favoured egalitarian policies.

The grounds for this doubt are as follows. First, and somewhat insubstantially, the conservatism of civil servants has been asserted by a number of people with first-hand experience of government, usually associated with the Labour Party, who claim that the reforming intention of the Party has been frustrated by the opposition and machinations of conservative civil servants.[64] The evidence for such assertations tends to be of a limited, anecdotal kind and — given the nature of our closed system of government — beyond rigorous testing. Of course, this does not mean that such assertions are untrue.

Second, and again somewhat insubstantially, the values that civil servants bring to bear on policy formation could be inferred from the social background from which they are recruited.[65] There is a wealth of evidence to show that civil servants are recruited from a restricted background. For example, Fulton showed that whereas social classes 1 and 2 make up 20 per cent of the population, 67 per cent of administrative class civil servants came from this background.[66] The educational background of the administrative class was also in marked contrast to that of the general population, in that 36 per cent had attended a public school and a further 19 per cent a direct-grant school. Only 1 per cent had attended a secondary modern school;[67] only 2 per cent had left school before the age of 16. The administrative class formed something of an elite within an elite, in that of those with degrees, 64 per cent had studied at Oxbridge. If anything, these figures understate the educational differences between those who now command the senior heights of the Civil Service and the general population, since the former were educated at a time when a much smaller proportion of the population than now experienced higher education. It will have been noted that these figures relate to the administrative class as a whole and not to the officials of the DES, but there are no grounds for assuming that DES officials are an atypical group of civil servants. Yet it is one thing to describe the likely social and educational background of

DES officials and quite another to impute conservative values to them on this basis. It is conceivable that a group of people drawn from such a privileged and atypical background is nevertheless wholeheartedly committed to advancing the interests of the educationally disadvantaged — if needs be, by securing a redistribution of educational resources at the expense of the advantaged — and the cause of state education in general. The probability that many senior DES officials do not send their children to the maintained comprehensive schools (for example)[68] need not be a basis for inferring a lack of diligence in advancing such schools. But is this likely? Is it so unreasonable to ask, with Halsey, 'whether those who use the private sector of education for their own children should at the same time serve in the DES?[69] This question, as Halsey was at pains to point out, implies no calculated neglect of the state system by civil servants, but 'it is not very plausible to suppose that you can always rely on a man steadfastly to act on behalf of other people's children as well as he will act on behalf of his own.'[70] By definition, the educationally disadvantaged are located in the state system, for the most part removed from the direct experience of senior civil servants. It is not unreasonable that this fact should give rise to some doubts about the strength of the advocacy of the state system on the part of DES officials of the disadvantaged.

Third, and most substantially, there is some evidence that the professed values behind DES policy-making are hostile to radical policies. In the terms of Sir William Pile, speaking as permanent secretary of the DES, the character of the Department is 'pragmatic, conservative and evolutionary, not theoretical, futurological and revolutionary'.[71] As the OECD report argues, the stance of the DES seems 'to preclude the possibility of interpreting the role of education as an agent for innovation and social progress'.[72] It might be argued that such matters as 'social progress' involve political choices and that civil servants are politically neutral. Yet, as we have already demonstrated, DES officials cannot be seen as simply concerned with 'means where ends have already been decided' (by politicians), as Pile would suggest. Civil servants have the power to determine ends: they fulfil a covert political function. Indeed, in Fowler's view, a Secretary of State 'will equally expect his officials to display political judgement in their own decisions'.[73] It appears that Fowler expects that such judgements will be made by strict reference to the political values of the Minister. Why this should necessarily be the case is not clear. Boyle concedes that the values of civil servants play a part in policy-making,[74] and there are no grounds for supposing that political values will somehow be expunged. Even if it were possible for civil servants to be 'neutral', neutrality is not an apolitical stance. To be neutral in the face of a fundamentally unequal education system is to adopt a posture conducive to the perpetuation of that system. Besides, Pile is open-handed about the stance of the DES. It is conservative.

A central feature of this conservatism is a style of policy-making that emphasizes the detection of lines of development from within the extant education system. This is what Boyle described by the phrase 'the logic of the education service as it was developing'[75] and recognized in the claim that 'the pressure of numbers was one constant determiner of policies.'[76] There is a similar recognition in Pile's evidence to the OECD examiners, when he stated that a major basis of policy was manifest demand and that planning should be essentially based on identified trends.[77] Thus the DES view has been quite literally just that — a view, a matter of perception, bland and uncontroversial, the legitimate issue of a basically sound education system, free of radical political choices and moral dilemma. Thus 'bad faith' is institutionalized. The DES responds to trends as a plant does to light (a reaction that botanists call tropism), within the limitations of such factors as the availability of resources that entail political choices about priorities, but of a kind restricted by an essentially conservative orthodoxy. Policy-making is benign 'tropism' and not a means by which we *preserve* inequality. It is important to recognize the essential conservatism of reacting to trends in this way. There is no reason why a trend should be sacrosanct, immutably given. The trends of an unequal education system are scarcely likely to possess authority in terms of social justice. What of those groups that do not have the pressure of numbers in their favour? There is nothing irrevocably given about the working-class demand for post-school education. If the demand lacks force of numbers, this is in large measure a product of rationing and stratification within the present system. An ideology of policy-making that precludes action to alter this system, and advocates passive recognition of marginal trends, makes for the unwarranted emasculation of the potential for progressive social action inherent in pluralistic democracy.

That 'going where the arithmetic leads'[78] — as Pile puts it — can be antithetical to educational equality can be illustrated by a consideration of the distribution of school building allocation. The greater part of this distribution derives from a policy of 'roofs over heads' — that is to say, giving precedence to building new schools in areas of expanding child population. Areas that attract sanction for capital investment tend, therefore, to be areas of suburban growth and/or areas of economic expansion. This has been the pattern of capital investment in schools since the Second World War. As was stated by the DES in evidence to the Expenditure Committee, 'the need to provide roofs over heads is an enduring and inescapable priority for all governments.'[79] But this means that areas of declining or stagnant population, such as inner urban areas or the Welsh valleys, tend not to attract such investment. In 1980 the chairman of Mid-Glamorgan education committee complained that 120 schools built before 1903 had 'outlived their usefulness'.[80] The County Council had submitted school building schemes for around £3 million but had been granted permission to spend only £1.6 million in 1979/80, of which £400,000 had to go on energy conservation. The Under-Secretary of State at the Welsh Office felt that Mid-Glamorgan had been given a fair allocation of the capital building programme for 1979-82, in the light of falling pupil numbers.[81] The DES view was that there was no alternative to 'roofs over heads', since 'given your statutory responsibilities to provide education for children of compulsory age, you *cannot* slant your building programmes towards the deprived areas to an extent which makes it impossible to provide schools in other areas.'[82] What this means in terms of figures is that the £126 million school building programme for 1977-8 allowed £114 million for basic needs (i.e., 'roofs over heads') and only £12 million for the replacement and improvement of old schools.

However, the demand for school places in expanding areas could be solved by means other than capital investment. Greater use could be made of the existing stock of buildings by recourse to larger classes. Accommodation could be rented, or hutted accommodation could even be deployed — recall the Hutting Operation for Raising the School Age after the Second World War. Thus it is not the case that we *cannot* slant the building programme to give priority to disadvantaged areas. It is a case of *choosing* not to do so. If the policy of 'roofs over heads' were abandoned, and recourse were made to 'Cox-and-Box' schemes to accommodate children in expanding areas, then those adversely affected (mainly middle-class parents) would be likely to organize political pressure to reverse the policy and would have unambiguous ways of demonstrating that the education of their children was deficient by 'normal' standards. By contrast, the working-class parents of children being educated in inadequate buildings that had 'outlived their usefulness' would be less able and willing to organize political pressure. The deprivations of such buildings are more unobtrusive and therefore less politically potent than any of the alternatives to 'roofs over heads' suggested above.

The DES's subordination to the allegedly compelling force of 'going with the arithmetic' is conceivably a far from neutral calculation of political expediency: that is, 'roofs over heads' will cause less political trouble than would favouring those being educated in inadequate buildings. Pile's 'cannot' is pre-eminently political, and the political choices of policy-makers tend not to favour the disadvantaged. Many would *choose* not to follow the alternative pattern of resource allocation that we have raised, and no doubt educational grounds could be adduced for not doing so. But *the fact of choice* cannot be denied, nor the desirability of a publicly accountable process by which arguments can be won and lost. A contrary view makes for the depoliticization of educational policy-making, which appears to be a primary tactic by which civil servants maintain their control of events and avoid the public language of priorities. The educational system has provided building resources for halls of residence so that mainly middle-class students can receive *non-compulsory* higher education away from their homes. At the same time we tolerate inadequate buildings for largely working-class children receiving *compulsory* education. If we cannot have both halls of residence and adequate primary schools, which should be given priority? This moral dilemma cannot be avoided by a style of policy-making that pleads subservience to 'going with arithmetic', which, if anything, serves to compound rather than counter educational disadvantage.

Educational policy-making as the recognition of trends leaves a number of important questions unanswered. Above all, by what social process is a trend recognized? Asked by the Expenditure Committee if there was any systematic way in which the DES identified a trend, Sir William Pile replied, 'We have no systematic way, but the "feel" [of education] is a very important bit of our trade.'[83] This depicts an exclusive, mysterious process, akin at first sight to Lawrentian 'blood-consciousness' and, at second sight, more prosaically, to secret bureaucracy of a classically Weberian kind. In further evidence to the Committee, Pile suggested that the source of these rather strange intimations about educational trends was participation in contemporary state education by senior DES officials *qua* parents. Pressed on this point, he conceded that his own children had attended public schools and that it was a fair assumption that not every high-ranking official at the DES sent his children to state schools, though many did.[84]

Of course, there is a greater rigour to the Department's recognition of trends than the mere esoteric exercise of the 'feel' of education. The Department does undertake concerted up-dating of major policies, but the terms of this activity — 'the facts of life', 'practicality'[85] — are synonymous with the central DES value of conservatism. In Pile's view, 'if you put people into back rooms they plan unrealistically. They do not have daily contact with problems, so you get into the flabby type of futurological day-dreaming . . . creative practical ideas [are] brought into focus and worked out' (when planning is done as an additional task by those who otherwise have a full-time job).[86] Thus planning is rooted in a day-to-day sense of the education system as it is or, rather, of what it is becoming. Educational options are narrowly defined within a frame of reference determined by the orthodoxy of the existing system: beyond the felt pulse of this system lies the error of futurological day-dreaming. It is clear that while the DES does have an ideology of change, perhaps best described as 'evolutionary pragmatism', this is not informed by a manifest concern with inequality and social justice, as is demonstrated by the absence of these issues from the DES's submission of evidence to the Expenditure Committee. Instead, the DES ideology of change is informed by three things — managerial efficiency, expansionism and consensus — none of which is necessarily conducive to change (in the sense of a radical redress of inequality).

By 'managerial efficiency' we mean a preoccupation with such problems as to how to obtain 'efficiency and value for money'.[87] This is an important and ubiquitous goal. But it should not become an alternative to, or substitute for, other goals, such as the reduction of inequality. There is no inconsistency in having both goals. Indeed, efficiency could facilitate reduced inequality. However, DES criteria of managerial efficiency are narrow and excessively concerned with the maintenance of the prevailing system. A prime yardstick of DES efficiency is the extent to which the education system can be said to be in a state of equilibrium, without blatant imbalances between the supply of, and demand for, educational facilities. When 'manifest demand' is in excess of supply, the DES takes this as an indictment of its stewardship. The 'departmental view' supported the expansion of universities because an increasing number of students qualified for university entrance by A-Levels were unable to obtain places, and this support is widely believed to have preceded the Robbins Report. Equally, when the birth rate dropped, teachers were held to be in too great supply: unemployed teachers were a massive indictment of departmental efficiency, so with great determination and alacrity the supply was reduced. Thus the criterion by which the management of the system is to be judged emanates from within the system itself — that is, in terms of the above examples, the disequilibrium of educational demand and supply. Insofar as external criteria obtain, they derive largely from the need to keep education in a state of consistency with the Treasury management of the economy. As the DES stressed in evidence to the Expenditure Committee, a depressed economy means that 'attention has to be concentrated on the short-term problem of distribution'[88] (it is tempting to add 'to the neglect of long-term problems of *redistribution*'). Such questions of social justice are not managerial problems. They are evaded by the myth of Civil Service neutrality in matters of value dilemma and by a preoccupation with managerial problems of administration in the technical pursuit of goals set by political masters.

Expansionism was the hallmark of educational development from the 1950s to the early 1970s. Change is that which is obtained by the acquisition of more resources for the education system. These are largely dependent on economic growth. Thus educational policy is the creature of economic policy. One civil servant's view of the expansionist document *Education: a Framework for Expansion,* published in 1972, was that it should be put in a glass case to show how such plans are destroyed by economic factors.[89] One view of expansionism as an ideology of change is that it may obstruct egalitarianism in three ways. First, it pre-empts consideration of the redistribution of resources by defining the resource problem as the question of how marginal increases in resources should be used rather than how we distribute existing resources between social classes. Second, it is wrongly assumed that simply spending more on education will correct inequality, whereas unless the pattern of the distribution of resources is altered, relativities between the educational experience of different social groups will be maintained, though at higher levels of provision overall. Third, it legitimates the primary managerial concern of improving standards for all; departmental aspirations become resolutely universalistic rather than particularistic, absolute not relative. The ideology of expansionism was a means by which the DES could accept managerial responsibility for the pursuit of new and better standards while at the same time ignoring that it presided over a system that delivered to different social classes a service that varied considerably in quality and quantity.

Against this view of educational expansion it might be argued that increased resources can provide an opportunity for the endowment of innovatory egalitarian policies. Clearly, such an endowment would be politically more acceptable than the redistribution of resources from existing programmes.

There can be no question that the DES's style of policy-making is perceived as consensual. This is proclaimed as the case by the DES and nearly all observers. As the OECD reported, the Department 'endeavours to identify in all situations a social consensus as to the priority issues which policy planning could be directed'.[90] Yet there is evidence to show significant scope for divergent opinions — ironically, supplied by leading protagonists of the consensual view of policy-making. Mulley, in evidence to the Expenditure Committee, argued against the idea of a standing Commission of Education because it would replicate existing contributions to the process of consultation. Also he argued: 'There would be no consensus.'[91] Sir Toby Weaver claimed:

> when I was in the DES one could go to seven different teacher associations and get seven different answers representing the views of teachers. There were five local authority associations in my day and often one would get not only five not identical answers but one particular association might say, 'We have asked our adviser to advise us on this question and here are five answers from them.'[92]

In addition, the consensus is as genuine as the process by which it is achieved, namely, consultation. We have already expressed some doubts about the social breadth of this process: those in what Vaizey might have called (but did not) 'the good ship DES' set their course from a severely limited range of bearings — what is more, bearings sometimes taken in haste. The DES has conceded that 'there was a general complaint that insufficient time was allowed for proper consideration and comment . . . the Department realizing that the effectiveness of consultation is reduced if those consulted are put under unreasonable pressure of time.'[93] The DES goes on to acknowledge that proper consideration and comment are particularly difficult 'when consultation started at the beginning of a holiday period'.[94] There has been a marked increase in consultative documents of one kind or another in recent years, possibly as a result of criticisms of this kind, but also as part of a general move towards more open government.

Arguably, the DES orchestrates, manufactures even, a so-called consensus. Halsey observed that 'as de facto policy-makers, the DES civil servants have an assailable authority because they lack secure knowledge.'[95] Conceivably, that authority is rendered unassailable by the cloak of a spurious collective wisdom derived from limited consultation. This consensus has had a narrow basis, not just because only a small fraction of the formally defined constituency of educational government has been consulted on any particular issue, but also because of the virtual absence of an organized voice for educationally disadvantaged. In areas of social policy such as housing and income maintenance there are groups that represent the disadvantaged. There is no national campaigning group to represent the interests of the educationally disadvantaged in an exclusive fashion. Furthermore, the DES style of consultation secures a consensus that avoids 'political sectarian opinions . . . confrontation and publicity battles'. Yet considerable, longstanding, class-based inequality in education should be a matter for political and public confrontation. How else in a democratic society can radical policy be forged? A departmentally managed consensus, or at best a consensus of the educationally advantaged, legitimates the sectarianism of the 'departmental view'. Kogan has argued that 'consensus was often the least line of resistance rather than the critical path determined analytically.'[96] Inevitably, the line of least resistance is that which does not threaten the *status quo*.

If the *status quo* is to be threatened, if we are to mount a serious assault on inequality, then change is called for in the structure of policy-making. Many outside the DES (and, we suspect, some inside) would argue that the present system of policy-making is unsatisfactory. Several reforms have been suggested in recent years. The Expenditure Committee recommended the creation of a Standing Education Commission that would have the authority and resources to contribute to strategic educational planning. Its staff would be appointed as individuals in their own right and not just as representatives of educational pressure groups, and one of its main aims would be to bring trade unionists, employers and ordinary citizens into the education debate.[97] The Government's response to the Expenditure Committee — a response that, in general, was disappointedly flaccid — rejected this proposal, since

> it is inevitable that the work of a Commission would be slower and less well informed than that of the DPO [the Department's own planning organization] and its findings would be likely, therefore, to lag behind events. The deliberations of the Commission would then be post-mortems and the Government do not believe that to establish such a body would be useful or attractive to the calibre of person it would be desirable to enlist in its membership.[98]

As an alternative to a Standing Commission, seminars and conferences on individual topics were recommended. The politics of this preference are obvious. Ad hoc seminars would be much easier for the DES to contain as a source of criticism than a Standing Commission. Unfortunately, the former would be less likely than the latter to provide a learning mechanism that ensured that past failures were not repeated. Many persons of high calibre *would* be attracted to the idea of conducting post-mortems on Government policy.

Since education is a massive industry, the NUT advocates a 'Little Neddy' as a forum where the three partners of education — the local authorities, teachers unions and the DES — could exchange views and discuss the planning of the DES.[99] Kogan has called for an 'action intelligentsia',[100] who must be political and evangelical as well as analytical, since 'there is no competent liberal or socialist intelligentsia that is feeding the political system with new concepts about the education system.'[101] This rather Fabian remedy was to some extent utilized, in an informal and ad hoc fashion, by the late

Tony Crosland. When he was Secretary of State for Education, he ·
invited a group of people, mostly academics, to visit his home to
discuss specific education issues when a decision was pending.[102]
An Institute for Education Policy Analysis, as a more formal device
for countering the DES's 'excessive power through its capacity to
collect and analyse information',[103] was considered by the Expenditure Committee but not recommended because of cost and the
undesirability of considering education in isolation from other
aspects of social policy. Instead the ideas was commended to
private foundations.

These solutions are largely intended to improve the process of
consultation and the means of acquiring knowledge as a basis for
better policy-making. Yet Maclure has argued that what is needed is
'not new machinery of consultation but willingness on the part of
the political heads of the Department to open up public discussion
on policy issues'.[104] And while it is understandable that academics
are likely to stress insufficient knowledge as an obstacle to policy-
making (and, to some extent, reasonably), it could be argued that
this misrepresents the nature of the problem. Our failure to act
against educational disadvantage is not simply a failure of
knowledge; it is a failure of political will. We have not forged a
political basis for acting against inequality. In fact, we have tended
to depoliticize educational policy. Value controversy has been
displaced by the myth of Civil Service neutrality, the identification
of self-evidently legitimate 'trends', the mystique of the mandarin
'feel' of education, limited consultation and the orchestration of a
pseudo-consensus. Raison can write: 'consensus is the key to the
success of the 1944 Act.'[105] If anything, it is the key to its failure to
provide equality of opportunity for all. The fundamental post-war
consensus persists: that is, that the education system is basically
sound; that, given a suitable economic climate, we should seek in
some vague way to improve educational standards for all; that we
should counter massive educational inequalities with marginal
programmes of positive discrimination; that a fundamental redistribution of educational resources is neither feasible nor desirable.

Various proposals have been made to bring educational policy
more surely within the arena of political discussion and scrutiny.
The Expenditure Committee declared that the 'programme chapters'
of the annual Public Expenditure White Paper will be examined, if
necessary with the aid of expert witnesses and additional evidence

from the DES and a report presented to the House of Commons. Additionally, the committee *requested* that it should be kept informed of any programme analysis review undertaken by the DES and that it should discuss such matters with the DES.[106] Such measures are suggested as means of securing more power for Parliament. Certainly, most observers have concluded that Parliament has little direct impact on educational policy-making. The advent of the new Select Committee on Education may have succeeded in giving Parliament a greater formal capacity to examine policy, but at the time of writing it is too soon to confirm this. Early attempts by the Committee to prevail upon the DES to reveal more of the process of policy-making and to become less secretive have not been successful. For example, the convention that official advice to Ministers is confidential has been maintained. The Expenditure Committee noted: 'the habit of secretiveness . . . grew up when Government was more autocratic and public opinion less well-informed; [it] served to prevent embarrassment.'[107] Educational inequality should be a political embarrassment so as to increase the likelihood of action. The Committee enviously ruminated on the way in which their opposite numbers in the Swedish Rikstag spent 'several days each week in sustained discussion of educational policies as they were produced by the Ministry of Education and the various Commissions'.[108] Without question, there is a case for subjecting educational policy-making to a more rigorous process of political scrutiny and contest.

The fact that the process is not more open to scrutiny and contest cannot be laid entirely at the door of civil servants — despite the fact that Lord Armstrong, formerly an eminent civil servant, has conceded that secrecy 'is comfortable, convenient, and one has to say it allows mistakes (and incompetence) to be covered up'.[109] Many Ministers of both major parties have been averse to open government. None has welcomed 'political embarrassment'. To some extent, officials and politicians act in complicity, preferring to advance within the political security of a consensus. This can have several dimensions all of which entail a conservatism beyond that which we have sought to delineate within the DES. Local authorities are important and generally conservative agents in the educational consensus. Furthermore, in a system of Cabinet government what DES officials or Ministers want to do will not necessarily happen. Cabinet government is generally conservative in its impact, and yet another form of consensus must emerge before anything can be done. Central to such a consensus is the limitation placed on policy by the Treasury.

Although we recognize the constraints on the actions of officials, we still wish to place them in a position of primary influence and to underscore the political character of this position. As Meacher notes, 'Examples abound of how the Civil Service uses both political parties to put through its own ideas or those of the wider Establishment.'[110] Sir Anthony Part, a former permanent secretary (at the Department of Industry), has openly declared the political character of official action in describing how senior civil servants seek to shift Ministers away from the extremes on to the common ground of British politics — 'unless the common ground is captured, policies do not last . . . it is the Civil Service trying to have a sense of what can succeed for Britain . . . in recent times neither of the main parties has been elected by a majority of the electorate.'[111] Here can be detected the emergence of dominant conservative values couched in terms such as 'the public interest', 'the general good'. Such values become a central point of allegiance between officials, part of the tissue of occupational culture that binds individuals to the 'departmental view' as opposed to the view of transient politicians, sometimes with minority electoral support.

Yet officials are not in any way licensed by the electoral process. The deliberations of the DES are not subject to any significant public political process at the stage of policy formation, and insofar as declared policy must stand the political test of Parliament and public acceptance, it does so as Government policy and not Civil Service policy. Officials are able to feel self-assured and protected.

This self-assurance has not been dented by the vigorous criticisms of the DES by the OECD and others. The management review of the DES set up in the wake of the OECD report wrote, for example, of planning — 'failures, we believe, are rarely caused by defects of organization but much more by shortages of time and by human fallibility.'[112] This ignores the prospect that a more open organization might help to counter defects of time pressure and human fallibility. The review expressed basic confidence in the informal style of DES management and planning but noted that informality had certain dangers, not the least of which was that important matters could be overlooked or misunderstood.

We therefore welcome the Permanent Secretary's intention that branches and H.M.I. should discuss with him annually their programmes of work. The annual public expenditure survey already provides a comprehensive review of policies but we agree a more broadly based look is needed which would deal with emerging policy issues and resources questions.[113]

It is to be doubted that an annual discussion between DES officials is an adequate reform of the system of policy-making to counter accepted 'dangers' and 'failures', still less the immense problem of entrenched inequality.

It would have been better had the Department abandoned its position of political privilege and conceded that politically neutral policy-making is as unattainable as a value-free language: policies are pre-eminently political choices between competing priorities. It is not scandalous that civil servants make such choices. Given their undoubted skills and knowledge, it would be scandalous if they did not. What is a scandal is that we tolerate the claim that they do not make policy, thus obviating the need to create contexts in which this activity can be rendered accountable. To deny the political and policy-making role of officials is to favour the emaciating depoliticization of educational policy, which, as a major strand of an ideology of conservative educational policy-making, renders radical change inconceivable by sleight of concept. There can be no prospect of adequate action against educational inequality until policy-making and the determination of priorities are open to debate and political conflict. Not to recognize this is to operate under the unnecessary constraints of a self-denying ordinance. It is to prefer, as Milton put it, 'bondage with ease than strenuous liberty'. A new commonwealth is needed, not, as the management review of the DES intends, a restoration of old ways.

3

Unions and Pressure Groups

So far we have examined the role of the official framework in which educational policies are formulated. We concluded that redistribution and the general advancement of the disadvantaged have not played a prominent role within this framework. We turn now to certain sources of external pressure on the politicians, civil servants and local authority administrators. We ask a similar question about this pressure. How far has it focused on redistribution? We have divided these sources of pressure into two main categories. They are the teachers' organizations and the ad hoc pressure groups. To cover all of these in one chapter would be an impossible task. For this reason we shall be highly selective in what we choose to examine. We shall look first at the NUT and its attitudes towards educational inequality and the policy case studies examined in chapter 2. Our justification for this is that it is by far the largest and most influential of the teachers' unions, and it has immersed itself in policy questions beyond those of pay and working conditions far more than have the other unions, including its closest rival the National Association of Schoolmasters and Union of Women Teachers (NAS/UWT). We shall look then at the Campaign for the Advancement of State Education (CASE). Because it is the most general and most universal in its coverage, it is the most interesting of the pressure groups from our point of view, though admittedly it is in some respects atypical just because of this. Neither CASE nor the NUT have shown very much interest in post-school education. For this reason we have excluded this — our last case study — and have concentrated on the other four.

The main difficulty we have faced in examining the role of the NUT and CASE in promoting equality in education is deciding what constitutes valid evidence. In the case of the NUT we have concentrated on an analysis of the content of its publications during the 1960s and 1970s and on conference resolutions and any other public statements of its position. We have not tried to piece together the less public activities in which the Union may have been involved, such as planted parliamentary questions or private meetings with Ministers or DES officials. One of the problems in relying on content analysis of the kind we have undertaken is that it focuses on printed comment. Absence of comment may itself constitute evidence too; so may all kinds of behind-the-scenes activities. Sometimes evidence may conflict. For example, in the written evidence that the NUT sent to the Tenth Expenditure Committee,[1] it suggested that it had a great deal of influence on policy-making. Yet in the oral evidence it gave to the same Committee it listed a number of examples of its lack of influence! As far as CASE was concerned, we were not able to rely as extensively on publications or even unpublished documents. While we were able to undertake a content analysis of its one regular publication, it was necessary to fill out the information thus provided with informal, unstructured interviews with members of the executive. Earlier documents had not been systematically filed and therefore provided a somewhat incomplete basis for reaching any conclusions.

In spite of the methodological difficulties just described, our view is that although there may be some disagreement about our interpretation in places, we have nevertheless sifted and presented enough evidence to be confident that our arguments are supported by the facts.

THE NUT

About half Britain's teachers belong to the NUT. The proportion of *unionized* teachers who belong to this particular teachers' union is, of course, higher. It draws its strength in particular from primary school teachers, most of whom are women, although the executive has tended to be dominated by male headteachers. At the secondary stage over the last twenty years it has lost some ground, in membership terms, to the NAS/UWT, which has substantially increased its members. However, in spite of the growing strength of the NAS/UWT and the growth in importance of the specialized associations such as the Secondary Heads' Association, few would deny the continuing predominance of the NUT. Yet there are a number of other teachers' associations, several of which have considerable strength. This lack of unity sometimes reduces the power of the NUT to influence policy. Indeed, the NUT, particularly under Sir Ronald Gould, a previous General Secretary, has favoured the creation of a single teachers' organization. Gould himself wrote in the early 1960s: 'If the administrative power in education which was once diffused is now being concentrated in the Minister, then the power of the teachers, which is at present diffused, should be concentrated too'.[2] But unity has not taken place, and the NUT's view that the teachers' potential influence is consequently dissipated still stands. However, the major disagreements between the teachers' organizations tend to focus on the handling and content of pay negotiations and conditions of service, not on questions of general educational policy. On such policy questions the NUT, largely because of its size, tends to have a near-monopoly when it comes to public statements. It is also rather more widely represented on various bodies directly or indirectly concerned with the making of educational policy than are the other associations. However, the DES consults them all on many questions of policy and consults, too, individual associations whose sectional interests may be at stake. Thus it certainly does not have an exclusive relationship with the NUT. In this sense the NUT might be accurately described as *primus inter pares* among the teachers' organizations.

It is difficult to trace the NUT's influence on educational policy. Ronald Manzer has described[3] the existence of an 'educational sub-government' in which the various parties, the DES, local authority associations and teachers' unions consult, bargain and negotiate until an educational consensus emerges. Much of this discussion takes place privately between officials. In certain circumstances, however, Manzer suggests,

> bargaining inside the education sub-government may break down and the participants have to appeal to the political system at large for a settlement. For educational pressure groups in England and Wales such an appeal is usually made with a 'public campaign'. The public campaign is an exceptional event in the politics of the education sub-government, however; and, in general, access to political as opposed to administrative arenas is definitely of secondary importance for all the groups in the sub-government.[4]

The methods that the NUT employs to influence policy are various. They include direct dealing with departmental officials, deputations to Ministers, planted parliamentary questions and membership of official working parties. At any one time it is likely to be represented on nearly a hundred bodies, including various unofficial groups as well as the more formal official ones. By this means it may exercise considerable influence on policy questions, sometimes obtrusively but, more often than not, in an unobtrusive way. It works through an extensive network of contacts, bringing pressure to bear on those with power or influence to get its views on a wide range of matters accepted. For example, there are a number of ex-teachers in the House of Commons, especially in the Labour Party. Moreover, the NUT actually sponsors several MPs. One instance of rare direct and visible NUT influence on educational developments is cited by Manzer. The publication in the early 1960s of a pamphlet entitled *Fair Play for Our Primary Schools* sparked off a parliamentary debate on the neglect of primary schools and probably contributed to the setting up of the Plowden Committee. For the most part, the process is less visible and, as a consequence, open to a variety of possible interpretations.

The degree to which the political arena is used may have grown somewhat in recent years, however. In the climate of rapid growth in educational expenditure which existed throughout the 1960s and the early 1970s there was less pressure on the teachers' unions to move out of the charmed circle of negotiations between the DES, the local authorities and themselves. Like Manzer, Coates argues:

Their [the teachers' unions'] additional reliance on parliamentary pressure and the mobilization of public opinion are secondary forms of behaviour (in which not all participate to the same degree), whose purpose ultimately is to affect the terms of reference within which that consultation with the Department takes place.[5]

Since the mid-1970s, however, the almost automatic assumption of high growth that existed before has been challenged by the circumstances. The harsh combination of public expenditure constraints, a declining birth rate and some disenchantment with the importance of educational expansion to achieve economic growth or redistribution has meant that cosy discussions about how best to spend a growing budget are over. There are already signs that to defend what they have already, all the teachers' unions are resorting to a more public and political role. Moreover, a concentration on fighting to retain the *status quo* may well detract from attempts to redistribute. It may also be the case that the DES has somewhat changed its style. The Department now consults more widely through the publication of Green Papers and consultative documents of one kind or another. This widens the debate beyond the 'education industry', makes it more public and may also serve to push the unions into a more overtly political arena.

Another aspect of the NUT's political position is its relationships with the major political parties. Manzer argues:

> on the whole the relationship between the Union and the parties is deeply inhibited, reflecting the low temperature of educational politics, the disinclination of the Union to become involved in party politics and the irrelevance of party educational policy to the overwhelming amount of national educational policy.[6]

In taking this point of view, he ignores the much closer connection the Union has with the Labour Party than with the Conservative Party and overstates the 'irrelevance' of party policy to national educational policy. Although it is true that there is some caution about identifying too closely with one or other political party (many of the union's ordinary members are Conservative voters), there is little doubt that most of the union's senior officials have an affinity with the Labour Party. Their contacts with Labour Members of Parliament, with members of the Labour Party's National Executive Committee's sub-committee on education and with Labour Ministers are likely to be closer and more extensive than those with their Tory equivalents. The Union's executive clearly draws its members from a range of political opinion. Two of its more prominent members over the last two decades have been members of the Communist Party, and there have been Conservative as well as Labour presidents. However, in general it is fair to say that the Union's political position has been to the left of centre rather than to the right, in terms of both its leadership and the policies it espouses.

This has implications for the stance that it is likely to take upon most questions of educational equality. The union is likely to attach some importance to achieving greater equality in general and, more specifically, greater equality through education. The Labour Party is committed to change in order to bring this about, while the Conservative Party on the whole is not, and Labour policies on education have been more in line with NUT policies than have Conservative educational policies. The Union has tried to influence the policies of both parties in government in order to create more equality. Its advocacy of certain policies may, however, have less to do with its commitment to such an ideal and more to do with self-interest. Cynics might argue that any espousal of greater equality has as much to do with trying to expand the system to create more jobs and more opportunities for promotion for teachers as with trying to improve the opportunities of certain groups of children. The real test comes, perhaps, when self-interest and moves designed to create greater equality conflict with each other. There are special tensions which are peculiar to 'professional' unions. On the one hand, they wish to represent the interests of their members with respect to pay, job opportunities and working conditions; on the other, they wish to be a responsible and influential force in the pursuit of wider aims concerning professional standards which they perceive to be in the national interest.

The rest of this section will examine the view that the NUT has taken of some of the relevant policy areas, namely, nursery education, positive discrimination, the abolition of selective schools and the raising of the school-leaving age. In so doing, it will from time to time touch on the professional/union conflict.

The union has long espoused the case for education for children under 5. Since the early 1960s it has produced several documents on the need to expand nursery schools and classes. The first of these involved a survey of maintained nursery education, carried out in 1962. It found that all the nursery schools in the sample, and most of the nursery classes, had long waiting lists. More than half of the schools had more names on their waiting lists than pupils in their schools. In the period leading up to the creation of the Plowden Committee, the Union was the first organization to emphasize the large gap between demand for, and supply of, nursery places and to stress the need to close the gap. In its own evidence to Plowden it recommended that nursery education should be available at the age of 3 and that 'there should be a statutory obligation on the local authority to provide facilities on the scale necessary to meet the full demand for such education in its area'. It explained the need for nursery education partly in terms of 'waste of ability' and 'differences of opportunity between one area and another', commenting particularly on the importance of the child's linguistic environment:

'Of all the cultural inequalities that widen the differences between child and child, it is the richness or poverty of its early linguistic development which demands most attention.' It went on to say that 'an adequate nursery-school system and the provision of infant school education from the age of 5 are both indicated if there is to be equal educational opportunity for all our children.'[7]

The emphasis was thus clearly on nursery education as an equalizer. There was no direct reference to its developmental role in early childhood outside the context of the elimination of inequality or deprivation. Although the references to cultural and linguistic disadvantage now seem crude and simplistic, they reflected the conventional wisdom of the time. Reference was made to work done in other countries, notably the USA, 'with its negro problem', and Israel, 'with its problem of the oriental Jewish immigrant'. There was also reference to high levels of provision in France, in spite of a later start to compulsory schooling there. The union's evidence rightly pointed to a third of 3-year-olds and two-thirds of 4-year-olds at school in France in the early 1960s. In an attempt, presumably, to draw the Plowden Committee's attention to the importance of employing fully trained teachers with this age group, it wrongly stated that French teachers in nursery schools had the same training as those in elementary schools, preference being given to those who had taken a special section concerned with very young children. In fact, although this was true of some French nursery teachers, many did not have the same training as primary teachers. Instead they took a more practical course with lower entry requirements and, probably, lower status.

The evidence also referred to the need to help parents of deprived children because of the strong link between early nurture and later ability to benefit from schooling. Interestingly, however, the document did not advocate bringing parents into the nursery schools but suggests instead the expansion of services available to mothers through child welfare clinics and education for parenthood in the secondary school curriculum. This may simply have reflected the view that intervention should take place only before the child starts school, or indeed before the child is even thought about. It may also have reflected the union's wariness of proposing that parents should be brought into the schools on a large scale. It did, however, suggest that informal contact between parents and teachers were important elsewhere in the report. It backed Parent-Teacher Associations but sounded a note of caution about their development replacing these informal contacts.

The document concluded by stating: 'we have emphasized but not, we think, over-emphasized the social role of the primary school as the great provider of equal opportunity for all our children.' To achieve this, it argued that it was essential that children should enjoy 'the benefits that highly skilled and therefore highly trained teachers can confer'. It went on to warn against any possible departure from this desideration for purely economic considerations.

To some extent, the Plowden Committee made just such a departure. It recommended a major expansion of nursery education along the lines proposed in the NUT's evidence, so that eventually it would be available for all children whose parents wanted it. However, the expansion was to be staffed in part by nursery assistants rather than entirely by fully qualified teachers. There would be a minimum of one teacher per two nursery classes, and the nursery assistants would work under her supervision and guidance. In its public response to Plowden, in a document in which it commented on the major issues of the report, the union said nothing about this recommendation. Indeed, its comments on the nursery education proposals were confined to three sentences. However, in its private negotiations with the Labour Government at the time the latter was considering the Plowden Report's recommendations, it strongly opposed the proposal to staff the expansion partly with nursery assistants. In a relatively recent series of lectures on aspects of government, Shirley Williams castigated the NUT for doing so.[8] She had been a Minister of State at the DES at the time and argued that the union's opposition prevented the Government from expanding nursery education at a time when there were still serious problems with teacher supply in primary schools, as well as constraints on public expenditure, making the cheaper nursery assistants doubly attractive. She put this forward as an example of the undesirability of excessive secrecy in British government. Had the union's opposition been made public, there would, she implied, have been a public outcry, which would have greatly strengthened the Government's hand in innovating in a way which the union opposed. Alternatively, the union might have been more constrained to avoid the embarrassment of public criticism. How far this was true is, of course, a matter for speculation. It is, however, hard to escape the conclusion that in this case the union's legitimate concern with the interests of the teaching profession was in some conflict with its desire to expand nursery education in order to equalize opportunity for all children. The case that no expansion was better than some expansion partly staffed by nursery assistants was and is hard to sustain. However, it can perhaps be understood in terms of a dilution of the quality of the professionals working with young children at the time when emphasis was being placed on imposing higher standards through, for example, longer and more demanding training.

The union persisted in its opposition to the employment of nursery assistants in the 1970s. In a comment on a DES Draft Administrative Memorandum on their employment, it stated that its attitude was governed 'by its long-standing policy that all teachers in primary and secondary schools, including nursery schools, should be qualified teachers'.[9] It went on to say:

> in welcoming the expansion of nursery education, [the union] was concerned that such expansion should not result in an increase in the number of unqualified persons employed as teachers in nursery schools and classes. Indeed this is one of the reasons why the union object so strongly to the proposal of the Secretary of State to cut down the number of places in colleges of education.[10]

It also continued to advocate nursery education expansion in order to alleviate inequality throughout the decade. It issued four different pamphlets. The first was a survey of nursery education in Wales.[11] The Welsh report stressed the importance of giving priority to areas of social need. Consistent with the Welsh tradition of an early start to primary education, it recommended provision from the age of 2. This was followed by another pamphlet on pre-school provision in England and Wales.[12] The pamphlet was marked by its attack on playgroups. By this time the playgroup movement had become an established form of provision rather than just a stop-gap, which was how it had been perceived in the 1960s. Moreover, it had a number of powerful advocates. Bridget Plowden had retracted from the commitment of her Report to nursery classes on the grounds that the participation of parents was crucial and that this could be more easily achieved in playgroups. A. H. Halsey, whose action research studies in educational priority areas had examined the work of playgroups,[13] was also giving them his support partly because of teacher opposition to parental help in schools. The NUT appears to have been willing to accept them as long as they were seen as a temporary expedient. As soon as they became more than this, it took a different view.

In a 1977 publication, *The Needs of the Under Fives*, the union again criticized playgroups, although perhaps a little less forcibly than before. It argued:

Playgroups are not educational establishments, and as voluntary organizations rely predominantly on fees charged and occasional grants from local authorities, nor can they always draw on the advisory help of local education departments. Playgroups are not established on the basis of nationally agreed criteria, nor do they all belong to the Pre-School Playgroups Association. This results in an haphazard distribution and great differences in the quality of the service and accommodation provided. The Union is concerned that little attempt has been made by either central or local government to monitor the standards and quality of playgroup provision.[14]

It went on to say:

The Union recognizes that the expansion of nursery education in the context of priorities for deprived areas means that there will continue to be a role for playgroups, particularly in more favoured areas, as an interim measure, while nursery education is being expanded. Nevertheless, we consider that there is a very real risk that any allocation of resources to playgroups would be prejudicial to the interests of nursery education and so to the children themselves.[15]

As far as the NUT was concerned, playgroups were second-best, stop-gap measures. This was partly because of a genuine belief that standards are higher where professionally trained staff are employed and partly, no doubt, to protect the role and status of nursery teachers.

Not only did the NUT oppose the expansion of nursery education using nursery assistants rather than teachers, but it also criticized the 1971 White Paper's proposals to expand provision by attaching nursery classes attached to primary schools.[16] It also criticizes the White Paper for failing to allocate sufficient financial resources to nursery education, claiming that it would cost more than anticipated.

Whether the union was correct about this or not, in general such criticism may well be counter-productive when governments are under severe public expenditure constraints, since it may serve to discourage them from expanding at all rather than encourage them to provide further funds. The union then argued: 'we strongly disagree with the almost total exclusion of nursery schools from the proposed provision.' It admitted the advantage of nursery classes, particularly that of greater continuity, then went on to claim that nursery schools had many advantages too. However, the only one it cited was that nursery classes were likely to be accommodated in mobile classrooms or in inadequately converted infant classes. Any objective observer would regard this as a somewhat weak claim for nursery schools. In fact, the real reason for the NUT preference for nursery schools was its belief that they provided better promotion prospects for nursery teachers. Although it did not reveal this in the 1974 document, it made the point quite clearly in *The Needs of the Under-Fives:*

> The Union believes that authorities should seek to ensure that nursery teachers have an opportunity to obtain promotion without necessarily having to apply outside of the nursery sector. This requires a restoration in the balance in the programme so that the number of places in nursery schools and nursery classes is nearly equal.[17]

Since nursery schools are considerably more expensive than nursery classes, their development might well have slowed up the expansion of the number of available places. This is another example of a conflict in the union between its goal to promote opportunities for its members and its genuine desire to obtain more nursery provision, especially for the disadvantaged child.

One further example of this concerns its views on parental participation, which have already been touched on. In the 1974 document it argued:

> Teachers welcome parental support and are prepared to put their training and experience at the disposal of parents. Nevertheless, we see dangers in that it may be assumed that such community of interest confers an unqualified right upon parents to intervene in the educational function of the school as and when they see fit . . . teachers are responsible for the welfare of all children and have to

hold a balance between the needs of the individual and the community, in a way parents do not normally have to bear in mind. The Union therefore believes that the Department of Education and Science and the local education authorities should give proper emphasis to this responsibility, and that they should institute further consultation on this matter with the teachers through their professional associations.[18]

Its attitude to parental participation was thus somewhat grudging. By 1977, however, its attitude seemed to have softened, although it is not clear why. In a section on home-school relations it endorsed parent education, suggesting guidance 'in techniques directed at the development of cognitive and perceptional skills'. The union also claimed: 'it is vitally important that all parents are conversant with techniques in child development and can make assessments of the child's progress.' It also reported, with apparent approval, the Red House project in the West Riding action research study,[19] where parents worked with small groups of children in the nursery school and accompanied them on neighbourhood visits. However, the union also warned that 'a lack of professional expertise among these adults can cause more problems than are solved', although it did not elaborate on how this happens.

The union has backed nursery education for many years, however. While in its 1977 statement it advocated expansion to meet the developmental needs of all children, it has consistently advocated priority for the disadvantaged child in the interests of equality and has castigated the DES for failing to provide the resources for this. In its response to the DES 1977 Green Paper it disputed the DES claim that there had been a big expansion in nursery education, rightly stating that it had been limited and uneven and advocating 'further substantial investment in this sector of education'.[20]

One of the more radical policies put forward over the last twenty years has been that of positive discrimination in education. The concept was first propounded by the Plowden Committee. The Committee had been influenced by the Poverty Program in the USA, which was trying to channel resources in the direction of the deprived or disadvantaged by a variety of different means. Under this influence, Plowden coined the term 'positive discrimination' and recommended that an attempt should be made to reverse the disadvantages suffered by various groups by discriminating in their favour in certain ways rather than against them, as normally happened. The development of positive discrimination is described in greater detail in chapter 5. It suffices to say here that it involved providing extra resources for certain schools (in the first instance, mainly primary but, later, secondary as well), mainly in the poorer areas of large cities. The policy was thus based to a large extent on a geographical theory of poverty, which emphasized the concentration of low incomes, low skills, poor housing, poor amenities and low educational standards in the inner city. The educational remedy centred on the idea of educational priority areas. Such areas would benefit from extra money for school building, and certain schools within these areas would be designated as schools with special needs operating in circumstances that became known in some LEAs as conditions of 'exceptional difficulty'. These schools would be given extra resources, including staff, and their teachers paid a special allowance. The main aim of the social priority allowance was to encourage teachers to remain in such schools and thus reduce the high teacher turnover which characterized these schools at the time. Lastly, the nursery education expansion programme was to give priority to areas with special needs.

In its published response to the Plowden proposals the NUT welcomed the principle of positive discontinuation, stating 'this has always been a feature of our educational system as applied to children with physical and mental handicaps, and we fully support its extension to those children whose deprivation is of a social, emotional and linguistic nature.'[21] The union also accepted that priority areas should have primary school classes reduced to thirty or below before other areas, though it emphasized the need to make the reduction universal. The union made surprisingly few other comments in this document on positive discrimination and priority areas. However, on the related subject of the integration of the school with the local community, to which Plowden attached particular importance in priority areas it took a more protective union stance as far as the teaching profession was concerned. Although accepting the need for close school-community links, the union stated: 'we believe that it could be unreasonable to base proposals of this kind, which might make inroads into the teacher's private life in excess of that required from other members of the community, on the assumption that they would be universally adopted.'[22] At the time it was also both complacent and half-hearted about the community use of school buildings. It argued that this was already 'not uncommon', and went on: 'many teachers have accepted the inconveniences arising from the dual use of buildings. We suggest, however, that the analogy of maximum utilization of industrial plant cannot be applied to a living community like a school . . .'[23]

The Plowden proposal for teachers' aides to help out teachers in the classroom was regarded with unequivocal hostility by the NUT. Again this was a reflection of the union's belief that teachers are the only adults suitable to work in the classroom with children and its wish to avoid a possible loss of status for teachers which might result from an inadequate definition of the boundaries between the roles of teachers and aides. However, opposition of this kind seems likely to have reduced the chance of increasing the manpower resources available to work in disadvantaged schools at that period, so it could be argued that the NUT's line did a disservice to those children it claimed it wished to see helped. In its anxiety to preserve the teacher as the only trained person working with children in the classroom, the union also opposed Plowden's proposals for the extension of training opportunities for aides. Instead it preferred on-the-job training in areas such as first aid and the maintenance of equipment for ancillaries. Since adults working in primary schools are bound to have a fair amount of direct contact with pupils, even if they never play formal pedagogic or instructional roles, the case for their understanding of children and their needs is a strong one. The NUT can therefore again be accused of failing to act in the best interests of pupils.

The recommendation to pay teachers in priority areas an extra allowance posed problems for the NUT. In its published response to Plowden it made no reference to this proposal, possibly because of divisions which existed within the union. One view held by some officials of the union was that it would have been better to allocate the extra funds to the schools rather than to teachers' salaries. Banting suggests:

> even before negotiations began, the representatives of both the teachers and the local authorities indicated coolness towards it. The NUT, however, was the major stumbling block. During the 1960s the union's primary goal was a much higher basic salary scale and it was not happy about the endless variety of special supplements that were

regularly proposed. They felt that such differentials created trouble-
some distinctions between teachers and drained away resources from
a higher basic scale.[24]

On the one hand, the proposal meant higher pay for teachers and, if
the policy worked, more and better teachers in areas of need and
lower teacher turnover there. On the other hand, it meant more pay
for only a minority of teachers. Hence the measure was seen as
potentially divisive within the profession and, possibly, as unpopular
with the majority of the union's members who would not benefit
from it. Moreover, difficulties about defining and identifying schools
in priority areas would probably have meant rough justice for some
teachers doing demanding jobs in poor areas in schools which just
missed qualifying for extra help. In the event, the union's initial
resistance to this recommendation declined, and it accepted a
modified version of the Plowden proposal. However, when the 1974
Labour Government wished to replace it with the Social Priority
Allowance for teachers, the union was again opposed on principle.
It argued that it was educationally unsound to channel extra
resources to deprived areas by this method (see chapter 5 for a
further discussion of these matters).

Racial minorities in Britain are not only at a disadvantage because
their members are concentrated in the lower socio-economic groups;
they are also at a disadvantage because they suffer from
discrimination. Another form of positive discrimination has been
the use of legislation to provide extra resources for schools with
high proportions of immigrant children. Under Section 11 of the
1966 Local Government Act, local authorities are able to claim 75
per cent of the cost of the staff who are employed to make special
provision for 'immigrants from the Commonwealth whose language
or customs differ from those of the indigenous community'. Any
local authority is eligible to make this claim if 2 per cent or more of
its school population are the children of Commonwealth immigrants.
In July 1978 the NUT issued a report which was critical of the
operation of this legislation.[25] Its criticisms were based on a survey
of local authorities, which revealed that the amount of grant claimed
varied enormously between authorities and that it bore little
relationship to the number of immigrants within their boundaries.
It also showed that staff employed under Section 11 were frequently
not being used to carry out specific tasks to help minority-group

children. Indeed, some headteachers did not even know that they had Section 11 staff.

The union put forward a number of positive proposals to improve both the Act and its implementation. These included abolishing certain limitations (such as those that restricted the application of the Act to people from the Commonwealth and those resident in the country for less than ten years) to take in all minority groups and some constructive suggestions on how much extra staff might be used. Among them were recommendations to use liaison officers between the community and the schools, to create education visitors to visit homes and to provide more resources for the teaching of English. It could be argued that in backing amendments to Section 11 and more effective use of the legislation, the union was in the enviable position of being able to support change which would benefit disadvantaged children and would also provide staff in schools 'extra to establishment' and thus benefit the teaching profession. In this case there was no conflict of interests. However, some of the NUT's proposals for use of Section 11 staff were unlikely to have a direct impact on reducing the burdens of the classroom teacher. It would therefore be unduly cynical, and rather unfair, to argue that this was the union's main goal with respect to Section 11.

A further report was produced the following year[26] in response to a Home Office Consultative Document on replacing Section 11 of the 1966 Local Government Act. This welcomed some of the Home Office's new proposals and reasserted the NUT's view that ethnic minorities must be given high priority in educational programmes within a wider strategy to deal with racial disadvantage. The second report confirms the view that the NUT has played a positive role in trying to improve educational opportunities for ethnic minorities.

There is further confirmation of its consistently concerned record in this area in two other publications. *All our Children,* published in 1978, summarized the way in which the union believes schools can contribute to a tolerant multi-racial society. In its conclusion it recommended that all teachers should 'champion the cause of social justice for all students in their classes, schools and communities'. It also suggested that the schools could and should be seen as agents of racial harmony. In this context it lacked a curriculum that recognized cultural diversity in schools. One practical outcome of this was a Schools Council project on need and innovation in multi-racial education, which the NUT proposed along with the National Foundation for Educational Research and the National Association for Multi-Racial Education. There was, however, a touch of complacency about the document's definition of the role of the school when the NUT quoted from its own evidence to the 1973 Select Committee on Race Relations: 'our educational system [is] non-discriminatory in intention and in fact.' The union went on to explain the fact that children separate into different minority groups as they get older and become more ethnically aware, or indeed intolerant, in reaction to pressures in the wider society. Such pressures are undeniable but do not mean that the educational system has nothing to answer for with respect to discrimination against minority groups. There was, in fact, no reference in this document to the need for positive discrimination towards minority group children. The DES argued at the time that general policies towards the disadvantaged would benefit black and brown children. The Department tended to down-play the extra dimension to the social and economic disadvantages from which these groups often suffer. Possibly to avoid stigmatization, it argued that policies should be geared not specifically towards minorities but towards the disadvantaged generally.[27] While the NUT did not actually say this, its omission of any reference to positive discrimination for ethnic minorities could mean that it accepted the DES line. However, it is perhaps dangerous to interpret lack of explicit comment as acquiescence. All the indications, including its strong stance on Section 11, are that the NUT has favoured positive discrimination for ethnic minorities.

One way in which the DES decided to tackle disadvantage was to found the Centre for Information and Advice on Educational Disadvantage. This was set up in 1975 as an independent body to promote good practice. The union gave the new centre strong backing in *All our Children.* However, it did not say anything in this pamphlet about its potential role with the disadvantaged among ethnic minorities. When the new Conservative Government took office in 1979 it embarked on an attempt to reduce greatly the number of QUANGOs. Although it was not especially successful and the great majority of QUANGOs remained intact, the Centre for Educational Disadvantage was one of the victims. The NUT roundly condemned the Government for its decision to close the

Centre. Max Morris, an ex-president of the union and vice-chairman of the Centre claimed that its valuable work on ethnic minorities and the 20 per cent of the school population who get no qualifications would be wiped out.[28]

The second document which demonstrates the NUT's commitment to minority groups is *Race Education and Intelligence: A Teacher's Guide to the Facts and the Issues,* also published in 1978. This pamphlet was commissioned by the NUT from biologists and psychologists at the Open University, including Steven Rose, a well-known critic of Jensen's and Eysenck's theories about racial differences and levels of intelligence. The pamphlet set out clearly for practising teachers the arguments against assuming any biological basis for differences that may occur. How much influence a document of this kind has is, of course, impossible to assess.

The third area of policy in which we wish to examine the NUT's position over the last fifteen years or so is the abolition of selective schools. The development of this policy is fully described in chapter 6. It is a policy that the NUT has forcefully advocated since the mid-1960s. Prior to this there is not much evidence of extensive NUT initiative to promote this cause. The reason for this is unclear. It perhaps reflects a tendency by the union to support certain changes when they become part of the political agenda rather than to fight for their inclusion on the agenda in the first place.

It was not until the election of a Labour Government in 1964 that the union apparently considered it worth devoting much time to the advocacy of comprehensive schools. In that year it published *The Reorganisation of Secondary Education.* This seems to have been designed as much to demand that certain conditions, such as adequate accommodation, should be fulfilled in the reorganization schemes as to make the case for reorganization. It was no doubt issued in an attempt to influence a new Labour Government not to proceed too fast *if* that meant that schemes would not be backed by extra resources and teachers would not be extensively consulted about the planned changes. The same year the NUT submitted its evidence to Plowden. In a long section on the transition from primary to secondary education it made its case for comprehensive schools. This case was not based on the socially divisive effects of failing to provide a common schooling for all at the secondary stage; it was based instead on the harsh effects of selection and failure on individual children and on the distorting effects of the 11-plus examination on the primary school curriculum. The emphasis was on psychological and educational matters rather than on the broader social and political implications of different forms of schooling, and the document listed

> the unreliability of the final results, the strain on the child, the tendency for the success of the school and its teachers to be judged by the number of children who gained places in selective schools, the inequalities resulting from coaching and homework and the effect on those children who failed the examination, and who suffered a loss of confidence and acquired a feeling of resentment as a result.[29]

The document argued that even where the methods of selection had been chosen with great care in the interests of maximizing fairness and reliability, many of the undesirable effects of selection remained. It recommended a system in which the primary school assessed the child and made a recommendation but considered that even this would not 'abolish completely the strain on children and parents'. Reference was also made, however, to the fact that secondary schools vary in the provision of amenities, standards of staffing and equipment, as well as in function: 'Such a position can be defended only on the assumptions either that some children do not need or deserve as good an educational opportunity as others, or that the nation cannot afford to find the money or the manpower to equalize opportunity.'[30] Both of these assumptions, it was implied, should be rejected.

A careful reading of the NUT's evidence to Plowden leaves little doubt that the union was in favour of the abolition of selection at the time. However, its view was often expressed in an oddly muted way. Whether this reduced the impact of what it said is hard to say. One example of its reticence and caution is as follows. The Plowden Committee had asked in its list of questions for those giving evidence whether selective education was desirable. In its reply the NUT said, 'In some ways we regret that we are called upon to answer the question at this particular time.' Because some authorities had already begun reorganizing 'in a very hasty and ill-considered way', decisions about this question were in some ways too late, it argued. At the same time, in some ways they were too early, it claimed. It was hoped that effects of Plowden's recommendations, including demonstration of the potential of all children, would help in the battle to persuade parents and teachers of the effect of environment upon the educational development of children (a surprising admission). This needed more time. In the light of all the evidence on this subject already available at that time, this is a strange statement. However, perhaps the findings of research had not yet percolated through to many teachers.

Although there is no doubt about where the union stood on this issue — it was in favour of comprehensive schools — its advocacy of the abolition of selection was certainly cautious and pragmatic rather than uncompromising and idealistic, perhaps because it was anxious to ensure that the reform would work. Its advocacy of change was hedged about with preconditions, notably those concerning buildings. Much emphasis was placed on the need for purpose-built accommodation. Constraints on new building were accepted as a reason why the tripartite system should continue in some areas. There are two possible interpretations of why the NUT placed so much emphasis on school buildings. The first is that it was anxious that comprehensive schools should succeed and therefore insisted that, for example, schemes which put together two schools on different sites should be avoided. There was not, however, much evidence to support the importance that it attached to buildings. The second interpretation was that it was primarily concerned with the job opportunities and working conditions of teachers and was anxious to protect these even at the risk of slowing down the development of comprehensive schooling. There were certainly fears that the senior posts in comprehensive schools would all go to ex-grammar school teachers and that ex-secondary modern teachers would suffer accordingly. After the publication of Circular 10/65, which invited local authorities to submit plans for the reorganization of secondary education, the NUT's house journal, the *Teacher,* came out in support of the Circular.[31] However, the editorial also criticized the Government for failing to provide extra money, which it claimed could delay the exercise by up to thirty years. It also indicated concern that reorganization would be at the expense of primary education, stating, 'the inequalities that the present tripartite system tends to encourage find their first beginnings in the primary school.' As many of the union's members were primary school teachers it was presumably politic to say this. However, if the Government had acted upon the criticism, there would have been even fewer resources for comprehensive schools and therefore, on the NUT's own argument, an even greater delay in establishing the new system.

By the end of the 1960s the NUT had adopted a tone of greater urgency about the implementation of secondary reorganization. Possibly fearing the return of a Conservative Government, which might have stopped further progress towards comprehensive schools, it began to demand legislation to enforce reorganization on local authorities. At the 1969 Conference it passed a resolution calling on the Government to provide the necessary money and to legislate in order to bring about comprehensive education. From then on practically every annual conference of the NUT has passed a resolution on comprehensive schools. During the 1970s there were only three years when such a resolution was not passed, and the topic was the subject of resolutions more often than any other. This perhaps indicates better than anything else the degree to which, by then, the NUT attached importance to the issue in spite of a somewhat cautious position earlier. Moreover, many of the Conference resolutions were phrased in terms of a belief that the comprehensive principle is the only basis for providing equal opportunity for all children. And by 1977 the demand was for 'an immediate end to all forms of selection'. Two years later Conference instructed the executive to encourage the membership to refuse co-operation in selection procedures. By the end of the 1970s, then, the union was taking a fairly militant position about selection.

Several possible reasons can be postulated to explain this change. First, the political climate was marked by a sharpening of the debate. With each change of Government there was an immediate attempt to change the policies of the previous Government. The NUT was drawn into this debate and could not easily sit on the fence. Second, there was probably a change in the general attitudes of the NUT's membership: teachers trained in the 1960s were exposed to educational research which demonstrated that social as well as academic selection was taking place. Third, dissatisfaction over the fairness and reliability of selection methods had probably grown.

Beside Conference resolutions, there are three documents, published between 1969 and 1979, which reveal a certain amount about the NUT's position on reorganization. One of the ambitions of Edward Short, who was Secretary of State for Education during the latter part of the 1966-70 Labour Government, was to produce a

new Education Act to replace the 1944 Act. His hopes were not
fulfilled. However, he did prompt others to think about what a new
Act should contain. Among them was the NUT, which produced a
document entitled *Into the Seventies,* in which it put forward its
ideas. In the introduction it made clear its views about the essentially
regressive nature of educational expenditure. The more privileged
the pupil, the more money is spent on him. Second, it identified
wastage.

> The outstanding characteristic of the system is its profligate waste of
> ability. There is waste of ability before the child enters school, waste
> at 11 +, waste at school leaving age . . . The present distribution of
> educational resources still very often means that the 'haves' receive
> positive discrimination in their favour, while the 'have nots' lose even
> the little that might be theirs.[32]

It went on to propose that the new Act should legislate for
comprehensive education over the whole of the compulsory age
range. It defined comprehensive education not just as a non-selective
system but also as a system in which each school has a
representative cross-section of the full ability range, and it admitted
that legislation might not be enough to secure this. It recognized
that it might also be necessary to limit parents' choice of school.
Since most parents have never been able to exercise such a choice, it
did not consider this restriction unacceptable. It also argued that
the advantages of comprehensive schools far outweighed the
disadvantage of some limitation of choice.

The second of the documents mentioned above addressed itself
specifically to attacking the Conservative Government's slowing
down of the process of going comprehensive in the early 1970s. In a
pamphlet provocatively entitled *What is Mrs Thatcher up to?* it
launched a personalized attack on the Secretary of State for
Education. It was more 'political' than any previous statement on
this subject published by the union. One of the devices it used was
to quote from Conservatives who had either made speeches or
written articles in support of comprehensive schooling. Lord Boyle,
a former Conservative Minister of Education was frequently quoted.
There were also quotations from Edward Heath and Rhodes Boyson,
at that time a comprehensive school head and since a Junior Minister
at the DES. The introduction noted that in successive deputations

to Mrs Thatcher when she was at the Department of Education the Union had failed to persuade her to change her policy. She was damned with faint praise for having proceeded with the raising of the school leaving age and the allocation of extra money for building primary schools but scornfully reproved for 'the outdated nature of her attitude and the harmful effect of certain of her decisions' on secondary education. She was tellingly contrasted with Lord Boyle, who was described as having shown 'a deep awareness of the way in which the organization of secondary education had to be reformed'.

The fact that many Conservative as well as Labour councils had rejected selection in favour of comprehensive schools was emphasized, and reference was made to the fact that in Margaret Thatcher's own constituency of Finchley a referendum of parents produced a four-to-one majority in favour of ending selection. The fact that 1000 comprehensive schools had been approved by the DES during Thatcher's term was attributed to the fact that she was unable to find any good reason for turning down LEA plans to establish them. The accusation was made that she used delaying tactics, that in some cases she gave only partial approval, thus leaving some authorities with a messy mixture of grammar and comprehensive schools and that she had no clear criteria or guiding principles for her decisions. The fact that grammar schools could not exist alongside comprehensive schools without the latter being no more than 'misnamed secondary schools' was stressed, with a quote from Rhodes Boyson saying just that.

What is Mrs Thatcher up to? is an example of political pamphleteering at its best. It is cleverly conceived, punchy and persuasive. If Mrs Thatcher were the kind of politician who could be embarrassed by attacks of this kind, it might have succeeded in making her feel uncomfortable. The third of the 1970s NUT pamphlets, entitled *Education in Schools,* which touched on secondary reorganization is in a quite different style, perhaps because it was published in a different political context. It listed and briefly commented on the main recommendations in the Government's Green Paper, *Education in Schools* (1977). This Green Paper followed the 'Great Debate' which was stimulated by the speech of the Prime Minister, James Callaghan, at Ruskin College, and it covered a wide range of issues. One of its many recommendations concerned secondary reorganization. It stated that comprehensive reorganization must be completed, though it was self-congratulatory about the substantial progress so far and went on to argue that what was needed in the wake of reorganization was a period of stability during which standards might be improved. The pamphlet questioned the Government's claims about the extent of the achievement so far. It suggested that although 75 per cent of pupils were nominally in comprehensive schools, this figure exaggerated the true proportion. It included pupils in schools where only those in the lower forms were in 'comprehensive' classes because of the recent nature of reorganization. It also included pupils in comprehensive schools which were coexisting with selective schools. The NUT went on to urge the implementation of the 1976 Education Act requiring all authorities to submit plans for reorganization. Only then, when recalcitrant authorities had been brought into line, would the period of stability be justified.

Thus by the end of the period we are considering the union was strongly committed to the abolition of selective schools, in strong contrast to its slightly tentative position a decade or so earlier. Its position on the raising of the school-leaving age to 16 seems to have been strong and consistent advocacy of it from the early 1960s. Some might argue that adding an extra compulsory year to secondary education greatly increased pupil numbers and therefore the demand for teachers, so that the union could hardly have advocated anything else. However, some teachers' organizations, notably the NAS, strongly opposed raising the leaving age significantly, to the detriment of existing pupils and their teachers. The NUT did not accept the arguments of the other associations. In a short paper stating its view of the issue the union explicitly attacked the argument that resources should be directed towards those who want to learn rather than those who are unwilling. It pointed out:

> views not so very dissimilar were being expressed a hundred years ago, when the principle of compulsion was being applied for the first time at a much earlier age. But more important, the fact that teachers were aware of the hostility of some of the present leavers, against the school and its ethos, should be taken as a criticism of our present attitudes and methods, rather than as a reason to welcome the departure from school of such youngsters at the earliest possible opportunity.[33]

It is difficult to detect exactly what position the NUT took on the question after the Crowther Report was published in 1959 recommending that the school-leaving age should be raised. However, once the Government had announced in 1964 that it would implement the recommendation, the union was active in encouraging preparation for it and in demanding extra resources for buildings, staff, in-service courses and curriculum development. However, its commitment to raising the school-leaving age was not sufficiently influential to prevent the Government from deciding in 1968 to postpone the measure by two years, from 1970-1 to 1972-3, as part of a package of public spending cuts. The NUT's Annual Conference in 1968 adopted a resolution deploring the decision to delay implementation. Among the reasons cited were that it would 'deny opportunities to underprivileged children' and would 'delay the satisfactory reorganization of secondary education', as well as restricting 'the output of better trained and skilled manpower'. Thus it emphasized both redistribution and manpower requirements. Voluntary staying on, which had increased, was thought to be insufficient; moreover, those who left early were most likely to be those who had already suffered other social disadvantages.

After this the union concentrated on the problem of how to implement the change, dismissing as irrelevant any further discussion of whether it should be introduced. It carried out a survey of all LEAs to find out what was being done to prepare for the raising of the leaving age and published its findings in a pamphlet entitled *16: Raising the School-Leaving Age*. The pamphlet claimed that many authorities complained of being hampered by inadequate resources, and as a consequence the union pleaded for greater generosity on the part of central government. However, it went on to say that there were substantial differences between LEAs in the quality of preparation, which had little to do with resources. One of the less obvious issues it touched on was the influence of examinations on the secondary school curriculum. The retention of all pupils until they were 16 would require that more thought be given to the examination system, though few authorities had apparently considered this. Finally, the pamphlet foresaw that the raising of the school-leaving age would strengthen the case for abolishing two separate systems of school-leaving examination. This is a policy which the union advocated as early as 1970 and has strongly espoused since then.[34]   One of the reasons it put forward in favour of a common system was that it would remove 'the divisive element implicit in the present dual system'.[35] In backing five years of compulsory secondary education for all children, the union did not explicitly anticipate the need for completely different forms of assessment, such as pupil profiles, which would be required if a substantial minority of pupils were not to be left without any form of paper qualifications whatsoever on leaving school.

The union's position on the raising of the school-leaving age can be summed up as the conventional liberal progressive one, which backed the measure strongly as a means of extending opportunities to less privileged children. Disparities in staying-on rates between different social groups and different parts of the country could be wiped out by this means. It did not question whether the extension of compulsion was desirable in principle. It did not consider whether the most obvious alternative method of extending opportunities in this age group — the expansion of part-time education for 15-18-year-olds, possibly on a compulsory basis — might be a more desirable use of the resources. It was, however, hardly in the NUT's interests to do so. The union represented schoolteachers, and the alternative policy would have meant expanding the further education sector rather than the secondary schools.

In this chapter so far we have examined the position that the NUT adopted on the key issues of policy designed to create greater equality, which we examine in greater depth later in the book. What conclusions can we draw about the NUT's influence? As we said in the introduction to this chapter, it is not possible to prove influence. We can only speculate on the basis of the fairly limited evidence we have available.

What we have said has been based largely on an analysis of NUT publications and Conference resolutions. What is difficult to ascertain is the impact of such publications. Who reads NUT pamphlets? How many people read them? How seriously are they taken by policy-makers in central and local government? How far do they influence ordinary NUT members? Are the members' attitudes and practices modified as a result of reading these pamphlets? If so, presumably this will have some indirect effect on policy formulation at the local level, and possibly at national levels, insofar as the teaching profession as a whole, rather than just its representatives, is seen to be strongly opposed or strongly in favour of particular changes.

Another important question is how closely the public position taken by the union in the pamphlets it produces accords with the position it takes up in the private negotiations it enters into with central government in particular. When attempting to put pressure on the Government through deputations to Education Ministers or through private discussions with senior officials, it may adopt a stance slightly different to the one it adopts publicly. It may feel able to take a more self-interested position than it would if its views were exposed to public scrutiny. In some circumstances the reverse may be true. It may feel more able to advocate policies in the interests of children, parents or the nation, rather than simply in the interest of teachers, when it is not exposed to its own members' scrutiny. Whichever is correct, it must be emphasized that the extent to which the union can privately depart from the public position it takes must be constrained. If it did so frequently and extensively, it would rapidly lose credibility with the 'insiders' in the decision-making process and would probably eventually lose some of its influence.

Where the union does adopt a somewhat different position in different contexts, this may not necessarily be the result of a cynical disregard for the principles of consistency and integrity. It may be because there are genuine differences of opinion between different sections of the union. So far we have assumed homogeneity. In fact, as in all large organizations concerned with political and policy issues, there are differences of opinion which are sometimes of a serious kind. Most of the work that goes into NUT publications is done by full-time officials, mainly in the Education Department. This work is scrutinized by members of the executive and its committees before being published. Hence it often represents a consensus and may mask differences of opinion that emerge elsewhere. However, in spite of all these provisos, it seems reasonable to assume that the publications are a fairly accurate reflection of the union's general position and that they are read by those responsible for making policy, who have to take into account the likely response of the teaching profession as a whole and of the NUT in particular.

Apart from the example of the pamphlet on primary schools mentioned at the beginning of the chapter and the 1970 proposals for a common examination at 16, there is no other evidence of the NUT's actually initiating new policies in the areas we are considering. Its mode is, in general, responsive rather than initiatory. Its opposition to particular proposals, such as the partial staffing of nursery classes with nursery assistants, may serve as an informal veto. Its opposition to extensive parental involvement is another example. Its views on this are in part a function of strongly-held professional values about freedom and autonomy in the classroom. Professionalism of this kind has undoubtedly produced tensions when certain kinds of change have been advocated. As the *Schoolmaster* stated with respect to the Beloe Report, 'it has always been a source of pride to the profession, and a very proper one, that in this country the teacher has the unalienable right to decide what to teach and how to teach it, and insofar as he is the best judge of the child's readiness to learn, when to teach.[36] On the other hand, its continual backing of certain policies may help to speed up their implementation. Its espousal, if a little belated, of the abolition of selection at the age of 11 over a number of years may have helped somewhat to reinforce the introduction of comprehensive schools.

We suggested earlier that the union's position has been on the radical side of the political spectrum rather than the conservative. (One result of this is that its public stance may vary a little according to which party is in power). However, Manzer has argued that 'in promoting the education of working-class children the NUT was part of a general movement in British society to improve the condition of the working class.'[37] He suggests there was a social idealism that was shared by administrators and teachers alike during the post-war years. He does not give the union any special credit for espousing the cause of equality. On the contrary, he claims that the NUT

must now be regarded as a powerful conservative influence in the politics of English education. This conservatism is explained by the Union's traditional professional concern for the education of the individual, its refusal to sacrifice long-standing educational ideals, the distractions created by divisions inside the teaching profession, and the threat to the collective role of teachers in the policy-making process posed by a more national orientation and centralization of educational policy.[38]

Does this judgement stand up in the light of our analysis of the NUT's position on our four policy issues? What has emerged shows

the NUT as both idealistic and self-interested, both conservative
and radical. In certain respects it has dragged its feet, as a
consequence possibly reducing the educational opportunities of
working-class children. In other respects it has fought hard to
expand educational opportunities for the less privileged members of
the community. Its record is by no means unblemished, as we have
indicated. Nevertheless, Manzer's assessment seems a little too
sweeping and harsh.

THE CAMPAIGN FOR THE ADVANCEMENT OF STATE EDUCATION

We turn now to a different kind of pressure group: the Campaign
for the Advancement of State Education (CASE). It differs from the
NUT in every conceivable respect, except that it shares with the
union a commitment to improving the quality of state education and
to extending to more children the opportunities that offers. Its
influence and importance are small compared to those of the NUT.
It has few resources, a much smaller membership and no teeth.

Its origins may be traced back to Cambridge in 1960. Like many
pressure groups, it began when a small group of people formed to
try to resolve a particular problem. Parents of children at an
individual primary school were united by the poor provision offered,
and they attempted to persuade the local authority to do something
about it. They were surprised to be told that their children were
fortunate. The conditions at many other primary schools were
much worse. As a result, the parents set up a pressure group to try
to improve matters. It became known as the Cambridge Association
for the Advancement of State Education. One of its members wrote
to the *Guardian* expressing concern. Soon after this a similar group
was set up in Oxford, sparked off, as in Cambridge, by poor
facilities in a particular primary school. The first secretary in
Oxford was Peter Newsam, who has since become the Chief
Education Officer in London. By coincidence, both primary schools
were called St Andrews. What is probably less coincidental is that
the first groups were formed in the university towns of Oxford and
Cambridge. Both these cities have an uncommonly high proportion
of upper-middle-class parents, who attach great importance to
education and many of whom send their children to local primary
schools, even though they may opt out of the state system at the
secondary stage. They belong to a highly articulate group, undeterred

by the barriers put up by local bureaucracy, well-informed and therefore well able to complain to some effect. Soon after the Oxford group was formed, new groups began to spring up elsewhere, predominantly but not exclusively in the middle-class areas of big cities (Hampstead and Richmond) or in middle-class towns (Chester and Stockport). By the middle of 1962 there were twenty-six groups in existence, and in the same year a national joint committee for the advancement of state education was formed.[39] This became known as the Confederation for the Advancement of State Education. Each local association was to have autonomy but to be affiliated to the national association; affiliation fees were to be related to size. The policy of the central association was to be made by the Annual Conference, with a small executive to implement it. CASE has retained all these features since its origins.

Its membership is predominantly middle-class. Many of its most active members have had some professional interest in education. This is reflected in the present national executive of twenty people, whose members include three college of education lecturers, two university lecturers, a primary headteacher and two ex-teachers. As one member of the executive put it, CASE has attracted those members of the teaching profession who are critical of existing organizations and the level of resources provided to support them and who presumably believe reform can and should be promoted from outside the system.

CASE operates largely at the local level. In this respect it is unlike most of the other educational pressure groups, such as the Advisory Centre for Education (ACE), the Campaign for Nursery Education (CNE) and the Campaign for Comprehensive Schools (CCE), which operate mainly at the national level, or the National Confederation of Parent-Teacher Associations (NCPTA), which operates mainly at school level.

In CASE the role of the national executive is confined largely to supporting the local groups by providing them with information about what is happening, notably with respect to central government policy. Its main independent role has been to secure an annual meeting initially with the Secretary of State, now with the Minister, to pass on National Conference resolutions. However, it has decided recently to maintain a higher profile and to try to sharpen its impact by examining a series of central policy questions on which it will produce a national CASE line by focusing on a number of issues. In this way the executive hopes to increase its influence nationally, which up until now has probably not been very extensive. It is exceedingly difficult to measure such influence. The hope is that the policy papers which emerge from examining the issue will in future serve as guidelines for local associations. Whether the local associations accept them will be entirely up to them. The local associations are totally autonomous — a state which they jealously guard. Thus greater control by the national executive would probably be resisted and might provoke some local associations to opt out. Basildon did so, not so much on the issue of autonomy as on political grounds; it considered the national executive's position on the reorganization of secondary schools and on subsidies to private schools too left-wing.

This example highlights the problems of a pressure group of this kind. As long as it keeps a low profile nationally, without stating too clearly the policies it advocates, it is able to hold together in a loose-knit confederation a fairly broad range of local activists anxious to improve state education. As soon as it becomes more precise and specific about the policies it advocates, it may lose some of its support. CASE altered its name from Confederation to Campaign in 1979, partly to give itself a clearer, more forceful and more militant image. The organization as a whole had in any case suffered some decline during the 1970s. Its officers believed that the attempts of a new Tory Government to cut expenditure on education increased the need for a national voice lobbying for state education across the whole social spectrum. One of the activities that the national body initiated at this time was a lobby of Members of Parliament against the cuts. It also arranged a meeting on the 1980 Education Bill with the Child Poverty Action Group (CPAG) and various trade unions, including the National Union of Public Employees (NUPE), the NUT and the National Association of Teachers in Further and Higher Education, (NATFHE), to which it invited all Members of Parliament. Its aim was to point out to MPs the undesirable aspects of the Bill and to provide them with ammunition with which to attack it.

In spite of such activities, it remains true that CASE's activities are concentrated at the local level. During the 1960s the number of local groups grew substantially, so that by the end of the decade there were about 120. By 1974 this had fallen to 105 and by the beginning of the 1980s to sixty. There are two possible explanations for this decline. The first is that a number of local associations were set up to fight for the reorganization of secondary education in their areas. When this was achieved, they collapsed. The second is that the arrival of a Labour Government in 1974 seemed to herald a commitment to various advances in state education, so that in some places complacency led to the collapse of associations.

The size of local associations has varied considerably. Some have 150 members, others as few as twenty. The largest has well over 200. They are concentrated in the south of England. Their style appears to vary considerably from the militant and radical to the more timid and conventional. Some groups have tried to widen their membership to achieve a broader representation of the community; many have remained strongly middle-class. Particular battles sometimes bring in a wider range of members. The campaign to retain the Inner London Education Authority (ILEA) was one example in the London area. Many parents did not want to see ILEA broken up and some of them were persuaded to join CASE, which was campaigning against the dismemberment of the authority.

Lack of funds has frequently been a constraint on activities at both local and national levels, as is the case with most pressure groups of this kind. Voluntary effort keeps the organization going. However, a small, non-renewable grant of £3500 per annum for three years was obtained from the DES in April 1979, which helps to pay for a part-time executive officer. The executive does not appear to believe that this will reduce its independence in any way. Another source of funds is the Home and Schools Council. This body was formed by CASE, ACE and NCPTA to publish pamphlets. Because of the political nature of its work, CASE cannot be classified as a charity, which reduces its access to funds. One way round this problem is to set up a separate charitable arm, whose brief is to seek additional funds mainly in order to carry out research. This happened in 1980. The presence of a number of different educational lobbies, all seeking funds, parallels in certain respects the existence of a number of different teacher unions. One proposed solution to the dissipation of effort that may take place is for a number of the pressure groups to get together and to share a simple set of premises, thereby reducing overheads and increasing contact between them. So far lack of capital has prevented this. A single building would not mean a single educational pressure group pursuing the expansion of educational opportunities. Many of those involved would advocate a more pluralistic system rather than the unification of CASE, ACE, CCE and CNE into a single body. However, a reform of this kind would probably reduce some duplication of effort, although it would leave out organizations such as the National Association of Governors and Managers (NAGM) and NCPTA, because their private-sector members would make them unacceptable to the other pressure groups.

CASE has attempted to co-operate rather than compete with these other pressure groups, although it is difficult to assess how successful it has been in this respect. Mutual suspicions do exist. For example, CASE has been suspicious of the consumer-orientated ideology of ACE and believes that ACE has been over-concerned with what it believes to be fringe issues, such as corporal punishment or the unavailability of school records to parents, as compared with the more important issues of the under-resourcing of education, the divisive nature of much of the educational structure and the lack of positive discrimination. ACE, for its part, has been suspicious of CASE, particularly on the grounds that it has not been critical enough of the teaching profession or of its authoritarian and secretive approach adopted in relation to parents. However, these suspicions have not prevented a certain amount of collaboration, nor have they prevented CASE from continuing to work with the teachers' organizations where possible. It does so because it believes that reform and advance are difficult without teacher commitment. There has been considerable antagonism between CASE and the NUT at certain times, however, notably on the issue of parent participation in the reform of school government. On the other hand, on such matters as the state's buying places in the private sector and cuts in educational expenditure there is strong agreement, so the Assisted Places Scheme is a target which brings the NUT and CASE together. Collaboration between rather different types of pressure groups, such as CASE and the NUT, is based in part on exchange and reciprocity.

In this particular exchange CASE is much the less significant partner. There is a sense in which it needs the NUT, but the NUT does not need CASE: that is, the NUT is one of the bodies CASE wishes to influence, whereas the reverse is not true to anything like the same extent.

The methods employed by CASE to get its views known and

accepted are similar to those used by other pressure groups. From the centre it publishes three times a year a newspaper, *Parents and Schools,* which is circulated to about 3000 subscribers. Rather surprisingly, it does not send this to those whom it is trying to influence. Its role, therefore, appears to be primarily to provide information and guidance for local members. Recent editors have started to devote themselves to particular themes, such as exemplary comprehensive schools, which demonstrate good practice across a number of different areas. The national officers of CASE try to make themselves generally available to the media and to respond to journalists positively. They write letters to the national newspapers. As already indicated, they meet the Minister for Education once a year. They lobby Parliament and have given evidence to the Select Committee on Education. CASE also submits evidence to government inquiries into education, and in the case of Plowden and Taylor two of its active members were appointed to the Committees.

At the local level the tactics are similar: letters to the local press, the use of local radio, public meetings, petitions, pressure on education committee members, discussions with chief education officers and their colleagues. Some local associations have also carried out surveys of various aspects of education. Three recent examples serve to illustrate this. In 1979 Oxford CASE carried out a survey of mixed-ability teaching in the middle age range.[40] It provided the facts about the extent of streaming, setting and mixed-ability teaching for 9- to 12-year-olds in Oxfordshire schools, which responded and listed the reasons given for different forms of organization. It made no judgements about the findings. The introduction to the report said: 'this report will provide a factual basis for informal discussion on the methods of organizing teaching at the middle age range in schools. We also hope that it will encourage parents to inquire about the system in use at schools their children are attending or are likely to attend.' In 1980 south-west Surrey CASE produced a pamphlet providing basic information about all the secondary schools in Guildford, in the hope that it would be 'useful to families moving into the area, to parents with children at middle schools, and all those interested in education generally'.[41] It is the kind of document that a local education authority might be expected to distribute to parents at the time of their children's transfer to secondary education. The third document is rather different. It is an attempt by the St Albans association to document the effects of cuts in the education budget during 1979-80. All the heads in the St Albans area were interviewed and their responses collated for each sector. The pamphlet concludes that 'basic educational standards, supposedly preserved despite budgetary cuts, have *already* fallen, particularly for children in need of remedial help.' It goes on to say:

> there will be increasing discrimination against children in poorer families because they may not be able to pay for services which have historically been provided as an integral part of their education. Since they will probably attend schools in poorer neighbourhoods, they will be at a great material disadvantage — soon.[42]

It is a much more political document than the other two. It implicitly criticizes the Government and the local authority, and it makes judgements about the quality of the education being provided.

The documents reveal the dual role of CASE at the local level. On the one hand, it is an information-providing service for parents, increasing knowledge and 'raising consciousness' about education. On the other hand, it is a campaigning body setting out to explore undesirable aspects of education and to fight for improvements. Some local associations appear to emphasize one role rather than the other; others seem to try to fulfil both roles, sometimes a little uneasily. The more traditional concentrate on uncontroversial activities, particularly in the sphere of home-school relations. These include holiday play schemes, 'meet the head' meetings, parent help on school outings and governor training. Some of the newer CASE groups born as a result of the cuts are more inclined to campaign directly in association with local branches of the NUT, NUPE or CPAG. The stance the national executive takes is to try to emphasize the organization's campaigning role. This is embodied in a policy statement produced in 1979, in which it listed its main aims. These included pressing for greater involvement of parents in education; campaigning for the abolition of the remaining forms of selection for secondary education and for the establishment of a 'genuinely comprehensive system'; campaigning for the extension of co-education; and pressing for the furtherance of community schools. It advocated the development of programmes to prepare young people for adult life and opposed corporal punishment, compulsory religious education and all subsidies to independent schools from public money. In its overall goal of increasing the quality and size of state education, CASE aimed to press for increased public expenditure in this area. It stated that it would campaign for higher expenditure on deprived areas, better provision for handicapped children, more opportunities for the education of children under 5 and for young people in higher and further education.

Thus its aims cover a wide range of educational issues. Undoubtedly, throughout the history of CASE two issues have been of dominant concern. These are the reorganization of secondary education and parental participation in education. It has sometimes been seen as a parents' group,[43] partly because of the emphasis it places on the second of these issues. However, as already indicated, professional educationalists are fairly prominent on its national executive committee, and it counts a substantial number of teachers among its members, although it is not possible to be precise about the numbers and how many of them are also parents. It asserts that it is not a parents' organization but welcomes as a member anyone who is dedicated to improving state education. Nevertheless, parent participation in decision-making has been one of its most important causes, which unites its members, unlike some of the other issues it has espoused, which have caused some dissension. One of its most prominent members over the years became a member of the Taylor Committee on School Government, where she fought for strong representation on school governing and managing bodies.

We will return to the issue of secondary reorganization below. Before discussing CASE's activities in this area, we will look at its position *vis-à-vis* the other case studies we have selected. In spite of its general backing for the expansion of nursery education and its inclusion of this in its list of policy aims, CASE does not appear to have given nursery education very high priority in its campaign activities. The existence of another pressure group exclusively devoted to this question may be the explanation. One of the difficulties CASE has faced in this area has been uncertainty about where it stands on the question of pre-school playgroups. The hard line or purist position has been to back state-financed and state-run nursery schools and classes and playgroups. But CASE draws many of its members from just the kind of social group which has been most prominent in the playgroups movement — middle-class mothers. Also its commitment to parent participation places it in a dilemma when it is argued that playgroups are model organizations in this respect. It is an area which demonstrates quite well the loose relationship between CASE at the centre and its local associations. The national executive has strongly backed state nursery education; many of the local associations have flirted a great deal with playgroups. In its guidelines the national executive gets round this as best it can. Guideline No. 6, on the early years of schooling, says:

> We recognize the valuable part played by pre-school playgroups, but do not consider them to be a substitute for adequate and properly equipped state provision. Some play groups have developed a high degree of parental involvement, and our ideal would be to see all under-5 provision fully involving parents on the lines of the best practice in both playgroups and nursery schools at present.

There is little evidence that CASE has advocated nursery education as an equalizer. In a leaflet entitled *The Kind of Nursery Education CASE Wants,* it lists 'many more nursery classes' but only points out that the first five years of a child's life 'are vital for his or her future development'. In a series of information sheets produced as guides for parents, one on nursery education is included.[44] Again, it concentrates on the developmental advantages of nursery education for all children rather than its social role for the less privileged sectors of society, although it makes passing reference to the needs of children in depressed neighbourhoods.

There is also relatively little reference to the Plowden policies of positive discrimination in CASE documents. Leading members of the national executive admitted when interviewed that this was partly a reflection of the organization's middle-class membership and the concentration of local associations in middle-class areas. 'Even nice people do not like giving up privilege' was the way one of them put it. The complexity of many of the issues involved in making positive discrimination work renders it a difficult area on which to campaign for a group such as CASE. Some of its own members have criticized the organization for mouthing the right sentiments but doing very little. One aspect of positive discrimination, to which it devoted an article in *Parents and Schools* in spring 1979, is multi-cultural education. It comments that both Section 11 of the 1966 Local Government Act and the Urban Programme 'were devised rather hurriedly'. Its criticisms of Section 11 are similar to those of the NUT: no monitoring of the use of additional staff appointed under it, no money for capital expenditure, too narrow criteria in the allocative procedure. It goes on to urge that the highest priority should be given to resources for multi-cultural education and lists various policies to improve it.

In the early years of its existence CASE backed the raising of the school-leaving age. However, it was not a policy for which CASE fought very hard. As one executive member put it, 'It swam with the tide.' Once the decision had been made, it did advocate thorough preparations, including an overhaul of courses to ensure that they would be an appropriate preparation for adult life. In a Parents and Schools Information Sheet[45] it reported on an essay competition on the extra year that the Richmond local association had organized for the first group of children affected. It wrote up their responses, which strongly emphasized a demand for vocational education, for more practical information about various aspects of adult life such as family finance and work experience. Its findings thus confirmed those of the earlier survey by the Schools Council.[46] It ought to be asked what purpose their publication would serve in a series of guides to parents, most of whose children would stay on at school anyway. We can only speculate that their inclusion in the series was to help persuade such parents that a purely academic curriculum for all 15-year-olds was not what was required.

It seems unlikely that CASE has had much influence in three out of four of our case studies. They are not issues on which it has joined battle very often. The last of them, secondary reorganization, is quite a different story, however. The reason why CASE has attached so much importance to this is not altogether clear. One suggested reason is 'agonized liberal consciences' among the liberal-radical membership. (If this is correct, it is hard to explain why these consciences have not been active with respect to positive discrimination.) It is possible that at least a minority of CASE members have had children or friends and relatives with children who failed the 11-plus and whose dissatisfaction with what secondary modern schools were offering has been vociferous. Among the more radical members there has been criticism of the 'old-fashioned' curricula of the grammar schools and a belief that comprehensive schools would offer a better education for all children, including their own, who were at or would go to grammar schools. The simple explanation is that the reorganization of secondary education on comprehensive lines has arguably been the most important issue facing state education during most of the period of CASE's existence. It is hardly surprising that an organization dedicated to improving the quality of state education for *all* children should have devoted a good deal of attention to it.

National CASE committed itself to supporting and fighting for a policy for a fully comprehensive system in 1966, about the same time as the NUT started to push hard for it. Since then it has campaigned consistently to achieve this. In 1971, perhaps rather surprisingly late in the day, it produced a Parents and Schools Information Sheet, *Going Comprehensive.*[47] This answered a series of questions which might have been put by doubting parents, such as 'What is wrong with the old system?' 'Why destroy the grammar schools?' 'Won't comprehensive schooling mean levelling down?' It also listed a series of points which parents might use as a check list when looking for a good comprehensive school. Its newspaper, *Parents and Schools,* has given the issue coverage. For example, it compiled a two-page item in 1976, at the time the Labour Government's legislation forcing LEAs to comply with the Government's policy in this area was going through, which included a progress report on the number of schools and authorities going comprehensive, implicit support for the legislation, as well as some criticism of various local anomalies in comprehensive schemes. More recently, CASE has produced a series of short discussion papers on various policy issues. One of these was on selection. It argued that selection is wrong because no tests can accurately measure a child's intelligence, because 'it is a competition for an arbitrary number of places available locally' and because it damages children's self-esteem and wastes talent.

> In some areas 'comprehensive' or 'all-ability' schools exist in name alongside selective practices. This is an abuse of language, since any schools which co-exist with a selective system are secondary moderns, whatever they are called. In some areas, like Kingston, the 11 + has become 'optional' which as well as adding social to academic selection, puts cruel burdens on the consciences of parents who are opposed to selection and therefore also opposed to second-rate alternatives.[48]

However, it is the local associations that have probably

campaigned most successfully for comprehensive schooling. Indeed, as suggested earlier, the decline in the number of local associations is partly a reflection of success in the area. Once an authority had decided to reorganize, for some members the main purpose of the association had vanished, and they drifted away, leaving behind a core which was not large enough to sustain the association's continuation. Nevertheless, a number of the most successful of the local associations have continued to exist. Perhaps the best example is Richmond. In what is a relatively right-wing Tory authority with a large middle-class population, the local CASE battled for a comprehensive system over a period of several years. It can justifiably claim that, along with Richmond Parents' Association, it got the authority to move from non-action to action, and the submission of plans, using a variety of tactics. These included persistent lobbying of councillors and officials and extensive exposure in the local press. Its success was based partly on its committed and determined leadership and partly on the breadth of its support. Its membership has been larger than that of most other CASE local associations. Success on one issue often spills over to others. Not only has Richmond CASE fought successfully for comprehensive schools, but it has also campaigned with success for the reform of school governing bodies (organizing a successful day training course for governors) and for the much more extensive consultation of parents.

In conclusion, there is little doubt that CASE has espoused the cause of greater equality in education. CASE believes that every child has a right to the facilities he needs to achieve his best. Those who start with disadvantages need more from schools. There are strong pressures in our society to concentrate on a 'quality education for a few', but 'we have paid dearly in the past for our failure to educate the majority', stated a CASE handout prepared for the 1979 election. It went on to say that CASE should urge 'extra help on a scale never before contemplated for schools in areas with special difficulties, so that children who most require it, for whatever reason, get more individual attention and learning aids'. These quotations reflect the national organization's general commitment to the cause of greater equality. They do not, of course, indicate how much campaigning effort has been put into pursuing them. We have suggested that of the four areas of policy we identified, CASE has not pushed very hard to initiate policies of positive discrimination, but it has fought hard to establish comprehensive education. This is also the area of policy in which it has had the greatest success.

Its very success in this area in a number of local campaigns has perhaps posed problems for it. For example, in certain local authorities, especially where Labour is in power, there have been invitations to CASE to put forward someone to take a place as a co-opted member of the education committee. Recognition of this kind is, in certain respects, a demonstration of success. Yet where such invitations are taken up CASE may become part of the local 'establishment', thereby losing its independence and capacity to criticize, thus jeopardizing its future success as a campaigning pressure group. Rick Rogers points to a rather different kind of problem that success may bring. He suggests that CASE has failed to capitalize on past success, notably in comprehensive reorganization, through a failure to identify other important issues so that local associations faded away.[49] He also suggests that middle-class loss of confidence in certain aspects of comprehensive schools, and thus in state education, may have contributed to the relative quiescence of CASE in the second half of the 1970s.

A Conservative Government bent on major cuts in educational expenditure may well change all this. It is possible that cuts will provide the rallying force needed for CASE to expand its network of local associations and their membership. It is possible that it may again become the source of considerable pressure in certain local areas, this time on the matter of cuts. There are signs that in this context it will collaborate with the NUT more than it has in the past to try to make any pressure that it exerts more effective. The more the local associations do this, the more likely it will be that any existing gaps between them and the central organization will close.

Both CASE and the NUT seem likely to go on being part of what Kogan has called 'the progressive consensus'. On past evidence neither seems likely to be innovative, in the sense of producing new ideas about educational policies which may enhance equality. The NUT has, however, probably had some impact in advancing existing policy proposals which have not yet been implemented. It may also act as a constraint on the introduction of other policies which it perceives to be in conflict with its general commitment to equal opportunities. Similarly, on a much smaller scale CASE has had some impact in certain areas in forcing local authorities to advance more quickly or to change the substance of their policies. But the influence of these pressure groups remains fairly small compared with the power wielded by central and local government on the policy areas with which we are concerned. However, as Maurice Kogan has eloquently put it, 'the sources of policy generation are so difficult to locate, let alone place in any logical pattern, that detecting the changes in values, or the pressures by which change is effected, is more a matter of art than of analysis.'[50] We take up some of these questions again in chapter 9.

4

Nursery Education

From its earliest origins in the nineteenth century right up to the present day, nursery education has been advocated as a way of increasing equality. It has always been conceived by some people as an important method of providing an environment in which the small child from a poor or deprived home can flourish; and insofar as the child flourishes, he acquires benefits which place him at less of a disadvantage in relation to his more privileged peers. There have been other motives, of course. These include child development, improving young children's health, supporting evacuation and releasing women for work, especially in wartime. These have often taken precedence over the arguments concerning equality, which in any case have often been addressed rather indirectly. When the time has been ripe to develop nursery education for other reasons, then the advantages it has in promoting greater equality have been cited. One of us has described at length the early development of nursery education, including the philosophical assumptions upon which it was based and the social and economic context which helped to shape it.[1] There is no need to rehearse these arguments here. Instead we will concentrate on defining the various ways in which it may increase equality in its present-day context. Having done this, we will examine in some depth the history of recent attempts to expand it and consider to what degree the policies have failed and why they have failed.

After some years of neglect from the late 1940s right through the decade of the 1950s, during which it was on the agenda of hardly any discussion about policy developments in education, nursery education re-emerged as an important issue. The turning-point was in the early 1960s. The rediscovery of poverty in the affluent society, and of child poverty in particular, and the dilemmas created by immigrant or minority groups judged to be underprivileged led to a search for methods to alleviate these problems. Nursery education was one of the remedies prescribed. It was argued (and still is) that it can attack the problems 'before it is too late'. In the early to mid 1960s, forms of pre-school provision began to be introduced on a large scale as part of the Poverty Program in the USA. A new programme, with the catchy title of Operation Headstart, was introduced on a nationwide basis. Its aim was to bring what were sometimes described as 'culturally disadvantaged' children into the schools before starting compulsory schooling. Entrance to the programme was based on the size of the family income. A great deal of emphasis was placed on recruiting minority-group children such as American blacks and Puerto Ricans. The programme began in a small way, in that they were confined to six weeks during the summer before the child started elementary school. However, they were eventually extended to run throughout the year, some children attending for as long as two or even three years. Later follow-through projects were introduced in the elementary schools. These American developments were influential in Britain, and led to demands for nursery education to help the poor and their children. Some emphasis was placed on the role it might play in improving the educational performance of this group.

These developments coincided with demands from middle-class women for nursery provision for their children. This demand was associated, among the educated and informed sectors of the population, with a growing awareness of the importance of a child's early years for his later development. It also coincided with the first stirrings of the revived feminist movement. The number of women graduates and of women with other forms of higher education and training was beginning to grow. Some of these women were not content to spend their entire time looking after their young children without an opportunity to pursue their own interests, whether at home or in the labour force. We will discuss pressure of this kind more fully below. Before doing so, we turn to the question of the role of nursery education in relation to the pursuit of equality.

There are several different ways in which nursery education might be conceived as a method of increasing equality. First, by simply exposing all children to a similar environment during the day, with similar material facilities and similar adult/child interactions, the great differences in their home environments will have a lesser impact. Second, some children are compensated for the vagaries or inadequacies of their home environments through the provision of extra facilities which are not made available to other children. Third, all women are released from the care of their young children for part of the day, which gives all mothers more time to do other things. Fourth, by allowing some poor and deprived women to work who otherwise would find it difficult to do so, lower family incomes may increase and draw closer to average incomes. Fifth, it increases the resources allocated to the non-selective part of the educational system, which is open to all, in relation to the post-school system, which is provided for a minority. How far these various methods do in practice contribute to increasing equality depends on many factors, including the actual form and quality of the provision made. It is worth while to discuss each of them in turn.

The uniformity of environment argument, if it is to be valid, must rest on the assumption that all of the children entering this shared environment will be equally able to benefit from it. In practice, it seems unlikely that this happens. Some children arrive, for example, with superior speech and language skills, superior physical co-ordination, more confidence or all of these. This may enable them to make better use of equipment and material designed to stimulate their intellectual and physical development and may increase their ability to attract the attention of teachers and other adult staff and to take up their time. The old story that privileged middle-class children may get more out of the educational system than some of their less well-off peers may apply as much to nursery education as to other stages; in fact, it may apply more, because of the informal and relatively unstructured style of teaching which, some have argued,[2] favours middle-class rather than working-class children. Nevertheless, in spite of potentially differential benefits for different groups of children, leading to a failure genuinely to equalize their environments, it may at least reduce inequalities somewhat. Thus if all the children were at home, the differences between their environments could be even greater. Moreover, the capacity of some of them to benefit from *primary* education might be smaller, (relative to others) without some pre-school provision than with it. Insofar as parents are also involved in the nursery experience of their children, some of them may learn more about their children's needs and how to respond to them, so that gaps between the awareness and responsiveness of different groups of parents are narrowed. Of course, if there is participation and learning only by those parents whose skills are already greater than others, the gap could widen rather than narrow. Last, it must be said that since much nursery education takes place on a part-time basis, for a small part of the day, the uniformity of environment case is weakened.

This brings us to the second way in which nursery education might increase equality. What have become known as 'compensatory programmes', offered only to certain designated categories of children may achieve this. Thus the majority may be excluded in order to allow those for whom the programme is designed to catch up. The concept of positive discrimination (see chapter 7 for a full discussion of this) is relevant here. Extra resources may be provided for certain areas, or certain schools, or even certain children. Criticisms have been made of the assumptions that are said to lie behind the notion of compensatory education. For example, it has been claimed that it treats children as 'little deficit systems',[3] when the real problem lies not in the individual child but in his treatment by society as a whole. This may well be the case. The question then becomes: can education do anything to alter the way in which society shapes the individual? As has already been made clear, the assumption on which many of the arguments in this book are based is that it can. It interacts with other influences and, in so doing, can play a role in modifying eventual outcomes. The aim of compensatory education becomes, in the light of this, to try to make up for deficiencies in the social system rather than in the individual. This does not necessarily mean that it cannot work through the individual. It may try to make up for some of the constraints and limitations imposed on that individual by his social circumstances rather than to correct for failings in him which can be ascribed to some fault or faults of his own.

If this is accepted, the next step is to consider whether nursery education is a viable form of compensatory education. Perhaps its greatest advantage is that it is not already provided on a universal basis, as are primary and secondary education. In principle at least, it could be expanded to provide for those most in need, excluding others thought to have a lesser claim. However, this would give rise to serious problems of a practical and political kind. There would be problems of defining and then identifying those most in need, and there would probably be vociferous protest from those excluded (namely, middle-class parents), who would generally be more articulate and would have more political clout than the deprived for

whom the service was being provided. The problem of how to
discriminate against the privileged is immensely difficult. It applies
to many other social services besides nursery education and is one
to which policy-makers and those who administer such services
have given too little attention. It may nevertheless be necessary,
however difficult, if the goal of greater equality is to be achieved.

One way in which nursery education might be able to play a
compensatory role more easily than could education at a later stage
is by providing full-time provision for the needy and part-time
provision only for the rest. This might reduce the political problems.
However, it would rest on the assumption that extending the hours
in which some children received the service was effective as a
method. That in turn would depend, at least in part, on the quality
of what was provided during those extra hours.

Finally, even if the problems of identifying the group and
providing the additional compensatory education were overcome
and gains were made by the children concerned, whether they were
intellectual, physical or emotional, there would remain the question
of whether they were lasting. Clearly, this would be rather unlikely
if no effort were put into following through the compensatory
programmes in the primary schools. Much effort — often
unsuccessful — has gone into trying to measure longer-term effects.
The findings are inconclusive, partly because of wide variations in
the results and partly because it is not in any case possible to come
to a firm conclusion because of the limitations of the measurements
used. In spite of these provisos, there is scope, certainly in theory
and probably in practice, to use nursery education to provide
compensatory programmes. Moreover, there is a case for judging
these programmes in terms of their immediate effects on parents'
and children's lives as well as the harder to measure long-term
effects.

This brings us to the third way in which nursery education might
increase equality. Commentators on the role of nursery education
sometimes neglect its potential in equalizing the position of mothers.
It is clear that most women with enough money to do so hire some
kind of help so that they are not totally tied to their children twenty-
four hours a day, seven days a week. In the case of the rich, this
help takes the form of a full-time nanny. In the case of the well-off it
may take the form of an *au pair*. Middle-class women who are

unable to afford help of this kind often make reciprocal arrangements with other mothers and occasionally leave their children in
each other's care. Arrangements of this kind require some
organization, however, and a good network of close contact with
other mothers. The very fact that nearly all women with the financial
or human resources to do so make such arrangements suggests that
most women feel the need for some escape from their small children.
The use of child-minders by working-class women may reflect this
need as well as economic pressures on them to work.

There is other evidence to suggest that the all-day care of young
children can give rise to severe problems for their mothers. Work
done on a sample of middle- and working-class mothers in south
London[4] showed that a high proportion of those studied, particularly
in the working-class sample, were suffering from clinically defined
depression. Apart from such serious effects as this, many women
report that they are lonely, isolated and sometimes miserable while
at home caring for their young children.[5]

Nursery education can provide welcome relief for mothers of 3-
and 4-year-old children. How far it succeeds in creating greater
equality in this respect depends on how far it is able to give priority
to those with least access to alternative forms of support. If women
in this category are always last on the waiting-list, and therefore
have the smallest chance of securing a place for their children, once
again the gap between the haves and the have-nots may be widened,
but if the system is successful at providing sufficient information
about the service, and thereby increasing take-up by those with
need, it may be successful in narrowing the gap. There remains the
problem of women living in remote rural areas, but their numbers in
the UK are relatively small. Perhaps more important are the
problems of urban dwellers who live some distance away from their
nearest nursery class or school and are without their own transport.
A woman who has one or two younger children as well as a child of
nursery age may find it too difficult to get the older child to school,
especially if she has few contacts with other women in a similar
position who might share the task. However, potentially at least,
nursery provision should make it possible for all women who want
it to have some respite from the demanding role of caring for young
children, which is patently not the case at present.

The fourth way in which nursery education might increase

equality is by making it possible for certain women to go out to work. The growth of the two-earner family is a relatively recent phenomenon. One of its consequences is that in many families in which there is only one earner, the standard of living is low relative to the average. This is particularly likely to be the case where a single earner is low-paid; thus semi- and unskilled men with a wife and several children to support may well have incomes little above the so-called 'poverty line' or that of similar families living on supplementary benefits. The case of the single-parent family, in which there is by definition only one earner, may be even more acute because opportunities for overtime are restricted and because it is difficult to seek work which is located at any distance from home. The provision of nursery education may allow both single parents and the second earner in the two-parent family to seek outside employment and thereby increase the family's income. In so doing, it may incidentally produce some off-setting savings either in family income supplement paid to poor families whose heads are in work or in supplementary benefits paid when the parents are unemployed. In practice, however, as we shall see below, the nature of nursery education, much of which is provided on a part-time basis only, may make it impossible for a parent responsible for young children to go out to work because the hours that he or she is free to do so are too short. In addition to the nursery classes in schools run by education authorities, there are day nurseries run by social services departments which operate for a full day, but because the number of places they offer at present is so small, only a small part of the demand from single parents or low-income families can be met. In principle, however, there is no reason why such provision should not be expanded, whether it is offered by education or social service departments. If this were to happen, with priority again being given to those in greatest need, this form of educational provision could help to reduce material inequalities. It could also reduce the inequalities of a less material kind from which single parents suffer, namely, their isolation and lack of contact with the adult world of work and the community in general.

Last, in that nursery education is provided for all children rather than for a minority of children selected on the basis of motivation and ability, its growth may redistribute educational resources from the privileged minority to the majority. This, however, assumes that any expansion of provision is, at least in part, at the expense of education for the post-school-age group rather than at the expense of primary education and secondary education up to the age of 16. If it were at the expense of the latter, there would be no such redistribution. However, a transfer of resources from higher education would certainly be non-regressive. Now is an opportune time to effect this, since it is in any case being asked to contract because of the decline in the size of the 18- to 21-year-old age groups during the second half of the 1980s. Insofar as the system of pre-school provision is able to give priority to those in need, there will be an even greater redistribution than if it simply provides for all on an equal basis.

There are, then, a number of ways in which nursery education may promote equality, but, as has already been intimated, the form in which provision is made will influence how far it achieves this. The way in which the target population is defined and identified will also be important. The kind of experience provided, in terms of the content of education, the relations between parents and teachers and the length of the school day, is also likely to be significant. In the next section we examine policies with regard to nursery education over the last twenty years. We then evaluate what they have achieved, focusing in particular on how far they reflect a concern for achieving greater equality.

The post-war period up until 1960 was one in which, as we have already mentioned, nursery education was rarely discussed. Moreover, it was also a period when there was little or no growth or development. It culminated in 1960 with the issue of a highly restrictive Circular which forbade any expansion of the number of places in either nursery schools or nursery classes and stated:

> No resources can at present be spared for the expansion of nursery education and in particular no teachers can be spared who might otherwise work with children of compulsory school age.
>
> At the same time the Minister values the excellent work being done in nursery schools and classes, and is anxious to ensure its continuance, both for its own sake and as a base for expansion in the future when the time comes for a full application of the principles set out in the 1944 Act.[6]

Authorities were recommended to maintain existing schools and classes at their current level. In addition a recommendation was

made that some of the existing full-time provision might become
part-time, which would allow a greater number of children some
pre-school education:

> During and immediately after the war one of the main purposes
> served by nursery schools and classes was to release mothers of
> young children for work of national importance. To serve this purpose
> it was necessary for nursery education to be full-time. The Minister
> believes that it is now widely understood that nursery education, in
> common with all primary and secondary education of which it forms
> a part, is provided in the interests of the children. The aim is always
> to meet the needs of the particular child.[7]

This rejection of any expansion of nursery education was based
on the view that children of compulsory school age deserved priority.
It was a period of severe teacher shortage in the primary schools,
and it was believed that any restriction on growth in pre-school
provision would prevent the problem from becoming more severe.
In arguing that the development of part-time nursery education was
desirable, the Circular made assumptions that 'normal' children
from 'normal' homes would not need more than a half-day
attendance. This emphasis on part-time provision meant that the
needs of the disadvantaged were likely to be played down, if not
ignored, although a proviso was made that some children might
continue to need a full day at school, partly because certain mothers
would be 'forced by circumstances' to work.

The Circular continued to be applicable until two addenda were
sent out, the first in July 1964 and the second in December 1965.
Their effect was to relax the restrictions on the expansion of nursery
classes; new provision would enable married women to return to
teaching who would otherwise be prevented from doing so through
lack of provision for their own children under 5. It is clear that the
purpose of these addenda was not to improve the lot of certain
disadvantaged women and children but to reduce teacher shortages.
The children who would benefit directly would be privileged and
middle-class, with parents in the teaching profession. The basis of
the policy was to use nursery education as a method of freeing
women for employment, as had happened during the Second World
War.

The next important event in the development of nursery education policy was the publication of the Plowden Report.[8] Chapter 9 of the Report was devoted to the subject of providing for children before compulsory education. In discussing the case for nursery education the Committee claimed: 'There is a wide measure of agreement among informed observers that nursery provision on a substantial scale is desirable, not only on educational grounds, but also for social health and welfare considerations. The case, we believe, is a strong one.'[9] It went on to describe various aspects of modern life which had increased the demand for nursery education and which pointed to the need to respond to that demand. These included new forms of housing in large cities, the increase in geographical mobility, leading to fewer extended families, and the growing numbers of married women at work. Implicitly it was argued that there was a case for nursery education for all children, given contemporary social and economic conditions. However, it also went on to claim:

Finally, there is evidence on the special needs of children from deprived or inadequate home backgrounds. Some homes have positive disadvantages: children from families in overcrowded or shared houses, or from broken homes, or even children of obsessive mothers may have few opportunities for normal and healthy development. Early help is also needed for handicapped children and for those with physically handicapped parents.[10]

The Committee clearly held the view that compensatory education should be introduced for children of this age group. Various pieces of research were cited in the Report to support this view. However, the Report admitted that the research evidence was somewhat unsubstantial with respect to support for nursery education for all. Instead they had relied, they said, 'on the overwhelming evidence of experienced educators'. In accepting the conclusions of educational opinion about its value for all children, it is possible that unwittingly the Committee may have reduced its impact over the last decade in helping those most in need. It is perhaps unfair to blame the Committee for this, since the case for introducing nursery education for all children is a good one, and it did produce proposals designed to give priority to certain categories of children. Thus, whereas most provision was to be part time, 15 per cent of places for both 3- and 4-year-olds were to be full-time. Moreover, it was suggested that the expansion of nursery education should have priority in deprived areas. With hindsight, perhaps the Committee might have been more forcible in its proposals for deprived areas, suggesting, for example, that *all* expansion should have been in such areas until need had been met there. It might have put more emphasis on the need for local authorities to instruct headteachers to give priority to certain categories of children, both in existing provision and in new schools or classes, rather than relying on the child's position on the waiting list as the main criterion for offering places.

The Report suggested that places should be provided for 90 per cent of 4-year-olds and 50 per cent of 3-year-olds. These figures were 'guesstimates' of the likely demand. In fact, the Report probably considerably underestimated the demand from parents of 3-year-old children. It suggested that the nurseries could be staffed by trained nursery assistants under the supervision of qualified teachers. At the time, when there was still a shortage of primary schoolteachers, this was clearly designed to deflect the argument that teachers could not be spared from the compulsory sector. In this respect the Report's proposals have been overtaken by events.

The Government's response to the Plowden Report could be described as welcoming but somewhat cautious as far as taking action was concerned. The proposals about nursery education in particular were welcomed. However, by the time the Government had changed hands in June 1970, little progress had been made in implementing the proposals. The Urban Programme (1968), designed to improve race relations and to decrease urban deprivation, had as one of its components some expansion of nursery education. However, the total number of extra places was relatively small. A second and rather different activity involving Plowden proposals on nursery education was the setting up of action research to examine the potential of positive discrimination. Proposals to do this came not from the Government itself but from Michael Young, who had been a member of the Plowden Committee, and from A. H. Halsey of Oxford University. In his preface to *Educational Priority,* the report that eventually emerged from this action research,[11] Halsey described the 'slow progress' of the obtaining of financial support to undertake it. Indeed, the Government was much less responsive than it might have been to a proposal of this kind, which was not particularly expensive and which could have had a substantial pay-off in terms of increasing the understanding of educational and social policy-makers of some of the problems associated with the development of new programmes designed to help the needy. However, it should perhaps be remembered that while the general climate favoured positive discrimination, there were powerful dissenting voices. For example, a *Daily Telegraph* leader suggested that such policies involved throwing away good money on poor material. Moreover, the pressure on local authorities to provide more pre-school education was very often exerted by articulate and militant middle-class women seeking provision for their own children.

It was left to the Conservative Government which followed to introduce proposals for a comprehensive expansion of nursery schools. In the DES planning document *Education: a Framework of Expansion,* which came out in 1972 as a White Paper, a chapter was devoted to the under-5s, from which it is worth quoting at some length:

> There is now considerable evidence pointing to the importance of the years before 5 in a child's education — and to the most effective ways of providing for the needs, and potential, which children display at this age. The Reports of the Central Advisory Council, under Lady Plowden and the late Professor Gittins, based practical proposals upon these idea. They recommended that most needs could be met by part-time nursery education and that places should be provided for all three and four year olds whose parents wished them to attend. The Plowden Council estimated that provision for 90 per cent of 4-year-olds and 50 per cent of 3-year-olds would be adequate to meet demand.
>
> The action the Government now propose will give effect to these recommendations. Their aim is that within the next ten years nursery education should become available without charge, within the limits of demand estimated by Plowden, to those children of 3 and 4 whose parents wish them to benefit from it. Circular 8/60 will be withdrawn.[12]

As well as suggesting that nursery education should be provided to permit the social and educational development of all young children, the document also argued:

> The opportunities which the new policy offers for families living in deprived areas — both urban and rural — in bringing up their young children will be particularly important. There, as elsewhere, the

Government believe that provision for the under-5s should build on, not supplant, parents' own efforts.[13]

It went on to suggest that such provision would make it easier to identify those children with special difficulties earlier and would make remedial measures more effective because they could be applied early. It accepted the Plowden targets, proposing that some 700 full-time equivalent places would probably be needed by 1981-2. The decline in the birth rate would mean that the accommodation in existing primary schools could be adapted for children under 5. However, the Government suggested that a substantial programme of purpose-built accommodation would also be required. It stated that it would give 'some priority' to deprived areas in allocating these capital resources. Exactly what 'some priority' entailed was not spelled out. It left to LEAs the question of how far their admissions policy should give priority to children with special needs, suggesting simply that this was something that they would no doubt consider.

So far in this chapter nursery education has been defined in terms of maintained nursery schools and classes. During the 1960s there was a substantial growth of playgroups run by parents and voluntary organizations in an attempt to fill the gap left by a very small number of maintained places. These playgroups, often run by voluntary effort on a self-help basis, clearly appealed to the philosophy of a Conservative Government. They also appealed to large numbers of other people who did not necessarily share that philosophy but believed that it was desirable to increase parental participation in the education of young children and to reduce the dominance of the professions, which, it was claimed, sometimes unwittingly reduced parents' confidence in their children's development. The playgroup movement received some Government support when Labour was in office. This was increased by the new Government. The 1972 White Paper, while clearly foreseeing expansion primarily in the maintained sector, expressed the hope that playgroups would continue to develop. It also specifically mentioned their development among socially deprived children, although it said little or nothing about how such development might take place.

At the time some commentators suggested privately that this ambitious programme would not be achieved. They believed that when the next round of public expenditure cuts took place, nursery education would be one of the prime victims, as has happened on various previous occasions during this century. Others took the view that the favourable demographic climate, the massive and manifest nature of the demand and the general consensus about the value of nursery education would protect it. Those who took this second view turned out to be wrong. A modest programme of expansion was begun early in 1973, after the publication of White Paper. Circular 2/73 encouraged the expansion of nursery classes attached to primary schools. The old restrictive Circular 8/60 was withdrawn. A building programme was initiated, mainly taking the form of additions to earlier works and block allocations for which local education authorities were requested to submit bids. Six months later the DES had received bids in England and Wales for some 165 new nursery schools and some 4900 nursery classes. At this point there was no lack of enthusiasm to expand nursery education on the part of local authorities.

The programme of expansion was continued by the new Government when it came into office early in 1974. In spite of the large expenditure cuts that were introduced in 1976 and the smaller ones of 1973 and 1974, the Government continued to give some backing to nursery education. Between 1974−5 and 1978−9 it authorized building programmes of more than £50 million for this sector. It also encouraged LEAs to take advantage of the declining primary school rolls to convert any surplus space for children under 5. However, by this time many of the local authorities were being squeezed by programme cuts and cash limits and were unwilling to take advantage of these opportunities on the capital side. The main reason was that they believed they could not spare money for additional recurrent expenditure. Thus many of them did not take up the allocations offered them. For example, one-third of authorities failed to make a bid for the 1979−80 allocation and seven failed to do so throughout 1974−9. As a consequence, by the end of Labour's period in office the target figures set by the Plowden Report were a long way from being reached. It is true that the number of children in nursery schools and classes rose from 140,000 in 1974 to about 210,000 in 1977. There were also some 270,000 under-5s attending infant classes at primary schools, but these figures meant that only 53 per cent of all 4-year-olds and only 15 per cent of all 3-year-olds were being educated in maintained schools.

The lesson to be learned from this experience is that if central government wishes to expand a sector of education run by local authorities which does not entail compulsory attendance at a time when there are public expenditure constraints, it cannot rely on the goodwill of the LEAs. It is hard to escape from the fact that officials at the DES at the time must have been well aware of this. However, the capital programme served to give the impression that something was being done by central government. One alternative which it does not appear to have considered would have been to introduce legislation giving children the right to nursery education and then insisting that this right must be met by a certain date. Local authorities would then have had to develop plans to expand their provision accordingly. In terms of real resources, there could have not been a better time than the late 1970s to have done this. The availability of places in primary schools (because of smaller numbers of children) was matched by the existence, for the first time this century, of unemployed teachers, many of whom had been trained to teach younger children in primary schools. Such legislation might have incorporated a system of priorities for certain groups, such as single-parent families or those qualifying for Family Income Supplement or free school meals, to ensure that such groups gained access to the provision before more privileged groups.

Perhaps the most important change in the wider social context affecting the demand for nursery education during the early 1970s was the large growth in the number of married women with children under 5 working outside the home. Between 1971 and 1976 the proportion increased from one-sixth to one-quarter. There were some 850,000 children under 5 whose mothers were in paid employment in 1976, although a high proportion of these women were only working part-time.[14] Pressure to increase provision was growing from various organizations representing women. The Equal Opportunities Commission, for example, said that it would like to see

the implementation of policies which maximize choices for both sexes and which make it feasible for parents who wish to do so to combine work and family, their domestic and their public lives. This applies not just to mothers, but to fathers who want to contribute more to the care of their children than is currently possible. . . .[15]

This suggests that another way in which nursery provision might increase equality is by reducing differences between the sexes as far as their opportunity to work was concerned. But men as well as women deserve more chance to exercise choice about their patterns of work. As the Commission points out, such choice is limited not just by the unavailability of child care but also by current norms with respect to aspects of employment and entitlement to state benefits. However, the expansion of nursery provision would certainly make it easier for large numbers of married women who wish to take part-time employment to do so.

The early pioneers of nursery education, such as Margaret McMillan, were well aware of the importance of providing care as well as education, but more recently it has often been claimed that nursery education has little or nothing to do with child care or with serving the needs of parents. The somewhat purist view taken is that its aim is to educate children and that it should not be concerned about such matters as women's need or wish to be employed. Even the Plowden Report reflected these views when it suggested that it is not the business of the educational system to encourage the mothers of young children to go out to work:

> We do not believe that full-time nursery places should be provided even for children who might tolerate separation without harm, except for exceptionally good reasons. We have no reason to suppose that working mothers, as a group, care any less about the well-being of their children than do mothers who do not work. . . . But some mothers who are not obliged to work may work full-time, regardless of their children's welfare. It is no business of the educational service to encourage these mothers to do so. It is true, unfortunately, that the refusal of full-time nursery places for their children may prompt some of them to make unsuitable arrangements for their children's care during working hours. All the same, we consider that mothers who cannot satisfy the authorities that they have exceptionally good reasons for working should have low priority for full-time nursery for their children.[16]

The climate has recently changed somewhat and most policy-makers and their advisers in this field would now accept that it is unrealistic to neglect the growing trend among mothers of small children to go out to work. In spite of this growing awareness of changing employment patterns, there is still some ambivalence about whether to take this trend directly into account and expand provision accordingly, or whether to continue to take the view that the trend can somehow be halted or reversed.

One consequence of the view that the role of nursery education is to provide an experience for *children,* to the exclusion of providing support for *parents* (in particular, support which enables them to take jobs more easily), is its separation from the provision of full-time day care. In the UK all-day, year-round care is provided in separate day nurseries run by social services departments locally and administered at the centre by the Department of Health and Social Security (DHSS). The number of places provided in this way is small, far below the actual and potential demand. Places are provided only in cases of need. These include some single-parent children, some children whose mothers are mentally or physically ill and some cases of severe family difficulties. In a number of European countries this split between educational provision and day-care facilities does not exist.[17]

Criticisms have been made of the split system and the failure to co-ordinate it adequately;[18] and one of us has suggested that provision for those aged 3 to 5 should be integrated, arguing:

> For some years, there has been concern about the quality of education provided in day nurseries, which are staffed by nurses and nursery assistants, never by teachers, and the Plowden Report rightly stated that children over 3 should be in educational institutions. This concern has led to action in many day nurseries so that educational goals are no longer secondary to health and hygiene. However, with the establishment of universal nursery education as a right for all children, would it be advisable for a small proportion of underprivileged children to remain outside the first schools in non-educational institutions, which could well become stigmatized because of their exclusive clientele of the most disadvantaged children in our society? Such children should be able to mix with their more fortunate peers and have the opportunity to benefit from trained teachers in these important years.[19]

Much of this case, put forward some seven years ago, is still valid today, in spite of the growth in the employment of nursery teachers in day nurseries. Integration for those aged 3 and over at the very least would also help to reduce the problems of co-ordination and duplication which exist at present between social service and education departments in local authorities. Were there two easily identifiable and clear-cut categories of children needing quite different types of care and education, there would be a good case for separate types of provision. In fact, no such categories exist. There is something more like a continuum, with at one extreme the children of mothers who are not working and have no social, economic or medical problems and, at the other extreme, children whose mothers work long hours or are chronically ill, whether physically or mentally. Between these extremes lie many variations of need, including the specific needs of children of the growing number of women who work part-time. The categories are also not distinct in the sense that individual circumstances vary over time; children may need the equivalent of day-nursery provision for a period, but later the shorter hours of nursery education may be adequate. An integrated system offers scope for more flexibility than does the present divided system, as well as eradicating the segregation of the most deprived from the rest.

While there has been some expansion of nursery education — although it has been slower than originally intended and certainly slower than reformers would have hoped — there has been very little expansion of day nurseries. A few were established under the Urban Programme, but since then the DHSS has not given them the priority they deserve. There are still a number of local authorities with no day nurseries at all; in 1976 only three authorities (all inner London boroughs) had places for more than 5 per cent of their population, and the *average* was less than 1 per cent. In 1976 just over 27,000 places were provided in England and Wales for a child population under 5 of about 3,250,000. And there has been little or no improvement since then. It can be argued that if policy-makers had taken the needs of underprivileged young children seriously, they would have accorded this service higher priority. Moreover, if integration with nursery education proved to be difficult for political or administrative reasons, then they might have begun by expanding the day nurseries, where the most desperate cases of need demanding places have been found, and then turned to nursery education later. In some local authorities the waiting list of desperate cases has run into several hundreds.

Instead they pursued various alternatives, apart from nursery education itself, in an effort to save costs. While it is only realistic to recognize that purpose-built day nurseries are an expensive service, and while it is legitimate to look at ways in which the service might be expanded more cheaply (for example, by accepting rather lower standards of accommodation), the wholesale rejection of institutional forms of care in favour of various forms of child-minding is probably unwise. In a paper prepared for its conference on low-cost day care, the DHSS noted that the capital cost of a day-nursery place at 1975 prices was £3000 and the annual running cost around £700 a place.[20] This compares with between £215 and £345 per year for a sponsored placement with a child-minder whose charge is paid by the authority, which also provides full support services to the minder. Since the minder's own home is used, there are, of course, no capital costs. In the light of such enormous differences in cost during a period of public expenditure constraint, it is hardly surprising that the DHSS espouses the cause of child-minders.

Its preference for child-minders is based on other factors besides costs. For many years the DHSS has been highly ambivalent about the day nursery as an institution. The dominant official view has been that day nurseries are places of last resort, to be avoided if at all possible. It perceives the environment with which they provide the young child as poor; among other things, there is insufficient continuity of care and, in some cases, generally low quality of care. Underlying this view is a belief that young children should be in their own homes and not in institutions, even those that they attend on a daily rather than a residential basis. When they cannot be at home, a 'substitute' home with a child-minder is usually more desirable because it will approximate more to 'normality' than will a day nursery. The model is the intimate one of the family, with the child or children minded in her own sitting-room. (Indeed, the American term used to describe child-minding is 'family day care'.)

While many child-minders undoubtedly provide a useful service and some provide high-quality care, a policy which relies on them has many disadvantages, in spite of the advantage of low cost. As one of us noted in 1973: 'there is a risk of discontinuities in care for the children if a child-minder decides to opt out of the scheme. The accommodation of the child-minder may not be altogether adequate, and there may be insufficient opportunities for the child's educational development.'[21] Since then a more extensive study of the quality of child-minding has been carried out than ever before. It is part of a major research programme on pre-school provision carried out under the direction of Professor Jerome Bruner of Oxford

University. In his summary of the various types of provision available, Bruner makes it clear that while the day nurseries he studied deserve considerable criticism, given that as many as a quarter of the children in them have severe social problems, they are tackling a difficult task, in some cases with a modest measure of success.[22] His description of child-minding based on a study carried out as part of the research programme in Oxfordshire,[23] makes gloomy reading. The researchers found that child-minding creates problems for at least one-third of children in this form of care, and perhaps for as many as half. Many of the children were withdrawn and mildly depressed, even when they were placed with minders who appeared 'qualified' and competent. Bruner describes the 'heart of the problem' as 'the discontinuity between home and the minder's for the child'. He goes on to say that the minder's 'is not a home away from home (however homelike it may be by conventional standards) but an empty time separated from home. In most instances there appears little the child-minder can do about it — save to let the child be'.[24] Communication between the child's mother and the minder is often limited and even awkward.

The findings of this study suggest that future policies should not rely on the expansion of child-minding as a reliable and suitable form of care for large numbers of children. To argue in favour of its benefits could easily be interpreted as a rationalization, when its only real benefit is its low cost. At the same time, in many cases a child-minder may be better than nothing. Moreover, the greater proportion of *full-time* provision takes this form at present. There were about 84,000 places with registered child-minders in 1976. Estimates for unregistered child-minders now range from 100,000 to as high as 300,000. Successive Governments and many local authorities have been anxious both to reduce the incidence of unregistered minding and to provide more support for registered minders. Since many deprived children are looked after by minders, such policies are crucial. However, they should be perceived as an accompaniment to the expansion of day nurseries rather than as an alternative, if the reduction of deprivation among poor families and their children and the pursuit of greater equality is to be taken seriously.

What distinguishes the expansion of provision for children under 5 from nearly all other recent issues in educational policy is the powerful consensus about its desirability. Both the main political parties have given it some prominence in recent election manifestos. The teaching profession appears united behind it; all the main teaching unions support it. As chapter 3 shows, the NUT has mounted a considerable campaign to try to secure its growth, publishing a series of pamphlets advocating it, including comments on the Plowden Committee's report in 1967[25] and three further publications in 1972, 1974 and 1977.[26] Its evidence submitted to the Plowden Committee,[27] the Bullock Committee[28] and the Warnock Committee[29] gave some prominence to the need for expansion. All these government inquiries into education also recommended it. Similar inquiries in other fields, such as the Finer Report on single-parent families[30] and the Court Report on child health[31] were also in favour of expansion. The TUC, the Equal Opportunities Commission and a variety of educational pressure groups have pressed for it. There may be some disagreement about the exact form that provision should take — whether in playgroups or nursery classes, in day nurseries or with child-minders, or in some form of unified provision — but there appears to be universal consensus about its need.

Successive Governments can therefore hardly blame political opposition to its growth for the failure to expand provision. The opposition comes from within government not outside it. It comes from a Treasury concerned to cut public expenditure and unwilling to make exceptions for this service. It comes from Ministers and civil servants in two main Departments who have not felt able to allocate it priority in the fight for additional funds or to redistribute resources from some other area. Thus whatever the potential of nursery education and day care to reduce inequality, it has not yet been fulfilled; many children remain without it, including some of the most needy. With every year that goes by, another generation of children misses out on the opportunities it offers.

If we return to the various ways in which nursery education might help to equalize opportunities that were outlined at the beginning of this chapter, we find that the methods employed to expand provision may not have been the most suitable possible to promote greater equality either.

The first was that by providing all children with a similar day-time environment, some of the environmental inequalities of their lives could be eliminated. This was one of the main arguments put forward for nursery education by the Labour Party in the 1920s

and 1930s. As we have already pointed out (see p. 90), the degree
to which this is likely to happen is probably more limited than some
of the early proponents of nursery education claimed. However,
there are three ways in which present policies have further reduced
the degree to which nursery education might contribute in this way.
The first is the very small number of hours in the school day (on
average about two and a half hours) because the great majority of
places are now part-time. A higher proportion of full-time places is
needed, particularly in socially deprived areas. Secondly, far more
encouragement of parental participation should be introduced. It
should be done sensitively, so that working-class parents do not feel
inadequate when faced by professional expertise. Evidence on ways
in which this can be achieved is available from a DES-funded
research project on parental participation in nursery education.[32]
Practitioners in nursery education have always prided themselves
on their accessibility to parents, but many teacher training courses
are inadequate when it comes to preparing nursery teachers to deal
with adults. There is plenty of circumstantial evidence to support
the contention that while nursery teachers may do better in this
respect than do some of their colleagues teaching older children, the
criticism made by the playgroup movement and others that mothers
(particularly working-class mothers) are kept at a distance may be
valid. Third, the training of teachers of young children needs to lay
greater emphasis on the need to provide additional help within the
classroom for children whose home environment may make it more
difficult for them to learn as fast as their more privileged peers.
There is a danger that teachers now *expect* such children to do less
well and consequently give them too little rather than too much
stimulation.

This brings us to the question of positive discrimination. The
Plowden Committee clearly expressed the need to give priority to
expanding nursery education in educational priority areas. Although
some authorities have tried to do this, others have expanded
provision in areas where need is not as great. Where there is excess
accommodation in a primary school in a middle-class area and the
space is easily convertible, it is, of course, tempting for local
authorities to set up nursery classes in such schools. Indeed, the
DES has encouraged them to make use of such space. In many
ways, to do so is rational. Yet if such a move entails nursery
provision for children who are already privileged in other respects,

while those in poorer parts of the authority are still unprovided for, it must be questioned whether this is the right use of recurrent expenditure, however rational in capital terms. There have always been large variations in the availability of places between different regions and different local authorities, as well as within them.[33] Though there is some association between public provision and need (inner London, for example, has a high proportion of places per child population), it is not very strong.[34]

One reason for the rather feeble application of positive discrimination in providing places is the acceptance of the principle of nursery education for all children. The assumption made by policy-makers and commentators alike is that it should be a universal service. The grounds for this are good. All children can benefit from it, socially, educationally and emotionally. All mothers can benefit from it. To exclude the majority permanently would certainly be politically unacceptable to the vast majority of parents. Yet in practice it is easy for this principle of universality to conflict with attempts to identify those in greatest need and to help them *first*. To run an entirely selective service in which income criteria are the basis for eligibility, as in the USA, has all the disadvantages of segregation of the poor and high administrative costs. To try to build some selectivity into a system which is intended to be universal is the challenge in the UK. Although, as we have already pointed out, there are difficulties in expanding provision in deprived areas first and in giving priority to individual children whose needs are greatest, they are not so overwhelming that they cannot be at least partially overcome. Some authorities have tried to develop indices based on the social and economic characteristics of the area to help them identify those schools that are most likely to need extra help or, for that matter, to merit a nursery class attachment. Though far from perfect, such measures are better than nothing or than relying on subjective judgements alone. But because even in the most deprived areas there is a substantial minority of families who are not deprived,[35] it is important that admission policies at the level of the school should be adjusted. This means that local authorities may have to work out a system of incentives to encourage headteachers to take poor children before their middle-class peers. Too few politicians or administrators have been willing to devote energy to devising schemes of this kind, and in recent years they have, regrettably, become unfashionable.

The third and fourth methods whereby nursery provision may increase equality concerned mothers. The expansion that has taken place has probably improved the quality of life of many young married women. Surveys of the demand for nursery education indicate that a high proportion of mothers would like at least part-time provision for their children.[36] Many of these women wish to work, but even those who do not wish to do so express considerable dissatisfaction with current levels of provision. Given the strong tendency on the part of surveys of public service to produce findings indicating considerable satisfaction (perhaps because of low expectations), this evidence on the strength of the demand is particularly noteworthy. Thus although some have been helped, recent policies have been inadequate in the sense that they still leave many dissatisfied.

For those who *need* to work they have failed most conspicuously. The provision of part-time nursery-class places (the main form of expansion) is obviously not sufficient for the single parent who needs and wants to work to support his or her family. It is not even sufficient for women with husbands on low incomes who wish to supplement those incomes by part-time work during the day. The hours are too short. In some areas there is evidence that take-up of part-time nursery places is poor for this reason. Mothers are forced to rely on child-minders instead. We have already noted the failure to expand day nurseries. Although there have been some experiments in providing an extended school day in nursery classes for the children of women who are working, they have not been implemented on a large scale. We have also noted doubts about child-minding as an acceptable alternative form of provision; even where registration takes place and there is some form of support or supervision, it has serious drawbacks.

The last sense in which nursery education might increase equality that we have identified concerns the automatic increase in resources devoted to the universal rather than the selective post-school sector that it entails. The average expenditure on a young person whose educational experience includes the sixth form and university is much higher than on a young person who leaves school at 16.[37] This is because the top end of the system is much more expensive than the bottom end. The average cost of a university place (£2400 in 1967) is eight times that of a primary school place (£300 in the same year). In this sense educational resources are not being fairly distributed. While a major expansion of nursery provision would by no means eliminate these inequalities in resource allocation, it would reduce them a little. But, as we have seen, the expansion has not taken place; nor has it concentrated sufficiently on those most in need.

In conclusion, the outlook for the future is bleak. The 1979 Conservative Government will not fulfil its manifesto commitment to nursery education. Its programme of massive public expenditure cuts will lead to fewer places rather than more. The history of nursery education over the last sixty years demonstrates clearly that it is one of the first items to suffer when cuts are imposed. As local authorities look around for ways to keep within their reduced budgets, many of them will select this service as an easier victim than many others. Those who espouse the cause of young children and their mothers and those who are concerned about inequality in this society will wring their hands, as their predecessors have done. Their protests will be heard politely. Sadly, it looks as if they will be ignored.

5

Positive Discrimination in Education

The advocacy and subsequent decline of positive discrimination in education epitomizes the ineffectiveness of attempts to deal with educational disadvantage by educational policy in the post-war period. The educational priority programme as a means of positive discrimination was long on rhetoric and short on coherent, positive, purposive action. The programme's planning, evaluation, co-ordination, resources, goals and time-scale of action, all reveal a dismal failure to devise a national policy to counter educational disadvantage.[1] In essence, the most salient definitions of positive discrimination as a principle were never radical. The enactment of the principle was more derisory than radical. Yet to say this is not to dismiss the notion of positive discrimination as insignificant. It was an important moral statement of a benign aspiration to correct the educational disadvantages experienced by working-class children. It raised vital questions about social justice in education and provided answers that, aside from their moral salience, occasioned valuable deliberation (together with some action, if only in the foothills) of the practicalities of fashioning cogent educational policy against disadvantage.[2] Furthermore, of equal significance to our general understanding of the failure of educational policy to correct inequality is the way in which positive discrimination was adapted, absorbed and ultimately neutralized by the conservatism of the education system.

The rise of positive discrimination in education, as a concern with deprivation in specific areas, can be first seen in the 1963 Newsom Report on secondary modern schools. Newsom was concerned about educational standards in what were described as 'schools in slums'.[3] But the Report was not clear as to the scale or nature of the problem. Unexceptionally, Newsom asserted that a slum was an area with an unusually high concentration of social problems, but did not advance beyond the conviction that there were no satisfactory objective criteria by which to define 'slums' or their schools. Consequently, the Report was tentative about the number of secondary modern schools that could be described as 'schools in slums'. Few schools of this kind had fallen within Newsom's 4 per cent sample of all secondary modern schools: in fact, because of this, an additional group of schools from deprived areas were especially selected and studied. Newsom's 'loose estimate'[4] of the proportion of secondary modern schools in slums was 7 per cent, with a further 13 per cent suffering many of the same disadvantages. There were some disturbing features about these schools. Seventy-nine per cent had buildings that were described as 'seriously inadequate',[5] which compared with a figure of 40 per cent for all secondary modern schools. However, since this last figure related to a representative sample and the previous figure did not, some caution must be used in estimating the relative frequency of inadequate school buildings in slum areas. Nevertheless, Newsom presented a stark picture of the social capital in slum areas. Quite understandably, such facts were taken to be related to poor educational attainment, as was the fact that in schools in these areas, on average only a third of women teachers and half of the men had been on the staff for more than three years.[6] If there could be uncertainty about the precise causes of low educational attainment, there could be no doubt about the fact of poor attainment. Newsom showed that the average reading age of fourth-year pupils in slum areas was seventeen months lower than the average for all secondary modern schools.[7]

As for solutions to educational disadvantage, Newsom argued that schools in slums required special consideration, whereas in the past such schools had been 'less expensive than average, and therefore pitifully inadequate'.[8] One aspect of this special consideration might be a particularly favourable staffing ratio. An appendix to the Report argued that as a matter of social justice children of average ability should be taught in the smallest classes by the best teachers.[9] This goal should be part of what was described as a positive teacher deployment policy, by which salary structures would be adjusted to match supply with the need for teachers. However, the policy was presented in terms more of principles than of practical proposals. The main text of the Newsom Report was dilatory about the means by which the aspiration of a favourable teaching ratio for schools in slums could be achieved. It mused on a 'change of wind' — which meant 'making it clear that professionally it is an asset to have served successfully in a difficult area'[10] — as an instrument of policy. This aim, and the inducement of providing good accommodation for teachers in problem areas, was ludicrously remote from the social and occupational aspirations of most teachers. Newsom made other proposals, which amounted not so much to an educational policy as a series of loosely formulated requests. For example, for a greater provision of social workers in slum areas and 'a bold building policy'.[11] This last item was said to be taking place.

Newsom's major significance was that it was a statement of concern. The Report made an amorphous plea for better treatment for disadvantaged working-class pupils, though it was vague about the nature of their disadvantage or the best remedy for it. In terms of principles, it is clear that Newsom wanted disadvantaged pupils to be given better treatment in future, relative to the standards enjoyed by the non-disadvantaged. This aspiration fell within the mainstream of long-standing reformist concern. Certainly, Newsom did not appear to be advocating a radical programme of redistribution in favour of the disadvantaged. Furthermore, an area approach to deprivation, while invested with the novel nomenclature of modernity, was rooted in a history that goes back at least to Victorian concern with the 'rookeries' of London. However, it might be argued that Newsom embodied the germ of redistribution policies, in that the Report underscored the importance of environmental factors in influencing the acquisition of intelligence; this seemed to enter the realm of political perception in Boyle's introduction to the Report and could conceivably have proved to be a stalking horse that invited more rigorous and radical solutions to the problem of disadvantage.

Four years after Newsom the Plowden Report on primary education was published. Plowden was a major — conceivably, *the* major — post-war document on primary schools. It was not concerned specifically with educational disadvantage but did consider the issue. Plowden expressed particular concern about standards of education for some working-class children and, like Newsom, argued that educational disadvantage was acute in certain areas. The Report proposed that these areas should be designated educational priority areas (EPAs) and given special treatment. This recommendation should be given 'absolute priority' over all others.[12] Though convinced that EPA criteria could not be exhaustive or definitive, Plowden was prepared to go beyond Newsom in offering indicators of disadvantage. The main social criteria by which EPA's were to be identified were the presence of a high proportion of unskilled and semi-skilled workers, large families, families in receipt of state benefits, families in overcrowded conditions and incomplete families. Educational criteria included school attendance rates, the proportion of retarded, disturbed or handicapped pupils in schools and the number of children unable to speak English.[13] Two things should be noted. First, the criteria of educational disadvantage were in large measure *social*. Like Newsom, Plowden assumed some ill-defined association between social and educational deprivation. Second, the criteria, individually and in sum, were no more than crude descriptions of an impoverished environment. For example, no attempt was made to rank EPA social criteria in order of importance; all were assumed to be related equally closely to educational disadvantage. Plowden was content to argue that experience would show which of the criteria was most useful, though without suggesting how 'usefulness' was to be defined or measured. Presumably, this was to be left to experience. The lack of precision in Plowden's proposals is highlighted by the following quotation: special treatment should be afforded '*schools* in *neighbourhoods* where *children* are most severely handicapped by *home conditions*'.[14] As a description of educational disadvantage and a guide to policy, this formulation is more inclusive than indicative, but perhaps it is too much to expect inquiries of this kind to work out the details of their recommendations.

What did Plowden think should be done about this vaguely defined problem of working-class educational disadvantage? The Report did make some powerful statements of general principle. EPAs should be the object of a policy of positive discrimination; that is, they should be favoured, 'going well beyond an attempt to *equalize* resources . . . the first step must be to raise the schools with low standards to the national average; the second, quite deliberately to *make them better*.'[15] This does have radical overtones. It argues for the reversal of a long-standing policy, tantamount to negative discrimination, that favours middle-class children, (though by no means exclusively) — what might be described as a policy advocating 'To those that have shall be given.' This interpretation is further strengthened by Plowden's view that a policy of positive discrimination 'calls for both some *redistribution* of resources devoted to education and, just as much, for an increase in their total volume'.[16] Yet it is not entirely clear at this point what stress Plowden was placing on redistribution as a means of securing positive discrimination. The phrase 'just as much' suggests that the Committee felt redistribution should be a major, integral part of positive discrimination — half its financial basis, even. On the other hand, '*some* redistribution' indicates that redistributive policies were not regarded by Plowden as the sole means of facilitating positive discrimination. This is made clear subsequently: 'it would be unreasonable and self-defeating — economically, professionally and politically — to try to do justice to the most deprived children by using only resources that can be diverted from more fortunate areas.'[17] A policy of aiding the disadvantaged must not be advanced 'simply by robbing more fortunate areas of all the opportunities for progress to which they have been looking forward; it can only succeed if a larger share of the nation's resources is devoted to education'.[18] Thus it appears that while Plowden wished to make EPA schools positively better than average, this goal was secondary to that of improving advantaged schools to some extent. The obvious tension between these two aims bordered on contradiction, and the equivocation typified a lack of commitment to advancing the interests of disadvantaged working-class children *above all else.* It appears that Plowden wanted to advance the cause of the educationally disadvantaged by means of a disproportionate share of additional resources, by redistribution at the margins of an expanding education budget — what might be called fairweather positive discrimination. Presumably the Committee also feared the possible political backlash of those who resented the transfer of resources from advantaged areas.

This slightly muted commitment to improving working-class education can be seen in some of Plowden's specific proposals. The Report argued that the most pressing need in EPAs was for better buildings and additional teachers. As to building resources, it might have been expected that had Plowden been committed to a radical redistributive policy of positive discrimination, the intention of making EPA standards better than average would have been the nub of distributional considerations. In fact, Plowden openly bowed to the fact that the greater part of building resources were earmarked for dealing with the rise in the birth rate and did no more than suggest that 'our criteria should be given great weight when determining which of the schools with old or out-of-date buildings is to be replaced first.'[19] Thus EPA criteria supported and guided a secondary, even peripheral, principle of distribution that was subservient to the wholly orthodox and non-redistributive principle of 'roofs over heads'. Undeniably, providing accommodation for areas of expanding child population was a problem. We have suggested elsewhere alternatives to the orthodox solution.[20] Here we simply note the conservative qualifications within which the apparently radical distributional principle of positive discrimination was advocated.

The proposals regarding teachers were equally unexceptional. Plowden wanted to bring experienced and successful teachers into EPAs and, to this end, recommended that the teacher quotas for these areas should be raised.[21] However, it was recognized that the problem in disadvantaged areas was not so much that they were prevented from employing teachers by the quota system but that these areas had difficulty in attracting and keeping teachers. Therefore Plowden recommended the payment of an additional £120 a year to teachers in EPA schools. As was shown above, this had been tentatively broached by Newsom and was recommended at the same time as Plowden by the Roberts Committee which was inquiring into the distribution of teachers in Scotland. In another area of social policy the principle of additional payments to attract doctors to poor areas had already been accepted by the Government. All this suggests that the EPA teacher allowance was not particularly new or radical proposal. Below we consider whether or not the implementation of the proposal had a radical impact.

What might be taken as innovatory was Plowden's plan of action against educational disadvantage,[22] which held out the prospect of large-scale, concerted endeavour in this field. It was proposed that, as a start, priority should be given to the top 2 per cent of most severely deprived pupils (not schools or areas?), increasing to 10 per cent in five years. Beyond this, when the best strategy had been identified, the programme was to be extended to a larger (unspecified) proportion of the population. Certain measures were to be taken in the period 1968–72: for example, the ratio of teachers to children in EPAs was to be improved so that no class exceeded thirty pupils. Teachers' aides should be provided for primary schools at a ratio of one to every two infant classes. £5000 should be allocated for minor works in each school.

In spite of the criticisms levelled at the Report above, Plowden displayed a manifest, forceful commitment to improving the education for the disadvantaged that was both imaginative and bold. Arguably, the report was the high point of expressed egalitarian concern in the post-war period. Reasonable criticism of Plowden should be tempered by the recognition that such a report cannot be expected to work out the detail of new policy. Plowden pointed in a new direction and recognized that an experimental, learning phase was necessary before Government could be expected to make a full commitment. Yet the importance of this phase should not be over-stressed. Enough was already known about the character and location of educational disadvantage to inform the deployment of resources. In essence, Plowden was not so much a plan of action as a plea for resources. And nothing could happen if resources were not forthcoming. Plowden took the view that LEAs would not be able to embark on positive discrimination until they knew what help they would get from central government.[23]

Obviously, central government would be wary of an open-ended commitment to provide additional resources to make EPA schools 'better than average'. All Governments are mindful of the political need to avoid generating demand for resources which may not be met. Without the key flux of additional resources, Plowden's programme would not start. Those who seek to advance working-class interests simply by asking for an increase in total resources indulge in a form of social piety — sighs in an oppressed world. Or, as Crosland remarked, from an altogether different ideological standpoint, we can all think of a thousand good ways to spend 0.1 per cent of the GNP. What he should have added, and what Plowden should have kept in mind, was that we are not as good at marshalling the political/administrative effort and imagination to devise a thousand ways of redistributing existing resources.

Since Plowden laid prime emphasis on more resources for EPAs, it is instructive to examine what changes were subsequently made in the distribution of resources. In fact, the major initial political response was to focus on the building resources aspect of the Report. As Banting argues, this was attractive to the Government, because an administrative framework existed through which a positive response could be implemented, and also the DES was acutely aware, from a study that it had itself undertaken, that school buildings were generally deficient.[24] Nevertheless, this question was construed in narrow terms by politicians. For example, Boyle claimed that 'much of the problem of EPAs is surely bound up with the need for a larger school building programme',[25] as if to rule out the possibility of changing priorities within the existing programme. And despite Crosland's conviction that positive discrimination was 'a radical recommendation, utterly convincing',[26] his enthusiasm for greater endowment of EPAs was bounded by the fact that priority would be given to the replacement of primary schools in EPAs when the basic need for new places had been met. He stated that the school-building programme for 1968—9 would include at least £3.5 million for projects in EPAs and that each year he would try to keep a school-building programme specifically for EPAs.[27] Thus the writ of the 'utterly convincing' radical recommendation of positive discrimination was to run within a miniscule fraction of the total building programme of almost £120 million. Most of the remainder was to be distributed on a non-radical, 'roofs over heads' basis. It is true that additional building resources, over and above the basic programme, were subsequently made available. For example, in July 1967 it was announced that £16 million would be provided for EPA schools over two years. This amount was not exclusively for the improvement of inadequate primary schools of the kind that had so concerned Plowden. Although Circular 11/67 expected that a major proportion of the resources would be spent on primary schools, it invited the submission of projects relating to secondary schools and quoted Newsom as justification for this.[28] This was not unreasonable, but it did mean that the resources were spread much more thinly than might have at first appeared to be the case. Also, this £16 million was not a 'new' resource being applied to disadvantage. Banting points out that it was a trade-off for Crosland's acceptance of an increase in the price of school meals.[29] However, in periods of public expenditure constraint there are few alternatives to trade-offs of this kind if resources are to be redistributed in favour of the needy. When Short, as Secretary of State for Education, was questioned about why the special building allocation for EPAs was not to be continued beyond 1969—70, he expressed the view that although the two-year programme was a valuable first step, he preferred to rely in future on those resources that could be spared from the general school-building programme. He noted that the programme was twice what it had been in the last year of the previous Conservative Government. From this he concluded that EPAs were getting a fair share of a very large building programme.[30] Of course, this does not necessarily follow. Admittedly, judgement about the fairness of the EPAs' share of resources is made difficult by the absence of clear yardsticks of need. Demand for buildings certainly exceeded supply. In response to the £16 million programme, LEAs submitted proposals totalling £43 million.[31] In 1971−2 a further £18 million was earmarked for buildings in deprived areas. The following year saw the start of a four-year programme to replace pre-1903 buildings, and in the first year priority was given to deprived areas.[32]

Despite the improvement that such resources brought to disadvantaged areas, the problem of inadequate buildings was by no means solved. A survey of school buildings undertaken in 1975 found that it would take some £1500 millions to bring all schools up to modern standards.[33] Obviously, this figure overstates the magnitude of deficiency in disadvantaged areas, since it refers to schools in all areas, but it does give some sense of the scale of the problem. The principle of positive discrimination does not appear to have had a fundamental or lasting impact in altering the distribution of building resources. What can be 'spared' from the main building programme, after provision for 'basic needs', is allocated to improving deficient schools. This practice preceded and has post-dated Plowden. The distribution of social capital still does not act strongly in favour of disadvantaged areas.

The second part of Plowden's two-pronged attack on educational disadvantage was to bring more and better teachers into EPAs. It would appear that EPAs did have something of a staffing problem. A survey of EPA teachers concluded that 'inner-city schools are staffed to a large extent by young teachers in their first job since leaving college' — 39 per cent of teachers in London and 36 per cent in Birmingham fell into this category.[34] Arguably, inexperienced staff detract from the quality of teaching in EPA schools. Also, as the above survey noted, this bias in composition makes for the likelihood of a high turnover of staff, as teachers leave in search of more attractive posts or to start families. A high turnover of staff can also detract from the quality of schooling. In two of the Birmingham EPA schools the median length of stay of staff was *one term*.[35] At the time EPAs had difficulty not only in retaining staff but also in attracting staff. Four out of seven priority schools in Birmingham and seven out of ten in the West Riding were worse off in terms of the pupil/teacher ratio than the average primary school[36] (though the London and Liverpool EPA schools had better than average ratios). Predictably, the teaching profession emphasized staffing issues in EPAs, as had Plowden. Headteachers in a London EPA, when asked to place Plowden's recommendations in rank order of importance, placed the desirability of classes of less than thirty at the top of the list; ranked third was the view that it should be easier for EPAs to obtain teachers.[37] The Government's solution to the staffing problem of EPAs was on the lines suggested by Plowden. In 1967 an EPA special allowance was awarded at a rate of £75 per annum (not £120, as Plowden had wanted). Also, the total amount allocated for this purpose was £400,000, which was a DES-determined, procrustean provision rather than a response to demand or need. For example, LEAs in the Black Country requested that 25 per cent of the schools in their areas be accorded EPA status, but only 8 per cent were so recognized. In Halsey's view, at least 15 per cent of those schools would have satisfied Plowden's criteria for positive discrimination.[38] On two counts — the rate and total expenditure — the EPA allowance was tardy, indicative of a minimal commitment to improving the quality of staffing in EPAs. However, it should not be forgotten that initially the NUT was suspicious of the special payment, which was held to compromise the pursuit of a higher basic salary (see chapter 3).

In fact, subsequent research was to show that the special allowance was largely ineffective.[39] The staff turnover in the seventy-eight ILEA schools receiving the allowance was compared with the next seventy-nine schools that were ranked immediately below on the ILEA EPA index but were not receiving the allowance. In the first full year in which the allowance was paid, teacher resignations dropped; using 1967—8 as a base year (index 100), resignations fell to 83.5. In schools not receiving the allowance, the index rose to 101.4. But in the second year the index for the former schools rose to 106.5; in the latter it fell to 104.2. Staff turnover remained a problem in inner-city areas. A DES report[40] showed that while high turnover was by no means an exclusively urban problem, some urban areas had an exceptional problem. In the ILEA the rate of staff turnover in primary schools was 33 per cent, compared with 22 per cent for all LEAs. No doubt the recent shortage of teaching posts has done a great deal to reduce teacher turnover in all schools, but this does not mean that EPAs no longer have staffing problems.

They may still not be able to recruit the best teachers, as Plowden had wished. Also teachers in EPA schools tend to be absent more frequently than do teachers in other schools — by as much as 15 per cent.[41] This *may* be compensated for, in quantitative terms, by the availability of supply teachers, but a high percentage of supply teachers could detract from the quality of teacher-pupil relationships. (We stress *may* because in response to current expenditure retrenchment, supply teaching is sometimes curtailed.) Differential rates of teacher absenteeism will adversely affect EPA schools. The staffing problem in EPAs is more complex than EPA staff policy permits, with its over-emphasis on special allowances flying in the face of the above research evidence.

Although it cannot be argued that the implementation of positive discrimination, in terms of both capital and recurrent expenditure, led to a significant alteration in the distribution of resources to the benefit of the disadvantaged, the evidence that we have presented so far understates the resources devoted to priority areas in the post-Plowden period. Some education projects were financed under the Urban Aid Programme (UAP). Government figures show that in the period 1969—72 nursery education under the UAP benefited by over £6 million and other education projects by £1 million.[42] A third phase of the UAP, which included some resources for education, lasted until 1976. Even when sums of this kind are taken into account, it does not alter the fact that the educational priority programme has been financed by miniscule resources. Admittedly, it would be difficult to establish exactly what level of resources would be needed to bring all EPA schools up to the national average and then make them better, as Plowden advocated. What is clear is that LEAs believed that considerable extra expenditure was needed. The evidence indicates that demand for special payment for teachers exceeded supply, as did the demand for building resources in response to the £16 million programme in 1967. Of course, demand for resources is not necessarily a totally reliable guide to need, but it is a useful pointer.

Another example can be taken from the UAP Circular 19/68: the first phase of the programme led to applications for aid that 'greatly exceeded the resources available'.[43] It should be remembered that this phase applied to only seventeen County Boroughs, ILEA and seventeen London Boroughs. Using evidence provided in reply to a parliamentary question, Meacher calculated that in 1972—3 positive discrimination expenditure amounted to 1 per cent of the total education budget.[44] This does not speak of the determined mobilization of resources to facilitate a national policy against disadvantage. In fact, it is inappropriate to describe the educational priority programme as a *national plan*. Crosland, who was responsible for the initial Government response to Plowden, seemed prepared to commit the Government to a national policy of positive discrimination only in the negative sense that the Government was to be the paymaster that decreed what additional resources could be spared for the priority programme. The Government was not prepared to devise a central plan for the implementation of positive discrimination. Crosland refused to designate EPAs using Plowden's criteria because he doubted that the Department could or should do this — 'many people would object in principle to the Government interfering by fiat in the responsibilities of local government in this way.'[45] This, the first major statement on Plowden, virtually abandoned the notion of a national policy. Not only did the Government refuse to designate EPAs, but the central guidelines by which LEAs were to identify EPAs were illustrative and impressionistic rather than directive. Circular 11/67 allowed much scope for LEAs to decide what comprised an EPA. Yet if LEAs used this freedom to make what central government regarded as inordinate claims for resources, the Circular embodied several vague principles that could be used to reject claims. For example, it would not be enough for a project to replace unsatisfactory schools that were 'old and in poor condition and sub-standard in relation to current building standards'; preference would be given to projects that facilitated 'the general redevelopment of the area'.[46] This elastic criterion bordered on the spurious, as did the proposal that favour would be shown to projects which could be shown to be 'related to planned educational development'.[47] This could mean whatever the DES saw fit, allowing for the near-arbitrary rejection of projects over the limit of resources fixed by political decision. The political subtlety of such an instrument as 11/67 should be underscored. Positive discrimination was a dangerous concept to the DES and to government. It might have engendered considerable demand for additional resources or raised the expectation of a redistribution of existing resources. Both outcomes would have been politically very sensitive. The issue has been partly desensitized by allowing it to pass from a national to a local level. But central government still needs to manage the demands for resources. This requirement is secured by administrative discretion in the application of vague, general principles of the kind to be found in Circular 11/67. The instruments of educational priority, such as Circular 11/67, make sense in terms of a political balancing act aimed at demonstrating a response to educational disadvantage (thus responding to reformist pressures from within and outside the education system), while at the same time containing demands for resources within, first, acceptable limits of political embarrassment that stem from a measure of unsanctioned projects and, second, the orthodoxy of Treasury economic policy. The 'Treasury factor' should never be lost sight of. As Peter Townsend has noted, 'The single source which can be said to have been most influential in shaping social policy throughout this period [1974-9] has been the Treasury.'[48]

The EPA instruments make less sense as concerted action against educational disadvantage if left mainly to LEAs. Inconsistency, inaction and sheer mish-mash could and did ensue as a consequence of allowing positive discrimination to pass from central to local government. The variation that resulted could not be explained in terms of differing local needs. We are left with the suspicion that the DES was only too happy to assign the concept of positive discrimination to the graveyard of the LEAs' unwillingness to act without central resources. Positive discrimination was applied to *current* expenditure by only a few LEAs, acting voluntarily and without central direction.[49] Gordon-Walker, as Secretary of State for Education, held the orthodox view that LEAs must have unfettered discretion about how they allocated resources. He implied that a barrier to positive discrimination was the fact that 'if [the LEAs] do concentrate more on [EPAs], they must take it away from something else.'[50] This was true. But it was not a barrier to positive discrimination: it was positive discrimination.

Far from being a national plan, the priority programme was more a series of disjointed, ineffective expedients. A good example of this is the allocation in 1974 of £10.8 million to special pay allowances in EPAs. This might be credited with significance as a development of the initial implementation of the Plowden proposal that we have already examined, notwithstanding the publication of evidence that the scheme was a failure. Perhaps the allocation of £10.8 million should be examined in the context of the Government's pay policy of the time. The Labour Government was seeking to impose Phase

Three of a pay policy and was also awaiting a Pay Board report on the special allowance for London teachers. It might be argued that in these circumstances to be able to point to a recent lump-sum endowment of the above order may have strengthened the Government's position in resisting pressure for a generous settlement on both basic salaries and the London allowance. However, this interpretation cannot be sustained by any evidence. Certainly, it was not the case that the Government's motive for the payment was a desire to respond to pressure for such payments from LEAs and teachers. An LEA representative, in evidence to the Tenth Expenditure Committee, claimed:

> What happened in this case was that teachers' salaries were being held down before the Houghton Committee, and the Secretary of State of the day had an opportunity to persuade his colleagues that he could allow £10 million that could go into teacher salaries at a time when it could not go in any other way. So he took an *opportunist* decision, as I see it, and said, all right, I will make £10 million available to the Burnham Committee for them to negotiate.[51]

LEA representatives were adamant that there had been no consultation about this lump sum, and they felt that it could have been spent in more advantageous ways in aid of EPAs. The NUT evidence to the same Committee claimed that not only was the development of special payments ad hoc, by Government directive, without consultation, but also policy towards the disadvantaged in general was of this order.[52] At the NUT's 1975 Annual Conference a motion was passed supporting a policy of switching money from special payments for teachers into school budgets. Special payments were attacked as divisive and the £10.8 million was seen as a diversion from the need to endow deprived areas with a much larger volume of resources. However, the motion was passed with only a small majority and against advice from the union's executive. The NUT was clearly ambivalent about the means, if not the principle, of EPA policy.

Thus this aspect of the priority programme was somewhat ill-conceived. It seems that there was insufficient consultation about the allocation. It was objected to by LEAs and teachers. Research had raised fundamental doubts about the efficiency of the EPA allowance. The allocation made no sense as a contribution to a subtle salary policy aimed at solving the staffing problems of EPAs. A coherent staffing policy might have considered such things as how salary structures could be reformed *within the limitations of existing resources* to see to it that the disadvantaged were protected from the consequences of teacher turnover — arguably, headteachers protect sixth forms and A streams — or how EPA schools could be compensated for high teacher absenteeism. Of course, this would entail a difficult move from an elitist to an egalitarian staffing policy; far simpler, politically and administratively, to spend £10 million on a gesture towards disadvantage within the trappings of a largely symbolic 'plan'.

Other aspects of the priority programme need to be considered in relation to the politics of immigration and the 'urban crisis'. Again, the Government was pushed into action by immediate events rather than developing a long-term strategy. Education provision in deprived urban areas was a significant part of the UAP, as we have already mentioned, and the UAP has been seen by some as an ad hoc response to the heightened sense of urban malaise occasioned by a number of factors such as Enoch Powell's 'rivers of blood' speech.[53] A central feature of the perceived urban crisis was the concentration of blacks in urban areas. Most politicians were at pains to point out that immigrants were neither the sole nor the main beneficiaries of the UAP, but they nevertheless loomed large in policy statements. James Callaghan, in introducing the policy to the House of Commons in 1968, stated: 'The Government have now completed the first stage of their study of urban areas facing acute social problems in fields of education, housing, health and welfare. Many of these areas include concentrations of immigrants.'[54] Education projects attracted resources within the UAP, not necessarily because this was a logical priority in the context of a comprehensive plan (although it might have been), but quite simply because money could be spent quickly in this area. Circular 19/68 explained that nursery classes or schools would be encouraged, since 'these categories can in general be planned and built more quickly than other schools.'[55] It was intended that the building programme be completed in two years. Circular 2/69 sustained this emphasis — 'priority will have to be given to projects . . . which are capable of producing a quick effect.'[56] All the Circulars were keen that money should be spent quickly. One considered it important 'to ensure an early start'[57] and noted that 'the Government want some

work on the programme to start at once.' Similar pace was evident
in a previous Circular:

> the Secretary of State recognized that in some cases it may be difficult
> to identify, plan and start new projects before 1968/9. . . . Some
> authorities may be well advanced in their planning of improvement
> projects already included in the 1969/70 programme and may
> therefore be well placed to bring them forward to 1968/9.[58]

Such was the haste, that legislation was introduced to allow
government grants to be paid retrospectively.[59] All this might be
considered to be commendable alacrity, but it stands in marked
contrast to the Government's dilatory response to Plowden.
Arguably, the intention was to spend limited sums of money as
quickly as possible, as a demonstration of action. Politicians like to
make statements about a certain number of millions having been
spent on a specific problem. But why in 1968 should anyone race to
spend money in two years? A general election was certain by 1971,
and in fact took place in 1970. The Labour Government wished to
embark on electioneering armed with evidence of action against the
urban crisis, especially given the political significance of Midlands
marginal constituencies, some of which were areas of social
disadvantage and immigrant communities. The time dimension of
the urban policy speaks of ad hoc political expediency, not sound,
long-term policy to counteract severe, long-standing educational
disadvantage.

Clearly, rectifying educational disadvantage will take a long time
and will require sustained action by powerful administrative
agencies. But the very apparatus of the educational priority
programme suggests a lack of commitment. Far from being located
at the heart of the policy-making system, where policy concerning
educational disadvantage must be placed if it is to be taken seriously,
it has been relegated to peripheral outposts. The money for EPA
teachers' allowances was dispersed by the Burnham Committee,
which was incapable of developing a staffing policy of the kind that
we have suggested is necessary. In fact, the very existence of
Burnham explains, in part, why £10.8 million was spent on teachers'
allowances. There was a ready-made administrative device for
allocating resources. This device meant that, having secured the

satisfactory management of resources in fixing the total cost of the allowances, the DES avoided *direct* responsibility for the detail of this aspect of the priority programme.

However, in other respects the issue of educational disadvantage did lead to administrative innovation. In response to the Select Committee on Race Relations and Immigration, the Government set up the Educational Disadvantage Unit (EDU). The Unit bore the major administrative burden of devising policy against disadvantage. It was set up with extensive terms of reference — 'to serve as a focal point for consideration of matters at all stages of education connected with educational disadvantage and the education of immigrants; to influence the allocation of resources in the interests of immigrants and those identified as suffering from educational disadvantage'.[60] Though this was a welcome development, the Unit did not subsequently make a significant contribution to the correction of disadvantage.

Another development was the creation of the Centre for Information and Advice on Educational Disadvantage. The Centre met a desire on the part of LEAs for more open dissemination of work and ideas relating to disadvantage. Yet the Centre tended to preoccupy itself with questions of good curriculum practice and internal school organization. Such matters are not unimportant, but they are politically much safer — if not with teachers, then in larger political terms — than are positive discrimination in resource allocation and the redistribution of resources. In this way the question of educational disadvantage becomes more a technical matter for professional teachers and less a political and moral matter for politicians, administrators and the public. The LEAs' implementation of technical solutions, in their very variety a celebration of local autonomy and the decentralized system, compounds the drift away from positive discrimination as a matter of national policy. Although the discovery of technical solutions to problems of good teaching practice is highly desirable, there is little evidence it has ever commanded, or will ever command, a major redistribution of resources, or that a non-political clearing house for good practice is likely to be a cogent base for radical change. Such change will require not only political will and sanction but also complex policies that span government Departments. In 1979 the Centre was abolished by the Conservative Government because it was a QUANGO (though, in fact, by this time the DES had become convinced that the Centre was not adequately fulfilling its functions).

Eighteen years ago Newsom advocated the setting up of an inter-departmental and inter-authority working party to consider the question of educational priority. Even this would be a limited forum, given the magnitude of the task. But it is still much more than we have achieved. Ad hoc, inadequate expedients are the hallmark of recent measures against disadvantage. The NUT was well justified in its concern, expressed to the Tenth Expenditure Committee, at the lack of consultation on educational disadvantage and the unwillingness of the Government to go beyond saying, 'there is a sum of money and you can spend it in a certain way.'[61] This is suggestive of the legerdemain of miniscule resources addressing massive educational problems to maximum political effect. It means that the educational priority programme can be reasonably cited as a good example of the Central Policy Review Staff's judgement that issues are dealt with individually, as they emerge with different departmental emphasis on different policy instruments, as opposed to being related to a broad framework of social policy.[62]

Plowden's proposals for dealing with educational disadvantage were realized in an altogether different framework — one of vested interests and concerns that utilized educational priority to further ends which, while not antithetical to the interests of working-class pupils, nevertheless meant that a centrifugal character was imposed on the education system's response to positive discrimination, thus inhibiting the emergence of an integrated policy. As one of us has written:

> There is now such a host of project workers, teacher/social workers, curriculum support teams, home-school relations officers, on- and off-site unit teams, that, as Shipman points out, 'it is difficult even to map where the various agencies are in the inner cities and impossible to account for their activities.'[63]

Professional self-interest is also a reality that all egalitarian policy must negotiate. Teachers, for example, took Plowden on board as a means of legitimating claims for more teachers and of developing aspects of professional territory, such as the school as an agency of care-giving, which made for the creation of further lines of career development and claims for more resources. Much of the work of the Centre for Educational Disadvantage was associated with the development of schools as agencies of care-giving, some of which is clearly concerned with the social control of disruptive and deviant working-class pupils.[64] In this way the terms of concern with educational disadvantage have been deflected from principles of resource distribution and towards the moral reform of the working class.

Tory politicians could adapt the notion of positive discrimination to mean selectivity in the social services,[65] while Labour could use the priority programme as a political instrument in response to the 'urban crisis' and as an ideological means of endorsing the cosmetic vision of a basically sound social system with some flaws that called for action. Thus educational priority (as EPAs) was politically transformed into something compatible with the idea of social deprivation as 'often scattered in relatively small pockets [that] require special help to meet their social needs and to bring their physical services to an adequate level'.[66] No mention here, it should be noted, of making these standards 'better than average', as Plowden wanted: not even a commitment to securing average levels, since 'adequate' might be less than average. Plowden's optimism about maxima for the deprived is on the way to being supplanted by the political 'realism' of minima.

The DES was prepared to accommodate the priority programme insofar as it endorsed policy preferences that already had support within the orthodoxy of the education system — for example, reducing class sizes, extending nursery education and, generally speaking, giving special ad hoc handouts to areas of disadvantage within the margins of extra resources. While not hostile to the principle of EPAs, the Department was not prepared to fashion a policy in pursuit of greater equality by considering how educational development priorities could be altered to favour the working-class through the redistribution of existing resources. This would have been anathema to the pragmatism and 'tropism' of the DES. Indeed, Pile, as permanent secretary of the DES, argued that the priority programme was merely an 'act of faith'.[67]

Unquestionably, the priority programme *was* an act of faith: positive discrimination was, and remains, a moral notion to be accepted or rejected, in the first instance, in terms of social justice, not the technical perfections or imperfections of the instruments of implementation, such as EPAs, about which there has been much dispute.[68] We need further and larger acts of faith. Admittedly, a limited case could be made for the proven success of past positive discrimination. The calculation of working-class gains is bedevilled, as Banting notes, in that elements of the priority programme would have taken place anyway.[69] The programme was to some extent simply a change of language. And Barnes concludes that school-based policies were most likely to benefit the children of non-manual workers born in the United Kingdom.[70] Nevertheless, one OECD conference[71] argued that in order to be successful, positive discrimination required more funds — 20 per cent more should be spent on children in need by a variety of means depending on the aim of the policy. Several dimensions of policy were suggested, including the levels of achievement of individual children and schools. The principle of positive discrimination could be systematically extended to embrace all areas of educational provision, including novel areas such as careers guidance. The case for doing this as a national policy is overwhelming, given what must now be regarded as the failure of the Government's response to Plowden's initiative, which relied heavily on LEA action. Successive Governments have been unwilling to set aside opposition to a centrally directed policy from teachers and LEAs. Whether or not central government does this by legislation — as Banting observes, 'legislation conferring additional power or establishing a specific grant could have been sought, as was done for the Urban Programme'[72] — or by incentives is a matter for debate and personal political values. What is beyond dispute is that without central direction positive discrimination is doomed to failure, especially as an essential dimension of any policy of this kind must be the correction of regional inequaiities. There is overwhelming public support for giving top priority to schools in poor districts by providing more teachers and better buildings and supplies. One poll found that 88 per cent of the population supported this idea,[73] though another poll found that only 33 per cent supported the idea of preferential treatment.[74] We should build on the political good will inherent in the first poll by promoting positive discrimination not as a form of preferential treatment but as a means by which to end negative discrimination. Negative discrimination dominates the present system of resource allocation, in that preferential treatment is given to the socially advantaged. There are firm grounds for the optimistic belief that this treatment can be countered. Much of it is to be found in the trenchant analysis of educational priority edited by Halsey.[75] But he is not quite right in claiming that 'the essential fact of twentieth-century education history is that egalitarian policies have failed.'[76] The essential fact is that egalitarian policies have not been devised and rigorously implemented.

6

The End of 11-Plus Selection

In 1965 the Labour Government issued Circular 10/65 to bring about comprehensive secondary education. In taking this course, Labour was seeking to counter the social-class bias that favoured the middle-class's access to grammar schools. This was by no means the only reason for comprehensivization; for example, the 11-plus was widely considered to have an undesirable, narrowing effect on primary schooling. But, unquestionably, secondary reorganization was regarded by Labour supporters, first and foremost, as fundamental action against educational inequality and, by extension, as social inequality. Indeed, it is not going too far to suggest that the reform of secondary schools was a major means by which Labour sought to implement its egalitarian commitment. It is against this background that the policy must be judged. Secondary school reform was about the pursuit of a central aim in Labour policy, not just a particular area of educational administration.

Yet in various statements that were made by Labour before the issue of 10/65, there was some ambiguity about precisely what it was that the Labour Government sought to achieve in secondary education. Michael Stewart, Secretary of State for Education, introduced the comprehensive policy to the House of Commons in 1964 in the following terms, in an oral response to a parliamentary question:

> It is the Government's policy to reorganize secondary education on comprehensive lines. The method and timing must vary from one area to another. In general, entry to grammar school will no longer be restricted to certain selected children at the age of 11-plus and the range of students will be widened. One aim of this policy is that what we all value in grammar school education shall be preserved for those children who now receive it and made available to more children.[1]

There is some difficulty in interpreting this statement. Stewart was clearly concerned to allay anxieties about the preservation of high standards in secondary education, which some people equated with grammar schools. Certainly, the Conservative Party at this time expressed grave concern about the wholesale abolition of the grammar schools and the threat that this was alleged to pose to academic standards. A parliamentary statement like Stewart's was thus as much a political statement seeking to defuse opposition as a statement of policy. Nevertheless, if words are to retain their meaning and politicians their credibility, it is not wholly inappropriate to consider the terms of 'political' statements from the standpoint of what they reveal (and conceal) about policy aims. The least that could be said of Stewart's statement is that it suggests a lack of clarity about Labour's policy. The implication of the statement is that in some sense grammar schools would remain but that access to them would be widened. This could be construed as a variant of a commitment to 'grammar schools for all', a remark attributed to Harold Wilson in the 1964 election, which echoed a comment that he had made the previous year, when he replied to the question 'Should the grammar schools be abolished?' as follows: 'My answer to this, as a former grammar-school boy, is: "Over my dead body. There may be some people who think it worth it, but I don't."'[2] These observations cannot be taken as considered statements of policy, and they did cause embarrassment and indignation in some Labour quarters at the time. Also, the notion of 'grammar schools for all' was to some Labour leaders the highest form of egalitarianism — that is, the extension of the best opportunities to all. This was very much in accord with the historical posture adopted by the Labour Party towards educational opportunity. Stewart offered some definition of the intended new system of secondary education: 'The essence of the comprehensive system is that no children will be in a position of being sent to a school that is accepted from the start as not possessing as good facilities as some other schools for advanced academic education.'[3] Here the evident concern is with what Stewart called 'separatism' — the allocation of children of high ability to a different type of school from that to which children of low ability are sent. All this suggests that Labour was more certain of what it wished to move away from than what it wished to move towards. There was little doubt that Labour wanted to get away from 11-plus selection and the rigid segregation of pupils into different *types* of schools. The alternative vision of comprehensive schools was less clear, apart from a wish to preserve the best in grammar *schooling* that probably reflected a genuine concern with maintaining standards and not just political expediency.

Labour decided to advance the policy by Circular rather than legislation. This decision merits examination. In his autobiography Michael Stewart makes it abundantly clear that he, and not his DES officials, wrote the Cabinet paper on how Labour should 'go comprehensive'. He concluded the paper 'by asking the Cabinet's approval for the issue of a circular *requiring* local authorities to submit appropriate plans, and for legislation in the next session both to deal with particular difficulties and, if necessary, to deal with unco-operative local authorities'.[4] This was not acceptable to the Cabinet. It was decided that Stewart should proceed under existing legislation but should make it clear that the Government was prepared to legislate if this proved necessary. Some light has been cast on this decision by Crossman, and Stewart has written that Crossman's account may well be right. According to Crossman, who was at that time Minister for Housing, he objected to legislation and communicated this view to the Prime Minister, Harold Wilson. Wilson concurred and requested that Crossman submit a paper to him expanding his argument. This Crossman did, deliberately concealing the fact from Stewart with the aid of George Wigg. At the Cabinet meeting Wilson argued against legislation, apparently in the terms of Crossman's paper. If Crossman's account is accurate, the idea of legislation was supported by 'the old schoolteachers like Fred Peart and Willie Ross'.[5] There is also a suggestion of further initial support in the statement: 'Even the other members of the Social Services Committee immediately withdrew when the Prime Minister made his point of view clear.'[6] Thus it seems that the Secretary of State for Education was denied his policy because of prime ministerial opposition, supported by Crossman and, presumably, a majority in the Cabinet.

Why Wilson took this line is not clear, though we do speculate about his reasons below. His own book on the period is unrevealing. Still, his remarks about the preservation of the grammar schools, quoted above, together with what was clearly a determining action in Cabinet, could be seen as suggestive of some reservation, or at least indecision, about comprehensives. Stewart found it remarkable that a man like Crossman, 'who had a reputation of being "left" ', should have 'acted as a brake on two important issues of party policy — land ownership and comprehensive secondary education'.[7] Stewart, to be consistent, would have to regard Wilson in the same light with regard to the latter issue. At this point we offer no judgement as to whether or not failure to obtain legislation was, in fact, a brake on the policy. This must await an exposition of subsequent events. We simply note that the Minister responsible for the policy felt that the lack of legislation was a brake. Crossman implies that Stewart was so dissatisfied with the Cabinet decision that in a House of Commons speech two days later he 'revealed his determination to use legislation'.[8] Crossman claimed that in doing this Stewart had failed to carry out the Cabinet decision — Wilson, Crossman states, agreed with this criticism. Stewart denies this. In his House of Commons speech Stewart said that he expected that there would be a very large measure of willing co-operation from the local authorities: 'I would not ask the House for legislative powers unless that were absolutely necessary for the continuation of the policy.'[9] In that Stewart did not say that he expected full co-operation, he could also be construed as saying that legislation would be inevitable. But it is hard to see that in what he actually said Stewart was departing from either the letter or the spirit of what is known about the Cabinet decision. Legislation, at some point, had not been ruled out by the Cabinet. Stewart had clearly not been deflected from his initial view that legislation would be inevitable in the end. The fact that he was not able to implement this judgement is an interesting example of the constraints on ministerial power. Notwithstanding the limitations of the auto-biographical material that we have used, the decision against legislation and in favour of Circular 10/65 is an intriguing, and possibly revealing, example of how educational policy is sometimes made.

Crossman's public explanation of why he preferred not to acquire legislative backing to reorganization is unconvincing. He states that it was not necessary, 'since our plans for encouraging the local authorities to go comprehensive of their own free will were going so well'.[10] At this point the Government had been in office for only a matter of months and could scarcely be said to have had any plans, still less to have had time to secure feedback from local authorities. An alternative explanation of the preference for a Circular rather

than legislation could be posited. It is sometimes pointed out that
the Government had a majority of only three. This meant that it
might have had difficulty in passing controversial legislation. While
true, this probably misses the real political point. A small majority
meant that an election could not be delayed for long. Indeed, the
period 1964-6 was one of almost constant electioneering, during
which policy decisions were not just political but also electoral. In
these circumstances Wilson would have been at pains to avoid
presenting issues in a way that might have focused political
opposition or aroused public concern. A Circular was one way to
advance a policy that would be approved by political supporters
without offering too exposed a profile to political opponents.
Legislation, in marked contrast to the administrative device of a
Circular, would have had to pass through Parliament, possibly to
orchestrated Tory opposition and media publicity. It is noteworthy
that a few days after the Cabinet decision to proceed by Circular,
the Tories used a supply day to debate the issue of secondary
reorganization and launched a strong attack on Labour policy. In
addition, the Government inherited a difficult economic situation
that made for firm control on public expenditure. From a resources
standpoint, legislation was less attractive than a Circular. Some
local authorities might have pressed the Government for resources
to meet statutory obligations. If the Government aroused expectations that it was unable to meet, this could have been politically
damaging. Factors like this meant that the Circular was a creature
of political finesse and not just a calculation of how best to
implement an educational policy. The political justification for this
stance was that if Labour were to lose the next election,
comprehensivization might have been slowed even more drastically,
possibly reversed.

Circular 10/65 requested LEAs to submit plans for comprehensive reorganization. Yet Stewart's paper to the Cabinet had used the
word 'requires' not 'requests'. Reg Prentice, then Junior Minister at
the DES, is known to have favoured the former word. Crosland,
Stewart's successor at the DES, claimed that his officials preferred
the word 'requests' and makes it clear that the choice between the
two words was a subject of much argument within the Department.[11]
It might be doubted that the choice of word had much, if any, effect
on the extent to which LEAs responded to the Circular. Whatever
words are used in a Circular, it remains an instrument of

administrative guidance from central to local government. As such, it does not have the force of law, and LEAs could not be compelled to respond. The most that might be argued is that since 'requires' sounds more commanding than 'requests', some LEAs might have been persuaded to comply with Labour's wishes. However, the impact that the choice of words had on the response to the Circular is beside the point; what matters is whose preference prevailed and what was the character of that preference. The preference of officials appears to have prevailed (though there can be no doubt that formal decision was Crosland's), with the result that Circular 10/65 came to have a persuasive rather than a directive tone. This could be said to have made for the dilution of the strength of purpose and commitment behind Stewart's initial Cabinet submission. Arguably, Stewart's defeat in Cabinet on the question of legislation meant that the substitution of 'requests' for 'requires' was not unreasonable, since, strictly speaking, *in law* Labour was not in a position to require LEAs to act. But *in terms of policy* Labour *did* require LEAs to act, in that Labour was not prepared to take no for an answer and would adopt legislation if necessary.

That 'request' replaced 'requires' could be seen not just as a semantic adjustment to legal reality; the choice of word implied a policy adjustment that put the threat of legislation on the shelf and the pace of reorganization firmly back in the hands of the LEAs — where, in fact, it had always been and where one suspects the DES wanted the issue to be located. Shirley Williams has claimed that in 1967, when she was first a Minister at the DES, the Department 'was still marked by the selective and meritocratic values of the 1944 Education Act. . . . Gradually the Department moved towards supporting the reform of secondary education on comprehensive lines.'[12] This journey had scarcely begun in 1965. At that time comprehensives were probably contrary both to the 'departmental view' of secondary education and the Department's stance on the 'partnership' between central and local government. A Circular that requested LEAs to act under a vague threat of legislative compulsion went a long way to reassert the 'departmental view' against the encroachment of Labour's political directive — unless and until LEAs demonstrated their willingness to act, when the DES would be prepared to follow a trend in keeping with its predominant style of policy-making.

The detail of 10/65 merits attention. Six forms of comprehensive system were considered. These were: schools with an age range of 11 to 18; three two-tier systems; comprehensive schools with an age range of 11 to 16, combined with sixth-form colleges; and a system of middle schools. These schemes were not all regarded as ideal. They were suggested with regard to the necessity for a period of transition during which reform was to be achieved largely with the aid of the existing stock of school buldings. The two-tier systems were described as 'interim arrangements'. Even so, evaluation of 10/65, especially as an alternative to legislation, must take into account the scope that the Circular afforded for the perpetuation of selection in some secondary schools. The first two-tier system proposed that 'all pupils on leaving primary school transfer to a junior comprehensive school, but at the age of 13 or 14 *some* pupils move on to a senior school while the remainder stay on in the same school'.[13] It was envisaged that some of the latter schools would keep pupils until they were 15 and would not provide public examinations; others would keep pupils until they were 16, provide GCE and CSE examinations and encourage transfer to sixth forms in the senior schools. The Circular noted that it was essential, if selection were not to be reintroduced at 13 or 14, that transfer to the senior school should be dictated by parents' choice. Parents should, it said, seek advice from several teachers, and parents from 'less educated homes'[14] in particular should be offered a full explanation of the opportunities open to their children. The Secretary of State was said to anticipate that these conditions would be observed. But what possibility was there that they would be? What sanctions could the Minister use if they were not? Would he even know whether or not there was adequate parental guidance? How should adequate guidance be defined? Even if parents were given what was agreed to be adequate guidance, it was still conceivable that covert selection would obtain. There was evidence to suggest that such guidance had not been free from social-class discrimination; hence working-class pupils might be 'cooled out'.[15]

Another proposed form of two-tier reorganization provided for junior comprehensive schools for pupils until the age of 13 or 14. Unlike the first scheme, no pupils would remain in these schools beyond these ages. Pupils would have a choice between senior schools designed for those who expected to stay 'well beyond the compulsory age'[16] and schools for those who did not. The objections that could be made to this scheme were similar to those that could be made to the previous one — for example, transfer at 13 or 14 could entail covert selection. Both schemes ran the risk of creating different categories of junior schools, or streams within these schools, that would act as 'feeder' units for the more prestigious forms of education, whose nature was not obscured by such euphemistic descriptions of their pupils as those that study 'well beyond the compulsory age'.[17]

A further proposed scheme, namely comprehensive schools from 11 to 16 followed by sixth-form colleges, allowed for selection. The Circular simply noted that two conceptions of transfer to the colleges had been put forward. In one, the colleges would cater for the educational needs of all pupils staying on beyond 16; in the other, entry would be conditional on the pupils' obtaining five O-Levels. This would clearly retain selection at 16-plus.

The Circular was rather vague about a number of issues other than the main forms of comprehensive organization. This lack of specificity was likely to impede the goal of comprehensivization. The existence of direct-grant schools would remove from the comprehensive system children of high ability, mostly (though by no means exclusively) from middle-class backgrounds. Thus 10/65 states that the Secretary of State

> looks to both LEAs and the Governors of direct-grant schools to consider ways of maintaining and developing co-operation . . . he hopes that authorities will study ways in which schools might be associated with their plans [and] asks that authorities should open discussions at an early stage.[18]

It is not at all clear what is meant by 'association' or how and when it should be achieved. Stewart had given some hint of what might be expected in a previous House of Commons statement. He considered 'whether possibly by widening the range of entry into the direct-grant schools they can preserve some of the special merit that exists in the direct-grant schools and at the same time make it possible for them to remain part of the comprehensive system'.[19] Arguably, the 'special merit' of the direct-grant schools — exclusivity of social class and ability — was irredeemably incompatible with comprehensive schools. It was an error of political judgement not to realize this and to rely on a policy (if it could be called this) of voluntary 'consultation' and 'association' — as has been said, it was rather like asking the Athenaeum to turn itself into a youth centre.[20] Ten years later a Labour Government recognized this truth and abolished the direct-grant schools.

The voluntary schools posed another stumbling block to the 10/65 policy. The Circular recognized that hitherto comprehensive reorganization had not embraced voluntary schools, but asked that the parties should enter discussions at the earliest practical stage in the preparation of plans. It was expected that in due course the voluntary schools would be as fully part of any comprehensive scheme as were county schools, though 'they need not follow an identical pattern and it may take longer for the necessary adjustment to be achieved.'[21] It was not clear how long the voluntary schools would be given to respond to Government expectations or what evidence suggested that the expectation of co-operation was reasonable.

The availability of resources was obviously important to the success of 10/65. The Circular recognized that the current stock of school buildings would have to remain in use for a considerable time and that this would influence, even determine, the shape of secondary reorganization. It was accepted that in some cases buildings would 'exhibit marked deficiencies if they are used for purposes for which they were not intended. Nevertheless the demand for new schools because of a larger school population, new house building and [the raising of the school-leaving age] must take precedence.'[22] The Circular concluded: 'it would not be realistic for authorities to plan on the basis that their individual programmes will be increased solely to take account of the need to adapt or remodel existing buildings on a scale which would not have been necessary but for reorganization.'[23] LEAs were invited to recast their building programmes for 1965/66 and 1966/67, but it was made clear that this should not raise the total cost beyond that already authorized. However, the Circular felt (wrongly, as it turned out) that there might be some scope for an increase in 1967/68, since the full programme for that year had not yet been determined. In Kogan's view, Crosland decided that secondary reorganization could be achieved from within the normal building allocation, plus that made available for the projected raising of the school-leaving age (though to some extent this programme was disrupted by the postponement of the latter for two years in 1968).[24]

The plan of action embodied within 10/65 was limited. The time scale of the policy was less clear than at first appeared to be the case. LEAs were to submit plans for reorganization within one year; only exceptionally would there be an extension of the period — or so the Circular stated. There was uncertainty about what was meant by 'interim' in relation to the two-tier arrangements described above and about how long direct-grant schools would be given to meet Labour's expectations. The plans were to include a detailed statement of each LEA's proposals, covering a three-year period starting not later than September 1967. This sounds forthright and positive. But it should not be construed as signifying that the Government expected LEAs to start reorganization within two years of 10/65 and that it would be completed by 1970. In effect, the Circular was doing no more than to request information about what changes in secondary education would be taking place in the period 1967 — 70. A longer time scale of change was hinted at when the Circular spoke of LEAs describing the futures of individual schools in terms of short- and long-term futures; of proposals for the period 1967 — 70 as *instalments* of a long-term plan; and of *interim* arrangements that were to be *modified* and *superseded*.

There was no firm indication of what period of time was envisaged by terms like 'long-term' or 'interim'. Substantial scope for a slow pace to change was suggested by the statement that while the Government wished progress to be 'as rapid as possible', this was not to be achieved 'by the adoption of plans whose educational advantages more than off-set the benefits which flow from the adoption of comprehensive schooling'.[25] This statement echoes a remark made by Stewart in the House of Commons — 'I would rather wait a bit for a good comprehensive system than to try to push a sham version in its place.'[26] Of course, no sensible person would argue for the hasty implementation of a 'bad' system. But what is important is the psychological impact that statements like Stewart's might have had on LEAs. Remember that the Circular recognized that a good system would require building resources that were not, in fact, to be made available by central government. Some LEAs would need little encouragement to justify 'going slow' by reference to their reluctance to view the educational disadvantages of 'sham' comprehensives.

Circular 10/65 clearly lacked rigour. 10/65 contained an invitation to inactivity. Much was uncertain. LEAs had innumerable options left open to them, not just as to the form of reorganization but also as to its pace. The Secretary of State 'urged', 'looked to', 'hoped', 'asked' and settled to 'wait a bit'. Indeed, it is difficult to see how 10/65 could describe itself as 'a clear statement of national policy'.[27] It was, rather, an unclear statement of local policy. LEAs could go comprehensive if they wanted to, as they wanted to, when they wanted to, with their own resources. If they did not act, there was no policy, just a declaration of governmental hope.

Against this it might be argued that the limitations of 10/65 that we have described were not evidence of ineffectiveness but indicated a genuine wish on the part of Labour to recognize the autonomy of local government. It is unreasonable to expect too much from a Circular. Circulars, while stating the broad terms of a national policy, can do no more than urge local authorities to act in certain ways. All Governments experience tension between their policy aims and varying degrees of commitment to local government autonomy, which alter as between Governments and policies. They also experience varying degrees of local government commitment to central government policy. In general, Governments do not expect to try to force the policy content of Circulars on local authorities. All this is true, but it is not a wholly convincing defence of Circular 10/65. In the first place, it need not have proffered so many alternative forms of comprehensive school, or been so uncertain as to the time scale of change, or embodied so many tacit grounds for LEA inertia. Second, a more directive, declaratory tone, implying less freedom of choice for LEAs, would not have been inappropriate. This was not just another Circular dealing with the small change of education: it was the foundation stone of a major policy. Furthermore, it was a policy in pursuit of which Labour was prepared to deny local autonomy.

Patently, the bedrock of Labour's policy was the conviction that LEAs would act, that they were already acting. 10/65 concluded: 'the spontaneous and exciting progress which has been made in this direction by so many authorities in recent years demonstrates that the [comprehensive] objective is not only practicable; it is also now widely accepted.'[28] The arithmetic of comprehensives was less convincing. On 12 November 1964, in response to a parliamentary question, Michael Stewart stated that in January 1964 there were 189 comprehensive schools in England and Wales (out of a total of nearly 6000 schools) and that thirty-nine LEAs had *some* secondary provision of a comprehensive type.[29] This gives a much clearer picture of the limited advance that comprehensive schools had made at that time. On this evidence it is not overwhelmingly apparent that the Government could reasonably expect that a totally comprehensive system would be established by an upsurge of LEA activity without any further action on its part beyond the issue of Circular 10/65.

Another reason why Labour might have felt that the policy had sufficient dynamism to carry it forward was the belief that a political consensus existed about the undesirability of the existing secondary system. Boyle argued:

> One of the historical myths is that comprehensive reorganization started with Circular 10/65. It didn't. It started a number of years before . . . one of the reasons why I never felt able to take quite so strong a position against 10/65 as some of my supporters would have liked was that I knew the spadework leading up to that Circular was the result of the replies to an inquiry that I had sanctioned in 1963.[30]

Naturally, there was no unanimity between the major parties on this issue, any more than there was within the parties (as Boyle's remark indicates). Boyle's view was subsequently echoed by Stewart. In defending 10/65, he claimed that he was 'only anticipating by twelve or eighteen months what Boyle would have done'.[31] Of course, Stewart may have had political reasons for implying a consensus of this kind. (For example, it would have added force to Circular 10/65.) Arguably, 10/65 was not so much the expression of political consensus as an instrument by which it could be constructed. Circular 10/65 might have created a consensus about the desirability of comprehensive reform within the conventional pattern of central-local government partnership in education. If it failed to do this, it might have created something of a consensus on a 'fall-back' position, namely, that the Government had duly tried to proceed by agreement, but, since that had not been forthcoming, it was now justified in turning to compulsion. After such a trial period, legislation and incursion into LEA autonomy would appear less draconian and certainly easier to defend politically — though in this, as in other respects, 10/65 was a hostage to political fortune.

Circular 10/66, published in March 1966, was the first to apply additional force to the policy adumbrated in 10/65. The Circular repeated what had been said about the constraints that the non-availability of building resources would place on comprehensivization. That being the case, 'it would be inconsistent with the Government's long-term objectives if future school-building programmes were to include new projects exclusively fitted for a separatist system of secondary education.'[32] Thereafter the Secretary of State would not approve secondary projects which were incompatible with non-selective secondary education. The effectiveness of this as a spur to comprehensivization is open to some doubt. Only a small proportion of building proposals would be manifestly incompatible with comprehensive schools: how else could the Government reasonably expect LEAs to redeploy the existing stock of non-purpose-built buildings if this were not the case? The DES recognized the difficulties it would encounter in making judgements about particular proposals, 'in cases where the Department did not yet have the necessary information about reorganization schemes',[33] by requesting that LEAs describe how each secondary proposal would, *or could,* fit into a comprehensive pattern. LEAs, acting in good faith, could easily show that school buildings could be adapted at some point, in some way, with some sort of comprehensive plan. Besides, 10/66 was a negative sanction. If LEAs were content to continue with their existing building stock, they could resist comprehensive reorganization, though, of course, those subject to pressures of expanding school population would have to give careful thought to their position.

Some indication of the progress towards reorganization secured by Circulars 10/65 and 10/66 can be gleaned from the following figures. By 1969 there were only 962 comprehensive schools out of a total of 5468. There were 772,612 pupils in comprehensive schools, 1,303,751 in secondary moderns and 531,948 in grammar schools.[34] Particularly noteworthy is the slow decline of grammar-school pupils, down by only 87,000 compared with 1965. Furthermore, critics of Labour's policy have doubted the extent to which the system could be described as truly comprehensive. Marsden argues that before the Labour Government left office in 1970, only 10 per cent of all schoolchildren were in schools with non-selective intake.[35] Many of the schools that were called comprehensive had as much as 20 per cent of the top ability range 'skimmed' for selective schools. Increasing pressure from Labour backbenchers and the Party beyond Westminster moved the

Government to further action. Another galvanizing factor was that control of LEAs had progressively passed to the Conservatives, who in some areas opposed reorganization.

Thus in February 1970 the Labour Government introduced an Education Bill that was intended to secure reorganization. Short, Secretary of State, in presenting the Bill to the House of Commons, argued that the Government 'could no longer tolerate that a minority of authorities and a minority of school governors are either ignoring or openly flouting national policy as laid down by this House'.[36] It was 'increasingly clear that unless the Government takes powers to require all authorities to change over to a full non-selective system . . . some would do nothing at all and many others would fail to complete their partial plans'.[37] Yet Short still sought to defend the previous policy. He claimed that it had produced excellent results and that 110 out of 163 LEAs had plans approved for all or most of their areas. This claim somewhat overstated the degree of co-operation that 10/65 and 10/66 had encountered, as the figures given above clearly reveal.

The Education Bill *required* local education authorities to have regard to the need for ensuring that secondary education was provided in non-selective schools and for ending the selection of pupils for admission to secondary education by reference to ability or aptitude. This represented a toughening of Labour's policy. The Bill now appeared to give the force of law to the Government's policy. The Secretary of State had the power to insist that five-year plans for reorganization be submitted. This was a more coherent approach to planning than the piecemeal, unrestricted submission of plans that had obtained, given the fact that hitherto the Government had had no powers to overcome non-co-operation from LEAs. However, there is a distinction between the submission of plans and their actual implementation.

The vital question is how far the Bill would have given the Government new powers to end 11-plus selection. Before considering this, it is worth noting that the Bill did not seek to abolish all selection in secondary education. Sixth forms were exempted from the requirement not to select, though Short had expressed his support for the notion of entry to the sixth form being open to all.[38] As to the central issue — would Labour now be in a position to compel LEAs to act? — grave doubts were expressed. Boyle raised fundamental doubts about the Bill.[39] The 1970 Bill was at one with the 1944 Education Act, which embodied a number of principles to which LEAs were to have regard — for example, the provision under Section 8 of the Act to provide education for children according to age, ability and aptitude. The 1970 Bill enshrined the further principle that LEAs should have regard to the need not to select. Boyle wondered what the legal position would be when the two principles conflicted. He felt that Section 8 might take precedence. It is beyond dispute that the Bill did not actually prohibit selection.

Thus in a number of respects the Bill appears to have been loosely drafted and ill-conceived. The problem of the direct-grant schools did not receive attention. Bacon, in acknowledging this fact, argued that it was implicit that LEAs that paid for children at direct-grant schools should have regard to the question of whether or not the school was comprehensive.[40] This was something of an evasion of the real issues. It suggested that LEAs should cease to pay for places at direct-grant schools that were not comprehensive, but said nothing of what the Government would do if the advice was ignored, as it had been in previous years. And in what sense could direct-grant schools become comprehensive without fundamentally altering their nature? Bacon was, in fact, advocating the abolition of direct-grant schools without taking steps to secure that end. Similarly, the Bill offered no action on the question of bringing the voluntary grammar schools within comprehensive reorganization.

The Bill was subject to bad parliamentary management. At a crucial meeting of the committee that was considering the Bill, three Labour MPs were absent, so that a vote was lost on the primary principle, that is, establishing reorganization by compulsion. The Bill was soon overtaken by events. The Government called for a general election, which it lost, and the Bill fell.

Margaret Thatcher was the Secretary of State for Education in the incoming Conservative administration, and she immediately issued Circular 10/70, which stated the following:

The Government's aim is to ensure that all pupils shall have full opportunities for secondary education suitable to their needs and abilities. The Government, however, believe it is wrong to impose a uniform pattern of secondary education organization on local education authorities by legislation or other means. Circular 10/65 is accordingly withdrawn. Consequential restraints on the character of secondary building projects will no longer apply.[41]

Thus it is clear that while the Conservatives did not seek to promote comprehensives, in the terms of the Circular at any rate, they sought neither to prohibit them nor to encourage LEAs to abandon them where they had already been established or were about to be established. As the Circular said:

> where a particular pattern of organization is working well and commanding general support, the Secretary of State does not wish to cause further change without good reason . . . authorities which have had reorganization plans approved may either proceed to operate them unchanged or notify the Department of their wish to modify them.[42]

Since this Circular was issued within days of Thatcher's attaining office, there could not have been any consultation with the educational world. Probably it was this fact, suggestive of the 'smack of firm government', as much as anything else, that led to what has been described as an 'immediate and sharp reaction' and the fact that 10/70 was seen 'as an attack on comprehensive education'.[43] If anything, the Circular was a statement of a belief in the possibility of the coexistence of comprehensives and grammar schools, together with a willingness to let the issue of secondary education find resolution at the local level. So it appeared.

In fact, through certain administrative decisions Thatcher obstructed comprehensive reorganization to a greater extent than might have been expected from the rather bland tones of 10/70. Section 13 of the 1944 Education Act was used to examine each school within a particular plan. By October 1972 Thatcher had refused LEAs permission to alter the character of ninety-two schools (for the most part, prestigious grammar schools) because of local protests, and she embarked on a policy of encouraging local defence of grammar schools.[44] Earlier that year, addressing the NUT Annual Conference, Thatcher had argued that since 1970 she had dealt with proposals relating to 1400 schools and that she had rejected only forty-six, that is, 3 per cent.[45] By the autumn of 1973 the rate of rejection had risen to 'only' 10 per cent (out of 3400 proposals), according to the DES, moved to present such (hoped-for) reassurance in response to criticism that proposals for comprehensive schools were being subjected to unwarranted alteration, delay or rejection.[46] Clearly, if a few grammar schools were excluded from a reorganization plan and remained selective, then the entire plan was vitiated. Benn and Simon argue that a pattern to the apparent non-policy of 10/70 soon emerged: 'what won approval for reorganization was enlargement of secondary modern schools as comprehensives, while what was disallowed were LEA requests for changes in grammar schools.'[47] Nevertheless, comprehensive schools, of a kind, continued to increase in number. In fact, between 1965 and 1970, the period in which Labour's policy of 10/65 was in operation, the number of comprehensive schools increased by 883, whereas in the period 1970 to 1974, when the Conservative withdrawal of 10/65 obtained, the number of comprehensive schools increased by 1128.[48]

In 1974 a Labour Government was returned to office. In April the Government issued Circular 4/74, thereby 10/70. This Circular stated the Government's intention of developing a 'fully comprehensive system' and of ending selection at 11-plus or at any other stage. There was no indication of what was meant by a 'fully comprehensive system'. Also, although the commitment to ending selection at any age after 11 amounted to something of a reformulation of Labour's policy, it was not clear what particular aspect of post-11 selection the Government was addressing. 10/65 had expressed concern about covert selection by means of guided choice in the interim two-tier forms of reorganization suggested to LEAs. Three types of organization were mentioned by 4/74: all through 11 – 18; 11 – 16, leading to separate colleges; middle schools, 8 – 12 or 9 – 13, leading to upper schools, 12/13 – 18. But there was no indication that transfer to the upper schools would be anything other than non-selective. Nor did the Circular refer to the mode of transfer to sixth-form colleges, which is puzzling given that the Government appeared to be mindful of the undesirable possibility of selection after 11 and the fact that entry to the sixth form had been a matter of debate in connection with the previous instruments of reorganization.

The Government did not intend to introduce legislation to secure comprehensivization. This represented an inexplicable reversal of policy in the light of the ill-fated 1970 Bill. At that time Labour was convinced, as Short argued (see above, p. 147), that some LEAs would continue to resist. It is not apparent what substantial evidence led to a change of view, and, as future events proved, the decision not to acquire legal backing for the policy was a mistaken judgement. The superficial evidence for relying on LEA co-operation is very clear. 4/74 talked of the 'substantial progress'[49] that had already been made. According to that Circular, by March 1974, of the 163 LEAs that existed before the reorganization of local government, seventy-two had received approval to reorganize totally on comprehensive lines, seventy-six had organized in part and only fifteen had not received approval to reorganize. Of the 104 LEAs in existence on 1 April 1974, only one had not reorganized any of the county schools in its area.[50] These figures were obviously presented in such a way as to highlight the degree of advance that had been made.

Thus the main strategy of the policy had not changed since 10/65, though Circular 4/74 did contain this stronger *sounding* sentence:

the Secretary of State requires [rather than requests] information as soon as possible and in any event not later than by the end of 1974 about the successive measures which will be taken to complete the process of reorganization in those areas where selection procedures are still operating.[51]

But, as we have explained above, a Circular is an administrative device that does not have the force of law behind it. The policy still assumed that LEA co-operation would be forthcoming. Even though the tempo of reorganization had apparently been stepped up, in that LEAs were only to be allowed a further eight months to submit plans, there was no deadline for their implementation, still less the creation of means by which this could be imposed by central government.

The Circular recalled that 10/65 requested that LEA plans should embrace voluntary schools, but noted that 'in some areas, the governors of voluntary schools have stood out against the wishes of their LEAs who maintain their schools to attain a fully comprehensive system.'[52] Yet despite this recognition, the Government intended to do no more than 'ask those governors to reconsider their attitude in the light of the Government's policy'.[53] If the governors did not co-operate, the DES would be powerless to act. There was one threat:

> governors cannot expect to continue to receive the substantial aid which their schools enjoy through being maintained by the local authority, if they are not prepared to co-operate with that authority in settling the general educational character of the school and its place in a local comprehensive system.[54]

But this was a toothless sanction. The Government gave no indication of how it would ensure that LEAs withdrew their financial support.

The section in the Circular relating to direct-grant schools could not have been more vacuous. The Circular simply stated that some direct-grant schools might fit into comprehensive reorganization, and if this was so, the fact that they were direct-grant schools should not be regarded as an obstacle. This non-policy was probably inspired by the fact that the phasing out of the schools was under active consideration; the process was initiated the following year.

Circular 4/74 implied that no special resources would be made available for reorganization. The Secretary of State was convinced that authorities and voluntary school governors could 'expedite the transformation of many existing schools *into parts* of a coherent and fully comprehensive system without special building alloca-tions'.[55] This suggests that the Government recognized that a lack of resources would inhibit the creation of a more than partially satisfactory system (in fact, 'parts of a coherent and fully comprehensive system' is a contradiction in terms), as does the remark that proposals for a school to function as an interim measure on more than one site would not be ruled out. Also, it is not altogether clear whether the full rigour of Circular 10/66's denial of building allocations for selective schools still obtained. Circular 4/74 stated that in considering proposals for individual major projects at secondary schools, the Secretary of State would take account of the contribution they would make to reorganization; projects would be allowed at grammar or secondary modern schools where they were necessary to enable the schools to become comprehensive.[56] Such projects were subsequently allowed, and it was not always clear how soon improved selective schools were to be absorbed within the comprehensivization programme or in what strict sense the building allocation had been a vital instrument of this transformation.

It is doubtful whether 4/74 was any more coherent as a statement of *national* policy than 10/65. In fact, in some respects it was less defensible. Nearly ten years' experience of voluntary reorganization should have convinced Labour (and the DES) that co-operation could not be assumed from some LEAs voluntary and direct-grant schools. Also, the move towards comprehensive reorganization, such as it was, had created new difficulties, chief among them being the wide variety of secondary education that had emerged following the Government's toleration of so many different forms of reorganization. This spoke more of anarchy than flexibility. Not only did comprehensives vary in form between areas, but the 1974 local government reorganization meant that there was variety even within LEAs. However, 4/74 simply stated: 'it is a matter for local choice whether the pattern should remain varied or whether within one authority's area a homogenous system should gradually be introduced.'[57] Yet again the Government failed to define, or pursue, a preferred form of comprehensive reorganization as part of a national policy. Indeed, it was soon readily apparent that 4/74 was an inadequate instrument for securing reorganization. In response to the Circular, sixty-seven LEAs out of 105 expected to have completed reorganization by the end of the decade (that is, after the next general election, which might have returned a Conservative Government committed to abandoning compulsory reorganization); thirty-one expressed commitment in principle, subject to available resources, which on past record were unlikely to be made available; and the remaining seven refused to commit themselves unless the law was changed to require them to do so. This determined the Government to introduce legislation, almost a decade after the start of its policy.

Before considering this legislation, it is instructive to examine the Tameside case. The Labour-controlled Tameside Metropolitan Borough Council, Greater Manchester, submitted plans for comprehensive reorganization in March 1975. They were accepted by the DES in November of that year and were due to be implemented in September 1976. However, in the local elections held in May 1976 the Conservatives were elected. As part of their election campaign, the Conservatives had committed themselves to retaining selective education. Accordingly, they abandoned the comprehensive plans of their predecessors. The Secretary of State, Fred Mulley, deemed that the Council was acting unreasonably. Mulley applied to the Divisional Court for an order of mandamus requiring the Council to comply with his direction under Section 68 of the 1944 Education Act. This was granted but was subsequently discharged by the Court of Appeal. The Secretary of State appealed to the House of Lords, but his appeal was dismissed. What emerges from the legal argument is that under the 1944 Act there are restrictions on the capacity of the Secretary of State to impose a national policy. Mr Justice May, in ruling in favour of the Minister at the first hearing, nevertheless observed that Section 68 gave power that was so wide that the court should be astute to ensure that the power was exercised lawfully; a Minister should not allow his decisions 'to be affected wholly or partially by his political views or considerations of policy'.[58] The Appeal Committee of the House of Lords argued that the test of whether an LEA was behaving unreasonably must be an objective one — that is, it must be judged to be acting in a way in which no reasonable LEA would act, rather than in a way with which the Minister merely disagreed or found to be in conflict with his own political views.[59] The Law Lords, in their ruling, stated that 'there might be a difference of policy between the Minister and the authority: the section [i.e., Section 68, 1944 Education Act] gave the Minister no power to make his policy prevail.'[60] Thus a Minister could not reasonably maintain that an LEA was acting unreasonably simply because its actions were contrary to national policy. It would be necessary to show that an LEA was acting in a way that no reasonable LEA would act — and opposing national policy by refusing to go comprehensive was not acting unreasonably. Clearly, national educational policy-making operates in a legal context that is highly conservative and restrictive. (Griffiths argues that judges tend to be conservative and to decide the meaning of subjective terms in statutes by 'the direction their political inclinations lead them'.)[61] The Tameside judgment suggested that the 1944 Education Act did not provide a statutory basis for the imposition of comprehensives as a national policy. The judgment was given on 21 October 1976. One month later the 1976 Education Act came into force, with the express purpose of providing legislative backing for comprehensive organization.

The Act says that

> local education authorities shall, in the exercise and performance of
> their duties relating to secondary education, have regard to the general
> principle that such education is to be provided only in schools where
> the arrangements for the admission of pupils are not based (wholly or
> partly) on selection by reference to ability or aptitude.[62]

There were doubts about the extent to which this would give power
to the Secretary of State to impose comprehensive schools. During
the Standing Committee stage of the Bill, Norman St John-Stevas,
Conservative Opposition spokesman, expressed doubts similar to
those expressed by Boyle in relation to the 1970 Bill.[63] The 1976
Act introduced a further principle alongside other principles
enshrined in the 1944 Education Act. In St John-Stevas's view, the
Act did not impose a duty on LEAs to end selection; it simply
required them *to have regard* to the general principle that secondary
school admission should not be selective.

Thus, an LEA, having regarded the principle, might decide not to
act on it and, in so doing, would not be in breach of a statutory duty,
which would mean that a Minister could react by seeking an order
of mandamus. However, the DES had no doubts about the power of
the Act to secure reorganization. It claimed that the Secretary of
State was able to require the submission of plans for comprehensives
by LEAs and voluntary school governors and to direct that proposals
come into effect within five years of being submitted. 'Once such
proposals have been approved, LEAs and governors or managers of
voluntary schools will be under a duty to implement them.'[64]

The Act did not resolve all the uncertainties about the Labour
Party's intentions regarding selection. In the debate on the Queen's
Speech which foreshadowed the Act, Mulley, the Secretary of State,
is supposed to have said, 'We are going to abolish selection, not just
at 11, but at 12, 13, *or any age.*'[65] Yet, as we have argued, Labour
policy with respect to selection at 16 has been somewhat inconsistent
with declarations of this kind, notwithstanding 4/74's commitment
to end selection at 11-plus or at any other stage.

It is true that the 1976 Act did not specifically exempt selection
for sixth-form colleges, as the 1970 Bill intended, but Fowler,
during the Standing Committee stage of the 1976 Bill, stated: 'we
would not in general wish to see the development of a selective
sixth-form college system, but where these colleges exist, we

recognize that it may be some years before it is possible to move to a different system.'[66] But the Government did not give a clear indication of when it intended to act. It appears to have been another example of Labour's waiting for LEAs to act, if and when they saw fit. In the Standing Committee that considered the 1970 Bill, Short, then Secretary of State for Education, argued:

> we believe that 11-plus selection is wrong, first because it measures social factors as well as the child's inherent ability and secondly because it closes the option for a child at much too early an age. But these factors do not operate at 16, or at any rate, not to the same extent.[67]

Short's observation that 11 is too early an age for selection cannot be gainsaid, though it could be argued that social factors are as much in evidence, if not more so, in selection at 16. It is clear that while the 1970 Bill sought to end selection, it extended some toleration to selection at 16-plus as did the 1976 Act — witness Fowler rather than Mulley.

When the Education Bill received the Royal Assent in November 1976, the Secretary of State, Shirley Williams, wrote to the eight LEAs that had not introduced comprehensive education and gave them six months to submit proposals. Seven of the eight did, or were about to, submit plans when the deadline expired. Tameside remained obdurate and was informed by the DES that unless plans were submitted in four months, the authority would be held to be in default of its statutory duty. Williams also wrote to thirty-eight other LEAs which had introduced partial comprehensivization and asked them to submit plans for full comprehensivization, again within six months. More than half did not do so, and the deadline was extended. In April 1978 Williams informed the House of Commons that of the thirty-eight LEAs required to submit proposals for all or part of their areas, only six had not complied. She intended taking legal action where necessary.[68] Williams defended herself against complaints about a lack of political will over comprehensive education by pointing out that 83 per cent of children were in comprehensive schools and that 503 proposals and schemes had been accepted since 1974. Slightly less persuasive figures were presented simultaneously by the DES which showed that forty-four LEAs (that is, less than half) were fully comprehensive, compared with twenty-two in 1976.[69]

Nevertheless, the fact remains that the secondary system had undergone major reform and the overwhelming majority of children were being educated in what could be described as comprehensive schools, notwithstanding dispute over whether or not this amounted to a 'truly comprehensive' system. Yet in assessing the significance of the transition, there are some difficulties with arguing that reorganization was the outcome of rapid, radical, egalitarian action on the part of Labour. This is evident from a number of standpoints, the first of which is a consideration of the resources that were deployed to facilitate the transition. Secondary reform was not an occasion for redistributive investment in working-class education.

Labour made the political choice initially of according low priority to reorganization as a claim on building allocations. For the most part, the capital basis of the policy was the normal building programme. As we have argued, this decision was biased against disadvantaged areas because they tend also to be areas of static declining population. Admittedly, the building programme associated with the raising of the school-leaving age was seen by the DES as facilitating the comprehensive policy, but it is extremely difficult to estimate how far the outcome of this policy could be seen as enrichment of working-class education. Some extra resources were made available for secondary reform. In Circular 8/75 the Government announced a special building allocation of £25 million specifically for reorganization. This was to be devoted to small extension projects rather than to the provision of complete new schools. It is difficult to measure this sum against some firm yardstick of the capital cost of reorganization. Boyson claimed that LEAs had asked for £68.5 million.[70] A DES report published in 1978 argued that the deficiencies in practical accommodation might critically inhibit the progress of comprehensive reorganization in some areas.[71] According to the report, about a quarter of state secondary schools were still not comprehensive, the buildings of almost all of which dated from before 1946. The cost of bringing them up to standard was estimated at £30 million. In all, a total of £70 million was required for basic improvements in order to complete comprehensive reorganization by 1986. In April 1978 the Government announced a further £20 million building programme for reorganization, to be divided between sixty-five LEAs. All LEAs might reasonably have been expected to have needs in this respect, but the programme was part of an economic strategy to counter unemployment, and it was this that determined the distribution, at least in part.[72] As so often happens, social policy was the creature of economic policy. How far lack of resources obstructed reorganization is open to debate, resources being neither a necessary nor a sufficient springboard for reform. Yet Alexander probably spoke for many in the LEA world when he said:

> This is the danger — doing it [reorganization] badly, with no resources, and having schools two or three miles apart and calling it a comprehensive school instead of a school properly organized, properly designed and properly staffed to this job . . . it will require substantial resources if it is to be well done.[73]

He might have cited as an extreme example the Thomas Calton School, Peckham, split as it was between *five* sites. In 1976 the *total* ILEA building allocation was nearly £0.5 million less than that requested by ILEA for the capital cost of a unified replacement for Thomas Calton alone.[74] The deficiencies in the resources made available for comprehensive reorganization stand in marked contrast to the plenitude that facilitated the expansion of higher education (see chapter 8). Perhaps the fundamental difference between the two policies — those of comprehensive reorganization and the expansion of higher education — was that the former *aspired* to enrich particularly, though not exclusively, working-class education; the latter, disproportionately, *did* enrich middle-class education.

But it could not be argued that this aspiration was the sole dynamic of secondary reform. Most explanations of the move from bipartite to comprehensive education make too much of the role of the Labour Government as an extrinsic agent of radical change and too little of intrinsic evolutionary forces within education that favoured reorganization. There was and is a dynamic to the education system — what Boyle called 'the logic of the education service as it was developing'.[75] To some extent reorganization was a 'logical' solution to some of the strains and tensions within secondary education: local administrative pragmatism was one reason for reorganization. Kogan argues that some Conservative authorities, such as Leicestershire, Shropshire, Staffordshire and Oxfordshire (all rural areas), made substantial advances towards integrating secondary education between 1951 and 1964, and that they were concerned not with ideological arguments for comprehensive education but with the practical problems of providing education other than in small, widely dispersed schools that would not provide an adequate range of subjects.[76] In Kogan's view,

> had Labour not come to power in 1964, there would have been a gradual extension of comprehensive education until the point would have been reached when a substantial minority of children would have remained in 'good' grammar schools, which the DES would have refused to allow to be closed.[77]

Even those who would dispute this — and we would — would probably concede that such a trend was at least a contributory factor in the impetus towards comprehensives.

Other factors were at work. The post-1956 'bulge' in the child population entered schools in the mid-1960s, thus increasing the demand for secondary education; the growing trend of staying on beyond the statutory leaving age had a similar effect. One could surmise that just as widely scattered populations in rural areas made comprehensives an attractive solution to problems of the costs of education, so the high cost of building land made large schools equally attractive in urban areas. Some debates about reorganization at a local level convey an *impression* — the evidence would not enable the point to be put any more strongly than this — that some chief education officers might have seen comprehensives as a convenient solution to practical problems. Batley argues that one chief education officer was convinced that it would be increasingly difficult to contain the phenomenal growth in sixth-form numbers at the boy's grammar school without building a completely new school.[78] This was one reason why it became necessary to examine the development of secondary education in the area. Arguably, in a context of such flux, comprehensives threatened less upheaval than they otherwise might have done. This is suggested by the fact that although 10/65 did give a significant boost to the submission of comprehensive plans, this continued between 1970 and 1974, while 10/65 was withdrawn.

Furthermore, it should not be forgotten that competition for entry to grammar schools was acute. In some areas it was undoubtedly the case that a majority of middle-class children failed the 11-plus. Their disaffected parents gave their support to reorganization not for egalitarian reasons but for reasons of self-interest, masked by spurious concern for social efficiency, modernity and the technocracy of the 1964 Wilsonian 'revolution'.

Thus to some extent the comprehensive policy served the interests of the middle classes rather than simply representing a diminution of their social influence. The same could be said of a previous major reform of secondary education — the establishment of free secondary schooling for all by the 1944 Education Act. In fact, the middle class gained in one respect because after 1944 it obtained free places for which hitherto it had paid. The existence of this middle-class social influence had two implications for the end of selection. The erosion of class-biased selection was likely to be contained and adapted within the inequalities of 'neighbourhood' schools, catchment area policies, house purchasing as a means of access to prestigious secondary schools and streaming within schools.

Neither did the instruments chosen to pursue the policy speak of radical rigour: the hallmark of the policy was a desperately slow-moving consensus. It is customary to speak of the 1970 Bill as marking the end of consensus; but the end of what was essentially a parliamentary consensus was not tantamount to a radical departure. To argue this would be to regard the fact of Conservative opposition as a sufficient presumption of radicalism. Indeed, as we have argued above, another and larger non-parliamentary consensus, of an essentially pragmatic kind, had developed by 1970. Labour had embarked on a conservative path of consensus with its decision in 1965 to proceed by Circular rather than by legislation. That this was probably an error of judgement is suggested by subsequent events. Yet this is not something that can be claimed just from hindsight alone — Stewart knew it when he asked the Cabinet to support his request for legislation. It is not convincing to argue, as so many have done, that the 1965 Labour Government could not obtain statutory powers at this time because it had a majority of only three in the House of Commons. In 1976 a minority Labour Government was able to secure what was believed to be statutory authority for reform, though by this time, when so many LEAs had gone comprehensive, legislation was an easier matter.

Through 10/65 the Government was seeking to alter the balance of authority between central and local government without embodying this shift of authority in statute. Civil servants probably played a significant part in determining this unsatisfactory course. They acted as a conservative influence on the terms and tone of

10/65 by substituting the word 'request' for 'require'. The adequacy of the advice given about the policy by DES officials also seems questionable — for example, in connection with the legal advice appertaining to the Tameside case and, before that, the drafting of the 1970 Bill. Short, the Minister responsible for the latter, is said to have left Whitehall feeling that officials had cheated him of his purpose. However, politicians are prone to blame officials for their own failings, and Stewart's major defeat was not at the hands of officials; it was inflicted by his political colleagues in the Cabinet.

The main problem was that the goals of the policy were neither consistently nor adequately defined and fluctuated between the end of selection, the end of the 11-plus and other (unstated) forms of selection and the creation of a 'truly comprehensive' system. Selection for sixth forms was specifically allowed in 1970 but was to be tolerated for an unstated period in 1976. Banding was definitely to be outlawed in 1970 but was allowed in 1976. Legislation was not considered necessary in 1965 but was necessary in 1970; it was not in 1974 but was in 1976. The evaluation of the policy seems to have been crudely concerned with quantitive aspects of the change and was, even within these limited terms, misleadingly optimistic insofar as it was made public. There is little impression to be gained of a well-thought-out policy being tested against experience and modified accordingly. The policy did change, but in a disjointed, sometimes inexplicable fashion; for example, 10/66 prohibited the provision of building resources for selective schools (inexplicably, after the reorganization policy had been in existence for a year), whereas 4/74 appeared to relax this as an expedient for the attainment of partial comprehensive systems. But the grounds for doing this and the prospects of successfully advancing the policy to its ultimate goal of full comprehensivization are obscure. Throughout, the issue of a time scale for achieving reform was either avoided or, if addressed, unresolved. The need to redistribute resources was not even defined as a nettle, still less grasped. Crosland said that the comprehensive policy was 'rooted in fundamental value judgements about equity and inequality of opportunity'.[79] To some extent it remained there, impervious to the need to change the educational world by coherent planning and executive discipline.

7

The Raising of the School-Leaving Age

In this chapter we examine the raising of the school-leaving age to 16 (RSLA). We offer some tentative explanation of why it happened. (We stress 'tentative' because of the limitations of the sources to which we have had access and, beyond that, because of the common difficulty of locating, let alone describing, let alone *explaining,* changes in educational policy.) The substance of the chapter is an evaluation of RSLA in terms of action taken against educational inequality. We consider how RSLA might be construed as of egalitarian intent and how far the implementation and outcomes of RSLA were also egalitarian. This consideration is prefaced by an account of the political context of RSLA.

RSLA took place in 1973. Almost thirty years before the 1944 Education Act had provided for the school-leaving age to be raised to 15, and to 16 when 'practicable'. Yet at the 1959 general election neither the Conservative nor the Labour Party had made a commitment to RSLA in its manifesto. Indeed, the Conservatives had implied that they relied on voluntary staying on: 'by 1965 we expect at least 40 per cent will be staying on after 15.'[1] However, RSLA was recommended by the Crowther Report (1959) and the Newsom Report (1963). The delay in achieving RSLA suggests political indifference towards it, or at least that low priority was attached to it by comparison with other educational aims.

In the House of Commons debate on the Crowther Report (which, significantly, took place after the 1959 election), Sir David Eccles (then Tory Education Minister) accepted RSLA in principle but declined to fix a date for the measure. This scarcely took the matter forward, since the RSLA principle had in effect been established in 1944. Eccles said that nearly 3 million pupils were in over-sized classes and argued: 'we shall not put any other advance before the elimination of over-sized classes.'[2] He also expressed doubts about the ability of teachers to hold the interest of 15-16-year-olds, especially since social and economic conditions that made for early maturity and robust independence had not run their full course. Furthermore, he thought it vital that public opinion should fully support RSLA: 'I am bound to say to the House that the public reaction to the Crowther Report has clearly shown that there are great misgivings about fixing a date now for adding another year to school life.'[3] Thus Eccles was content to adopt the posture implied in the 1959 manifesto. Fortified by inspectors' frequent reports of areas in which voluntary staying on had 'suddenly become fashionable', he felt: 'this is the most practical way of raising the school age while teachers are still in such short supply.'[4]

Greenwood, replying for the Labour Opposition, cited Crowther's argument:

> the problem of educational advance is often represented as a difficult choice between smaller classes on the one hand and some single step forward on the other, such as raising the school-leaving age . . . this seems to us to be a wrong antithesis. A reduction in the size of classes is, or ought to be, a continuing process until the optimum size is reached. Whenever a major reform is introduced, there is bound to be a temporary worsening of the pupil-teacher ratio, but this deterioration should only be of short duration.[5]

Neither was the choice simply between RSLA or a reduction in the number of over-sized classes. The range of choice was broader, involving other options, such as the expansion of higher education. Eccles expressed concern that the sixth form, in which 'the nation's leaders are taught',[6] were forced into excessive specialization because of competition for university entrance — 'the conclusion is inescapable. Many more university places must be available.'[7] He affirmed his Government's commitment to such an expansion. Thus it was not reasonable to argue that in the late 1950s RSLA was impracticable. Practicability is often a matter of political choice. Eccles chose to put the nation's leaders before RSLA children.

By 1964, after the Newsom Report had made yet another plea for RSLA, the Conservative Government was prepared to specify a date for RSLA. It could not be said that this change of heart came about because in some final sense the problem of teacher supply and over-sized classes had been solved. Both remained, despite an improvement in teacher supply. Boyle, in announcing a commitment to RSLA in 1971, related Crowther's expectations that there would be a dip in school numbers in the late 1960s, when RSLA could take place without seriously worsening staffing standards. The dip would not transpire, which meant 'we have either to postpone setting a date for RSLA almost indefinitely; or else we have to accept a period in which staffing standards will not be what we would like to see.'[8] He acknowledged that RSLA would lower staffing standards in primary schools. Why, then, this conversion? The most cynical explanation is that a general election was approaching. Willey, a Labour MP who played a prominent part in the House of Commons debate on RSLA, argued: 'for years we have ben saying that the Government would not make a statement [about RSLA] until the eve of the general election.'[9] This suggests that the Government saw RSLA as something of a vote-catcher. There may be something in this, though it is difficult to be certain. When political appeal is not in the eye of the politician-beholder, it is obscured from view by the thirty-year rule. Politically speaking, a commitment to RSLA was probably more tangible and dramatic than (say) one to reduce over-sized classes. Labour was pressing for RSLA, and therefore the Conservative move conceivably 'stole Labour's clothing'. Also, RSLA may have been an apparent counterweight to the Conservative's contemporary commitment to expand higher education — RSLA for the less able (working-class?), university expansion for the able (predominantly middle-class?). On the other hand, such evidence as there is (see below) does not suggest that RSLA would necessarily have been electorally popular with those parents affected by it.

A less cynical explanation for the 1964 commitment to RSLA would be that Edward Boyle's personal views played a significant role and that he influenced the acceptance of RSLA. He had recently written a sympathetic and progressive Foreword to the Newsom Report. Furthermore, contrary to both Eccles and the Conservative 1959 manifesto, he did not believe that a reliance on voluntary staying on was sufficient. He pointed out that by 1970, if the present national trend continued, only 40 per cent would stay on voluntarily to 16.[10] However, it is doubtful whether Boyle's personal influence is a sufficient explanation for the acceptance of RSLA. Nevertheless, it should be remembered that the Conservatives had held office for thirteen years before announcing a date for RSLA, and by 1979, after RSLA had been implemented and Boyle had withdrawn from Parliament, it was the case that Mark Carlisle, as Opposition education spokesman, advocated that disruptive, non-academic children should be free, in certain conditions, to leave school at 15. This did not amount to a wish to reverse RSLA, but it does suggest a commitment of a different order from that which appears to have motivated Boyle. In this, and in other educational respects, Boyle was probably ahead of his Party, (certainly, sections of it at least), which confirms the likelihood of his personal influence over the 1964 commitment to RSLA.

As we have already implied, the Labour Opposition of 1964 was in favour of RSLA. Indeed, Boyle's announcement of his Government's commitment to RSLA was made in response to a Labour censure motion condemning the Government for having failed for more than four years, since the Crowther Report, to take a decision on RSLA.[11] However, in 1968 a Labour Government postponed RSLA from 1971 to 1973, as part of a public-expenditure cuts package, so as to save £33 million in 1968/69 and £48 million in 1969/70, principally in the school-building programme. Harold Wilson described this postponement to the House of Commons as 'difficult, indeed repugnant'.[12] This 'repugnant' measure appears to have been part of a list of economy proposals presented to the Cabinet by the Treasury, presumably with the reluctant acquiescence of the DES. The economy measures were presented to the Cabinet in mid-November 1967 as an accompaniment to devaluation. 'All the accompanying [economy] measures were agreed to after considerable discussion, with the exception of the postponement of RSLA which we left to fuller and calmer evaluation.'[13] The 'calmer evaluation', which lasted two months, does not appear to have involved educational considerations or the educational world: it was more a case of devising an economy package with the right political balance to pass through the Cabinet and the Parliamentary Labour Party.

If Boyle's personal influence might be held to have been instrumental in the initial commitment to RSLA by 1971 Patrick Walker's lack of such influence (as Education Minister) might equally be held to have been a factor in the postponement of RSLA until 1973. Crossman's account of the Cabinet debate on the matter suggests considerable opposition to postponing RSLA from senior

Ministers. He cites Brown, Gunter, Callaghan, Crosland and Gardiner as defenders of RSLA.[14] (It must also be assumed that Lord Longford opposed the measure, since he resigned because of it.) And he states that 'it was obvious that if there was a majority on Roy's [Jenkins] side, it was very small.'[15] Yet 'Gordon Walker sat through this debate, speechless and obviously trembling . . . [until] Harold [Wilson] said that Gordon Walker should tell Cabinet what his view was. "It's an agonizing decision," he replied, "but in the last resort I must accept a two-year postponement."'[16] If Crossman is correct, the failure by the Minister responsible for the policy to defend it in Cabinet made it likely that RSLA would be postponed: an undefended educational policy, whose main beneficiaries were children from unskilled, working-class backgrounds, was readily made subservient to the political expediency of short-term economic management. The parliamentary defence of this expediency fell to Jenkins. He argued that postponement was not abandonment — a weak defence, since it would have been politically impossible for a Labour Government to abandon a commitment of this kind that had already been made by a Conservative Government. Neither was his observation that the cohorts of 1968-71 would not in any event have received the extra year a convincing argument for not providing it for the 1971-3 cohorts. Clearly, two cohorts of RSLA children were judged to be politically expendable.

Innovatory educational policy is politically vulnerable,[17] since established vested interests obstruct the redistribution of resources from other sectors of the education service, and orthodox economic management in an era of 'stagflation' inhibits the creation of new resources. The Conservative Opposition suggested that instead of postponing RSLA, the price of school meals should be raised: this was rejected, since the measure would, it was claimed, have raised the cost of living and thus undermined the prices and incomes policies of the day.[18] The merits of this specific proposal matter less than the general and vital point that educational policy is always the outcome of political choice. In the area of political choice RSLA was vulnerable, as the near-thirty years' delay in realizing the 1944 commitment and the 1968 postponement indicate. The causes of this vulnerability went beyond those related above.

It could not be said that RSLA enjoyed the support of an active, broadly based public constituency. Parents who wished their children to have a five-year secondary education could keep them at school anyway. Of those parents who did not so choose, some were indifferent, others hostile, to RSLA. A Schools Council report, *Enquiry 1* found that only about one-third of parents of children who were expected to leave at 15 were completely in favour of RSLA.[19] Of the pupils in the sample, 44 per cent expected to leave at 15. Clearly, RSLA entailed a significant degree of coercion of both parents and pupils.

The attitude of the teaching profession to RSLA was variable. While the NUT has supported the policy (see chapter 3), the NAS called for the school-leaving age to be returned to 15. The National Association of Head Teachers, at the 1974 Annual Conference,[20] passed by 7000 to 4000 votes a resolution that called for a complete reappraisal of RSLA. Given the power that headteachers enjoy, this was particularly noteworthy, suggesting a significant antipathy to the measure. Indeed, an extensive survey undertaken by the *Times Educational Supplement* in the same year found that a majority of teachers were against RSLA: 77 per cent in primary schools and 75 per cent in secondary schools.[21] This negative attitude had been foreshadowed in *Enquiry 1.* Only 13 per cent of teachers in the sample thought that all RSLA pupils would benefit from the extra year.[22] The teachers most despondent about RSLA were those who taught the less able children — i.e., those most likely to teach RSLA children — 30 per cent of whom saw RSLA as providing 'only problems and no opportunities'.[23] As for RSLA parents a majority of teachers (66 per cent) thought they 'were not interested' in what the schools were trying to achieve.[24]

This lack of enthusiasm among teachers must raise doubts about the value of the extra year for some children. It conflicts markedly with the spirit and energetic optimism displayed by educational entrepreneurs in the divers discussion documents that preceded RSLA. It further suggests that the teaching profession was not an important lobby for RSLA. The official NUT stance, which strongly supported RSLA, was less significant than at first might appear to be the case because it was not wholly congruent with the views of its membership. Arguably, RSLA was used by the union, which claimed the facile legitimation that more education is necessarily a good thing, as a vehicle for justifying extra staff resources — for example, teachers to fill 'posts of special responsibility for RSLA'. The union argued for recognition of these 'additional responsibilities' in the form of Burnham increments and, in some cases, head of department status. 'Some authorities have appointed education officers or advisers to have specific responsibility for co-ordinating RSLA preparations.'[25] There is always a danger that extra resources end up by benefiting the teachers and allied staff[26] more than the children concerned. It can be argued that pressures for change of this kind are part of a larger process by which social reform is manipulated by the 'producers' of social services in the pursuit of vested interest.

Yet, ostensibly, RSLA was an egalitarian measure that extended to all children a full five-year secondary education: prior to 1964 a minority of children had remained in school until the age of 16. It is true that in the post-war decades the size of this minority grew significantly. In 1955 26.7 per cent of pupils (in maintained schools) stayed at school beyond the age of 15; by 1963, 39.8 per cent did so.[27] This led some to argue that the trend towards voluntary extended schooling made RSLA unnecessary; but the trend might not have secured 16 as the universal school-leaving age until the end of the century. It would have been unwise to assume a steady increase in the numbers of pupils voluntarily remaining at school — certainly at the rate implied by the above figures. Children from school-resistant cultures would obviously have been less readily enticed to stay on voluntarily than would those children of the skilled working class and the middle classes who had been denied grammar-school places in the 1950s and 1960s but whose parents sought to exact some compensation by way of a five-year secondary-modern schooling. Such children were the willing volunteers in what has been called an 'explosion in demand'.[28] Furthermore, the trend towards extended schooling might not have been irreversible; reductions in the numbers of pupils voluntarily staying at school are not unknown. Between 1927 and 1930 the percentage of grammar-school pupils leaving before 16 rose from 27.3 per cent to 32.7 per cent.[29] Arguably, in times of economic depression the instrumental worth of extended education is called into question. Conceivably, this could have happened again, stemming — albeit temporarily — the trend of voluntary staying on. Thus the RSLA decision was of considerable moment and not an inconsequential submission to a compelling trend. Far from affecting a marginal number of pupils, RSLA meant 'retaining in school for a fifth year of secondary education some 60 per cent more of an age group than [stayed] on voluntarily'.[30]

RSLA was significant for other reasons. First, a disproportionate number of those children who left secondary school after only four years were working-class. In one sample 92 per cent of the sons of unskilled workers left school at 15, compared with 25 per cent of the sons of professional and managerial workers.[31] Douglas claims: 'the heavy losses through early leaving occurred largely in the manual working classes — only 36 per cent of the lower manual working-class pupils remained at school after the statutory leaving age.'[32] This meant that upper-middle-class pupils were two and a half times as likely to stay on after the minimum leaving age as were lower manual working-class pupils.[33] It might be argued that the social-class differentials were a product of the fact that working-class children were less able than middle-class children. But even accepting the validity of the criteria of academic ability — and suppressing doubts about the cultural bias of schooling and school assessment — it is clear that this was not a sufficient explanation of class differentials in the context of early leaving. The *Early Leaving* report found that working-class pupils of high ability (who had secured a grammar-school place) were prone to leave school before their middle-class peers. Of the high-ability children of unskilled workers, those who were in the top third of ability on admission to grammar school, 54 per cent either completed a five-year course without a School Certificate (or more than three GCE O-Level passes) or left school before 16. In fact, of the 1621 children of semi-skilled and unskilled workers in the sample, 520 had left before the end of their fifth year.[34] Almost a decade after the *Early Leaving* report Douglas produced findings which suggested that measured ability was not a sufficient explanation of variations in the length of school life. When measured ability was held constant, the date of school leaving differed between pupils from different social classes. Of those children of lower manual workers who came within the top 16 per cent of measured ability,[35] 20 per cent did not complete their fifth year of secondary schooling, compared with 3 per cent of high-ability children of the upper middle class. In the second-highest bracket of ability the differential was even more significant. Fifty-four per cent of the children of lower manual workers did not complete their fifth year, compared with 7 per cent of the children of upper-middle-class workers.[36] Indeed, about half of the entire sample of pupils left school at the earliest opportunity (in the case of this sample, at Easter 1961). The date is significant for two reasons. It underlines the fact that a decision to raise the school-leaving age taken a few years later affected a significant number of pupils. Further, it highlights the consequence of early leaving — not so much (in this instance) that children do not receive a further term's schooling as that they are unlikely to sit for a major public examination and are thus denied a chance to gain certificates that would pave the way to getting a job. Given the above pattern of early leaving, RSLA had a disproportionate impact on working-class children, who were held to be the main beneficiaries in terms of receiving both additional education and an enhanced opportunity to obtain formal qualifications in the race for prestigious employment.

Secondly, prior to RSLA there were distinct regional variations in the age at which children left school. In 1965 the national average figure for children staying at school beyond the statutory leaving age was 40.2 per cent. However, in the same year the figure for the North region was 27.4 per cent and for the South-East 50.7 per cent (respectively, the lowest and the highest percentages for the country).[37] While the difference between the North and the South-East has been reduced by 1973 from 23.3 per cent to 15.5 per cent, the gap was still considerable.

There were intra- as well as inter-regional variations in the percentages of pupils remaining at school beyond the statutory leaving age. For example, in 1972 in Wales the range of pupils aged 16 (expressed as a percentage of those aged 13 three years previously) extended from 49.4 per cent in Cardiganshire to 32.9 per cent in Radnorshire. For the city of Cardiff the figure was 34.5 per cent, compared with that of 42.7 per cent for the city of Swansea. In the London area the 56.5 per cent of Bromley contrasted sharply with the 24.5 per cent of Barking.[38]

Thirdly, before RSLA girls were less likely than boys to remain at school beyond the statutory leaving age.[39] Such differences were sometimes marginal.[40] Nevertheless, RSLA meant that in formal terms both sexes would receive five years' secondary education.[41]

Thus, it might be contended, these regional, sex and social class differentials in the completion of secondary education were countered at a stroke by the egalitarianism of RSLA.[42] However, we have referred to RSLA as only 'ostensibly' an egalitarian measure: this now requires explanation.

Themes other than egalitarianism were addressed in the debate that preceded RSLA. A particularly strident theme was the way in which RSLA would aid the economic well-being of the country. (Such economic justifications are often the most politically potent terms of the advocacy of development in social policy.) Boyle argued: '[given] the more complex patterns of production that are a feature of so many modern and developing industries, we shall need a better level of general education among those employed in industry and commerce, not only at the top levels but at the lower levels also.'[43] This reflected much of what had already been said. Newsom noted that in the United States two-thirds of the population are at high schools until the age of 18 and that France had raised the school-leaving age to 16 in 1959 — 'in the national economic interest we cannot afford to go on waiting.'[44] This sentiment was an echo of the Crowther Report, which had said of RSLA: 'we find it difficult to conceive that there could be any other application of money giving a larger or more certain return in the quickening of enterprise, in the stimulation of invention or in the general sharpening of those wits by which a trading nation in a crowded island can hope to make its living.'[45] Crowther's case for RSLA as 'investment in national efficiency'[46] included calculations about the wastage of ability as a result of premature withdrawal from school. It was shown that half of the respondents in a sample of National Servicemen in the two highest ability groups had left school at 15.[47] (Furthermore, among National Service recruits to the Army who came from families of manual workers, two-thirds of those in the two highest ability groups had left school at 15.)[48] These facts moved Crowther to remark that 'the country's economic welfare demands, at the very least, that the whole of the first [ability] group and a substantial section of the second should have had a secondary education until 16.'[49]

Crowther developed another argument for why RSLA was necessary to secure the optimum use of manpower. 'The great increase in higher positions, and the much wider access to higher education, have between them deprived the middling jobs in industry and business of the level of ability they formerly attracted.'[50] Since under-utilization of manpower would ensue if such jobs were performed 'by people of superior ability', it was imperative that an extended education be provided for 'people of only average intelligence'.[51] As the Report observed, 'it is not only at the top but almost to the bottom of the pyramid that the scientific revolution of our times needs to be reflected in a longer educational process.'[52]

Indeed, the predominant tone of the Report suggests pressing concern not with known social-class differences in connection with the age of school-leaving but with the wastage of ability amid *some* early leavers, notably 'the very important group of skilled workers' sons, who provide nearly half of the two highest ability groups'.[53] At several points in the Report the characteristics and needs of these groups are subjected to special analysis and comment. The narrowness of the concern is indicated by the fact that very able sons of manual workers represented only 16 per cent of all children who left school aged 15 or under.

Crowther was concerned essentially with a minority of potential 'blue-collar' workers — the 'enablers' of the new technocracy — whose economic ability could not be exploited soon enough through mere dependence on voluntary staying on. 'How hard that road would be,' Crowther commented.[54] It would have been impossible to compel extended schooling for this minority other than through the universality of RSLA. How far economic growth can be fostered by extended schooling is disputable. (Crowther's expectation in this regard, though unquestionably more grandiloquent than sensible, was congruent with the rhetoric of the 'technological revolution' of the early 1960s.) What is indisputable is that a preoccupation with the able 16 per cent minority was in some respects more elitist than egalitarian.

In fact, the RSLA debate in general posed few — and muted — egalitarian questions. The emphasis was not so much on such things as the social-class-based inequalities in the distribution of educational resources (i.e., the deficiencies of the education service) as on why certain groups did not take full advantage of proffered educational opportunities. Thus early leaving, as a problem, was personalized and rooted in the cultural inadequacies of working-class parents and pupils.

Newsom viewed the early leavers as those 'who most readily succumb to the attractions of the pay packet and the bright lights that it commands'.[55] According to the *Early Leaving* report, even the more intelligent leavers withdrew in part because they found, 'the full grammar-school curriculum and methods of teaching too arduous'.[56] More recently, the main beneficiaries of RSLA were described as those 'with backgrounds which militate against rational choices regarding the length of school careers'.[57]

Some parents of early leavers are portrayed in a negative fashion. One report, in seeking to explain early leaving, expressed the view that 'educational sub-normality in parents may play a part'.[58] Another report described parents as regarding 'an additional year of education . . . like a football pool in which you lose your stake unless you win a cash prize — and not, as [they] should, like a premium bond in which your capital is safe whether you win an additional prize or not'.[59] Thus the causes of early leaving have been variously attributed to a moth-like adolescent inability to resist neon lights, academic weakness, irrationality and lack of support from indecisive, ill-informed gamblers.

Ironically, this negative image of pupils and parents is juxtaposed with evidence about early leavers which does not support it. While the *Early Leaving* report claimed that early leavers were not able to keep up with the pace of grammar schooling (see above), the evidence presented by the report suggested that some of these children had been in the top ability group on entering grammar school.[60] Furthermore, while early leaving was associated with social class, finding school work difficult as a reason for leaving appears not to have been. 20.1 per cent of the sons of professional and managerial parents gave this as a reason for leaving school, compared with 16.9 per cent and 21.3 per cent of the sons of semi-skilled and unskilled workers respectively.[61]

Enquiry 1 showed that 15-year-old leavers attended schools with a slightly higher staff turnover and that

> the most marked variation in the school staffing situations experienced by pupils leaving school at different ages was in the pupil-teacher ratio. Only 7 per cent of 15-year-old leavers were in schools in which there were sixteen or fewer pupils to a teacher, compared with 23 per cent of 16-year-old and 43 per cent of 17- to 18-year-old leavers.[62]

In addition, '80 per cent of 15-year-old leavers on entry to secondary school went into classes which were in some degree streamed by ability, [compared] with 62 per cent of 16-year-old and 36 per cent of 17- to 18-year-old leavers.'[63] Factors of this kind, although crude measures of variations in schooling, suggest that schools may have contributed to early leaving to an extent understated in inquiries that concentrated on the contribution of pupil and parental inadequacies.

Apart from being an insufficient explanation of early leaving, the dominant terms of the RSLA debate were also stigmatizing. Examples have already been given of the negative image of early leavers and their parents. Although Crowther valued the early leavers as an economic resource, they were simultaneously devalued. They were people of 'marginal talents' and 'the bottom of the pyramid'.[64] A DES report noted that in one instance the new teaching spaces for RSLA children had been made 'as unlike conventional classrooms as ingenuity can make them'[65] (presumably, for children who were unlike conventional pupils). Indeed, the stereotype of the RSLA child is one manifestation of a more general tendency to stigmatize working-class children.

The lineage of this tendency may be traced back to the nineteenth-century conception of elementary education for working-class children. The intention to ensure their capacity to calculate a shop bill and understand a plain sermon speaks with derision of the educability of such children. This inferiority was formalized in the Codes issued by the Board of Education in 1904. The Elementary Code suggested that elementary schools should aim

> to give [the pupils] *some* power over language as an instrument of thought and expression, and, while making them *conscious of the limitations of their knowledge,* to develop in them such a taste for good reading and thoughtful study as will enable them to increase their knowledge in after years by their own efforts.[66]

Insofar as these children were educable during their school life, the emphasis was to be placed on practical work and manual instruction. Too much cannot be made of such limited evidence, but it does suggest the minimal nature of elementary education and hence the inferior educational identity bestowed on children who received this form of education. By contrast, the Regulation for Secondary Schools, 1904, prescribed for a superior kind of pupil a superior kind of education, 'of wider scope and more advanced degree than that in Elementary Schools'.[67] The child of the 1904 Elementary Code reappears in the Norwood Report, 1943, in which he is depicted as being able to deal more easily

> with concrete things than with ideas . . . abstractions mean little to him . . . his horizon is near and within a limited area his movement is

generally slow . . . he is interested only in the moment . . . he finds little attraction in the past or in the slow disentanglement of causes or movements.[68]

The grammar-school pupil, however,

can grasp an argument or follow a piece of connected reasoning . . . [He] cares to know how things came to be as well as how they are . . . he is interested in the relatedness of related things . . . he can take a long view and hold his mind in suspense.[69]

The Newsom child — 'half our future' — was heir, in some respects, to the unfortunate mantle of the less able child as perceived by Norwood. With many well-meaning phrases and some acknowledgement of ability ('*a substantial proportion* of the "average" and "below average" pupils are *sufficiently* educable'),[70] Newsom added, especially through his call for less demanding, non-examinable courses, to the construction of a sub-type of pupil. Arguably, the RSLA child is the most recent scion of this tradition. Indeed, in its most extreme form the stigmatization has gone beyond the imputation of a marred educational identity to the assertion of criminal tendencies. It has been claimed that RSLA may have created 'a new sub-criminal class, living on their wits and shoplifting, worthy of the pen of Dickens'.[71] Doubtless, this is an extreme example of the RSLA stereotype, but the fact of a stereotype has been conceded by the DES (arguably, in understated terms): 'it is clear that in some cases the danger of creating a distinct "RSLA group" somehow outside the corporate life of the school has not entirely been avoided.'[72]

Why does all this matter? It matters for a number of reasons. First, such perceptions as those shown above can be the terms by which a coercive element in social policy is justified. Since RSLA parents were depicted as feckless, indecisive, unaware of what was best for their children or country, they could not be allowed freedom of choice, and compulsion was readily justifiable. As Crowther patronizingly and manipulatively remarked, 'they will cheerfully acquiesce in [RSLA] and benefit from it once the decision is off their shoulders and their parents'.[73] Secondly, stigmatization is important because it is part of what might be called the stratification of publicly bestowed identities. The fact that the social services contribute to mental as well as material welfare is often neglected. The education service is a major distributor of personal identities. The identity 'RSLA pupil' is less desirable than that of 'A-stream pupil'. The labelling process involved in RSLA is a form of psychological inegalitarianism. It perpetuates inequalities in self-image. Thirdly, negative definitions are the very stuff of unequal resource allocations; children of limited educability do not 'need' expensive laboratory equipment, etc. Finally, and most important, RSLA curricula are a derivative of the 'non-academic', 'limited potential' definitions of RSLA children.

The spectre of the 'RSLA pupil' has been the cornerstone of the curriculum response to the extra year. The implications of this fact require elaboration. With the RSLA announcement, the Schools Council declared: 'RSLA presents schools with the opportunity to redesign the curriculum for the young school leaver.'[74] The underlying assumptions of this redesign are noteworthy. To start with, it is assumed that the humanities and social studies could take up as much as one-third of the weekly timetable, yet many pupils will not take even a CSE exam in these areas. Though it may be desirable that to some extent traditional academic subjects linked to public examinations have given way to courses concerned with things such as social education (and no doubt all pupils would benefit from such courses), it is important to maintain a balance between the traditional and the new to ensure both breadth of educational experience and vocational opportunities. Arguably, RSLA curricula are unbalanced since pride of place has been given to the humanities, for social education, and to non-examined 'interest'-based courses. This is the outcome of the perceptions of the RSLA pupils shown above. The stereotype of RSLA girls has led one account of RSLA preparation to claim: 'our aim has been to make the last year these girls spend at school relevant to their future lives, remembering that in the immediate future they will be working girls and in a few years they will be wives and mothers.'[75] By contrast, the predominantly middle-class girls of the A streams, though they too will be wives and mothers, follow a curriculum that places more emphasis on certificates and access to prestigious employment and higher education[76] — the 'hard currency' of school life. (Nor should it go without remark that boys will be husbands and fathers.) Another account asks the question 'Do we pay enough attention to education for leisure? Next to promotion of literacy, this would be the most important pursuit for them [non-examination RSLA pupils].'[77] What, one might ask, of numeracy? The negative image of the RSLA pupils has engendered limited expectations on the part of those responsible for planning RSLA curricula. They look for modest gains — for example, 'the ability to discriminate between pop music which is mawkish, sentimental or boorish and that which evokes, however crudely, genuine human feeling, represents a gain in sensitivity that is worth having.'[78] *Perhaps* the appreciation of pop music, of whatever sort, has a place in a secondary curriculum, but this is not argued for. It is an unreflective derivative of the RSLA pupil homuncule. In such ways stratification by subject within schools replaces stratification by the 11-plus examination between schools.

What appears to be the dominant form of RSLA curriculum is not desired by RSLA pupils or parents. It has been conceded that 'many pupils who leave school at 16 (or before) have very little good to say for what they have learnt in those subjects which are concerned with the understanding of human nature and human institutions'[79] and that 'the early leaver is at best apathetic, at worst resentful and rebellious'[80] towards history, geography and religious education. These opinions are supported by the survey of pupils published in *Enquiry 1*: 93 per cent of boys (15-year-old leavers) thought that mathematics was a useful subject, and 90 per cent thought the same of English; whereas the figure for current affairs/social studies was 56 per cent, history, 29 per cent and religious instruction, 22 per cent. The figures for girls were similar. When pupils were asked which subjects were interesting, metal-work/engineering found favour with 76 per cent of boys. Only 47 per cent of boys found current affairs/social studies interesting.[81] The yardstick for judging a subject was the extent to which it provided 'basic skills which were essential for obtaining and holding satisfactory jobs and for getting on in life generally'.[82] Another survey asked pupils how they would wish to spend the extra year. Seventy-seven per cent endorsed the statement 'I should like to be taught the beginning of a trade or career', and 75 per cent 'I should like to take only those subjects which will help me in the job I hope to have.'[83] The parents of 15-year-olds have also been shown to be similarly influential with respect to their attitude to the extra year. In one survey 63 per cent cited 'better qualifications, better job prospects for youngsters' as their reason for favouring RSLA — it

was, in fact, the most frequently cited reason.[84] Such expectations
are unlikely to have been met, since

> teachers very generally rejected the achievement of vocational success
> as a major objective of education . . . [they] considered that very
> important areas of school life should be to develop the characters and
> personalities of pupils, to teach them ethical values and to help them
> to become mature, confident and successful in their personal
> relationships.[85]

— that is, we would say, to compensate for their personal
inadequacies, rather than to equip them with the skills they seek as
a route to occupational success. The hallmark of these 'very
important areas' is a concern with social control.

RSLA courses are intended 'to give [RSLA pupils] the right
approach to life'.[86] This approach is essentially quietest, implicitly
encouraging pupils to adjust to the facts of their social location. As
one Schools Council document put it, 'older pupils will all too soon
be *forced* to find a way *of coping* with the complex social and
economic and political order which demands some degree of
understanding of its purposes and operation if life is to be
tolerable.'[87] The aim is for people 'to know themselves' as more than
the playthings of impersonal forces and 'to make sense of' the
business of living, but in a manner that is suggestive more of
personal adjustment to the social order than of political action to
change that order.

A further dimension of social control can be seen in Crowther's
justification of RSLA as a means of ensuring (among the unskilled
occupations) 'that [industrial] responsibility does not fall into
irresponsible hands'.[88] How this might be achieved is illustrated by
the following example from a Schools Council Working Paper[89]
showing how the topic 'The Organization of Labour' might be
approached:

> It might be wise to eschew the historical approach. Here is a chance to
> show young adults that this is not a clear-cut picture of the virtuous
> worker against the wicked capitalist, or the idle workman breaking
> the heart of the sympathetic employer, that the picture has changed
> greatly since their parents' day, and to leave them with the idea that
> this is one field at least where their own responsibility or
> irresponsibility as future workpeople would make or destroy not only

themselves and their families, but their union, their trade and even their nation.

As White argues, 'the aims [of RSLA curricula] are what the aim of working-class education has been since the 1870 Education Act and before: in one word, obedience.'[90] What has changed is the means by which these aims are obtained. White claims that obedience is no longer inculcated by explicit preaching but by interest-based indoctrination, through which identification with desired values is achieved by the presentation of material that contains 'presupposed attitudes'.

Furthermore, some RSLA courses are concerned with fitting working-class pupils into working-class jobs — with 'getting the child to see that he is naturally fitted to be a man of Bronze'.[91] Similarly, the work-experience component of the final year, in some cases, may delimit occupational horizons by, as one document put it, giving 'greater reality' to the school course.[92] (Neither will the extra year do much to provide RSLA children with the requisite certificates for entry into 'good' jobs — see below.)

In terms of social control, RSLA might also be construed as a facet of the constraining response to the 'moral panic' engendered by contemporary youth. To some an extra year is a means of combating juvenile delinquency. In Crowther's view, 'delinquency may arise, not because boys are at school, but because they are not at school enough.'[93] As was argued above, this view has stigmatized some RSLA pupils and has neglected the role of schools in generating deviancy. For others the extra year has afforded an opportunity to counter the ill-disciplined, non-discriminating, 'follow-my-leader activities' of smoking, drinking, drugs and promiscuity,[94] which, while less threatening than delinquency, have nevertheless advanced the pleasure ethic rather than the work ethic of the dominant culture of elders (aside from which, this is a clumsy, indefensible stigmatization of working-class youth culture). The dominant culture is opposed not to pleasure but rather to instant gratification, that is, to pleasure without work — the work of discrimination (for example, between music that is 'mawkish' and 'boorish' as opposed to that which expresses 'genuine human feeling': see above).

Even if the *dominant* terms of RSLA curricula were acceptable, doubt still remains about the adequacy of the curricula preparation for RSLA. It had been argued that simply adding another year to the four-year secondary programme was not enough. It was expected that RSLA would not be 'just another year at school': 'The whole school course will be refashioned to give a wider and deeper education.'[95] Boyle, when announcing the date for RSLA, argued that 'with only a four-year course you cannot provide much more than an improved version of the old senior elementary curriculum . . . with a five year course . . . [there is a] possibility of reconstructing the entire course so as to give an education that is truly secondary.'[96] Yet according to an NUT survey, only 17 per cent of LEAs had planned a complete reorganization of the curriculum.[97] The general picture conveyed by the survey was that in terms of curriculum development, the schools were insufficiently prepared for RSLA. This evidence stood in marked contrast to the DES's claim of 'a general picture of considerable activity and soundly based preparations'.[98] The evidence adduced to support this claim was nothing more than a geographia of trivia, which, while clearly intended to give an impression of nationwide activity, only served to show the 'soft currency' of some RSLA courses: for example, 'in Grimsby, a course in "cosmetology" (the analysis and production of cosmetics) is very popular with girls, while in Birkenhead and Chester courses based on the study of personal relationships have developed.'[99]

In sum, the content of the extra year has been dominated by an exaggerated response to an allegedly ineducable, recalcitrant element, so that for the majority of RSLA pupils education has been subordinated to social control; insofar as the RSLA curriculum is taken up with non-examinable courses tantamount to social training, it is not action against inequality but rather a form of inequality, both educational and (incipiently) social.

Last, it should be noted that the RSLA curriculum debate is of a larger significance precisely because it was to the fore as an issue of debate after the commitment to RSLA in 1964. This was because from the outset the RSLA problematic was the nature of the RSLA pupil; as *Enquiry 1* noted, 'the most frequently mentioned reason for teachers' doubts [about RSLA] lay in the pupils' attitudes to school.'[100] Thus the RSLA 'problem' was personalized and apolitical, unconcerned with the redistribution of educational resources and opportunities (certainly, redistributive concerns were not even mentioned by a single teacher in *Enquiry 1*'s large sample). Given that the problem was the nature of the RSLA child, a series of questions were then posed which asked in effect 'How should we act on RSLA pupils?' — that is, the 'stark and fundamental' issue was 'what to teach and how to teach it'.[101] Put this way, the problem of RSLA was more amorphous than 'stark', more peripheral than 'fundamental'. The debate inevitably foundered on questions of technique or fetishism of method, in connection with which the loquacity of professional pretensions can so easily become a substitute for action. In this way the debate is deflected from such 'stark and fundamental' issues as how we take away from the privileged and give to the underprivileged. What resources do we divert from predominantly middle-class university students to predominantly working-class RSLA pupils? The apolitical way in which the debate was formulated by most people precluded questions of this kind. (It is noteworthy that the great education debate launched by Mr Callaghan in 1976 had a similar emphasis, to the neglect of stark redistributive issues.)

Beyond the content of the extra year, the adequacy of the resources provided for RSLA is central to a consideration of the egalitarianism of the policy. Some idea of the scale of resources necessitated by RSLA can be gained from *Enquiry 1*. Teachers in nine subject areas were asked whether they felt that accommodation was inadequate for teaching the sort of pupils who left school at 15. A substantial majority in all subject areas replied that they did, ranging from 82 per cent of teachers of practical/expressive subjects to 62 per cent of teachers of foreign languages.[102] A further dearth was recorded regarding equipment needs. A majority of teachers in eight out of nine subject areas stated that their present equipment was inadequate for teaching RSLA children.[103] (This evidence must be treated with caution, since to some extent teachers always want 'more' and/or 'better' facilities.) *Enquiry 1* also observed: 'one-fifth of the boy 15-year-old leavers in the sample were in schools which lacked either a gymnasium or playing fields, and one-tenth were in schools which were without both facilities.'[104] It is likely, therefore, that a disproportionate number of RSLA pupils attended schools which were inadequate even without the demands of the extra year.[105]

In 1966 it was announced that a building programme for RSLA would commence in 1968/69. It was expected at the time of the announcement that RSLA would take place in 1971. The 1968/69 school-building programme included an allocation of £33 million for RSLA projects, as did the 1969/70 programme. A further £33 million was anticipated in the 1970/71 programme. A small (unspecified) instalment in 1971/72 was expected to bring the total allocation to over £100 million.[106] This programme was disrupted by the decision to postpone RSLA to 1973 which we have already described (see p. 165). Announcing the decision, Wilson claimed that it would mean a saving of £33 million in 1968/69 and £48 million in 1969/70, principally in the school-building programme.[107] A subsequent DES document recounted a building programme of £125 million during the years 1970/73.[108] It is difficult to gauge the adequacy of this programme. It was substantial, in that when first announced the annual allocations amounted to about a quarter of the total school-building programme. But there was no clear measure of need. The *Enquiry 1* evidence of need is of extremely limited worth. Nor is it certain that RSLA resources were entirely devoted to the exclusive needs of RSLA children. An NUT survey found that only ten LEAs (of the seventy that gave information) were concentrating additional facilities on the age group affected by RSLA. Other LEAs were spending additional resources across the secondary schools, and a substantial minority (twenty-six LEAs) stated that they were considering RSLA in the context of a wider reorganization of secondary education.[109] This picture is to some extent reflected in the DES account of how the RSLA building allocation was utilized: for example, Northampton used all of its allocation to provide one new upper school. In some areas part of the RSLA allocation was used on primary schools or prospective middle schools to facilitate comprehensive reorganization.[110] Doubtless, in such cases accommodation was released which could have been used for RSLA children. However, it is conceivable that the impact of RSLA resources on RSLA pupils was diluted, so that their claim on resources was in fact less sure than appears to be the case at first sight.

Certainly, the occasion of RSLA did not pass without severe criticism of the adequacy of the provision for the extra year. An NAS questionnaire to members elicited the criticism that 'in some areas not enough extra classrooms had been added and in others there was not enough extra money for books, materials, school visits and other outside activities which were essential to maintain the interest of reluctant pupils.'[111] NAS members threatened to refuse to take RSLA classes in eleven English counties and parts of

Wales. At the union's 1973 Annual Conference it was reported that 'the main grievance was that not enough extra teachers had been employed to make teaching groups small enough to handle properly.'[112] Thus an earlier NUT survey appears to have been prophetic in arguing that although most LEAs expected to maintain staff-pupil ratios, 'the failure of most LEAs to improve their staffing ratios . . . could jeopardize the ultimate success of RSLA . . . smaller classes are essential if the majority of pupils are to benefit from RSLA and it would appear that the majority of LEAs do not expect to be able to provide them.'[113] By contrast, a DES report argued that 'in general, staffing has been sufficient to allow the implementation of plans dealing with the extra pupils', though it was conceded that 'pressures [on teachers] have been exacerbated in some areas by a high turnover of staff, an undue dependence on probationary and supply teachers and in some inner city areas an acute shortage of experienced staff.'[114] Since RSLA pupils have low standing when judged by the prevailing school standard of academic excellence, it would not be surprising if, in the main, they have been taught by a changing population of less experienced teachers.

About this and other resource aspects of the adequacy of RSLA provision one can merely conjecture, since the quality of evidence prohibits conclusive judgement. Yet it could be reasonably maintained that RSLA was not the occasion of a major redistribution of resources in favour of the educationally disadvantaged. The direct cost of RSLA was officially estimated at £60 million a year — a very small part of the total education budget.[115] In 1964 Boyle stated that RSLA would effect 350,000 pupils[116] (at an estimated cost of £60 million per annum) and that acceptance of the Robbins Report would cost £3,500 million over ten years[117] (for an extra 174,000 students by 1973/4).[118] Thus in *crude terms* over a ten-year period the Robbins commitment meant spending nearly six times the RSLA resources. Furthermore, the notion of positive discrimination was virtually absent from the RSLA issue. The implementation of RSLA appears not to have overthrown the pattern of unequal resource allocation identified by Byrne[119] — arguably, RSLA pupils will remain at the end of the resources queue.

RSLA could be criticized from another standpoint, namely, that it was not accompanied by other measures that dealt adequately with the fact that poor families were deprived of the earnings of 15-year-olds. There is evidence that casts doubt on the blandness of

Crowther's assertion that reduced family size meant that most manual workers could look at education until the age of 16 from the same sort of perspective as non-manual workers.[120] Crowther showed that of the grammar-school boys who left at 15 but wanted to stay at school, 34 per cent gave as their reason for leaving 'wanted, or needed to earn money': the equivalent figure for girls was 43 per cent.[121] In both cases this was the most frequently cited reason for leaving school. Admittedly, the conflation of 'wanted, or needed' is confusing. Crowther's sample of National Servicemen showed that 18 per cent and 21 per cent of Army and RAF respondents respectively left school at 15 because 'money [was] short at home.'[122] The *Early Leaving* report found that 17.4 per cent of the sons of unskilled workers left school at 15 because their families could not afford to keep them at school.[123] *Enquiry 1* produced evidence of similar reasons why parents did not support RSLA: '41 per cent of parents of 15-year-old leavers who were against compulsory raising of the school-leaving age mentioned financial problems.'[124]

Indeed, Wynn has gone so far as to argue that the 'largest contribution to the cost of RSLA (£70 million a year for the upkeep of the children involved) will be paid by a quite small minority of parents . . . generally the larger and poorer families whose children would not otherwise continue at school beyond the age of 15-plus'.[125] However, it should be remembered that child benefit is paid for 15/16-year-olds. More might have been done — for example, higher rates of Family Income Supplement for parents with children in this age group.

Other social welfare aspects of RSLA seem to have been generally neglected. A DES report noted:

a few authorities mention that close consideration is being given to the implications of RSLA for their school welfare services. Manchester, for example, consider that they will need additional welfare officers, and they are also planning to strengthen the psychological and child guidance services.[126]

But why only 'a few authorities'? Perhaps Manchester was atypical, but the fact that not all authorities were reported to be taking similar steps shows patchiness in the preparation for RSLA. This was an important deficiency, since extended school welfare facilities might have made a significant contribution to the success of RSLA, especially in terms of combating truancy. It is difficult to be precise about the extent of truancy among RSLA pupils, but a Welsh Office working party on truancy concluded that 'absence from schools is an old problem which has been aggravated by RSLA.'[127] Given that the instrumental expectations of RSLA pupils and parents were subordinated to the teaching profession's view of the extra year as an opportunity for liberal education, this is not surprising (see above). Truancy might be regarded as RSLA pupils voting with their feet (though, clearly, this is an insufficient explanation of truancy).

A further, though limited, yardstick by which to judge the egalitarianism of RSLA is the extent to which it has improved the educational attainment of disadvantaged pupils. As measured by examination performance, there is some evidence to show that RSLA has secured gains. Since 1973 the number of pupils in England leaving school without any certificate has declined — from 19 per cent in 1973 to 13 per cent in 1978.[128] The percentage obtaining between one and four GCE O-Levels grades A-C or CSE at grade 1 has increased from 25 to 27 per cent, and the number obtaining one or more GCE O-Levels grades D and E or CSE grades 2-5 has risen from 31 to 34 per cent.[129] Clearly, these figures demonstrate only marginal advance at the bottom levels of attainment. The percentage of pupils obtaining five O-Levels (grades A-C) has remained virtually constant through the period, as has the percentage obtaining three A-Levels.[130] Also, there has been very little change since RSLA in the percentage of all English school leavers who left school in the year in which they reached the minimum school-leaving age.[131]

The very fact that such small gains are as much as one might have reasonably expected from RSLA underscores the limitations of RSLA as egalitarian action. More should have been done to extend educational opportunity for working-class youth. RSLA was a defensible first step, but it should surely have been followed, even accompanied, by the introduction of a legal right to part-time further education for 16- to 19-year-olds. RSLA and part-time education have long been considered to belong to a common frame, sometimes as alternatives, it is true, but more often (and more correctly, in our view) as complementary. Crowther dismissed the idea of part-time further education as an alternative to RSLA, chiefly because a full secondary education was taken to be an essential basis for subsequent part-time education.[132] And Butler had promised 'to tighten the [1944 Education] Bill to make the establishment of county colleges a duty for LEAs within three years of a leaving age of 15'.[133] Yet further education has been very much neglected in the post-war period, as we demonstrate in chapter 8. Given this neglect, RSLA was inevitably something of a half-measure.

Nevertheless, since RSLA has provided further schooling and some certification largely for working-class children, it can be held to have reduced educational inequality. Despite the criticisms that we have made, RSLA merits strong support. But the burden of the evidence presented above detracts from the egalitarianism of the policy. It was an accretion to a thoroughly unequal system, bearing all the hallmarks of a rather tepid piece of 'disjointed incrementalism'. The DES view — that the most successful schools were offering RSLA pupils 'equal but realistic opportunities',[134] is an honest summation only if the stress is not placed on 'equal'. Even then, one is tempted to say of this realism what Orwell said of realism — 'it used to be called dishonesty.'[135]

8

Post-School Education

This chapter is about education beyond the statutory school-leaving age. It is divided into two parts. First, we consider provision for 16- to 19-year-olds, largely in terms of further education, though with some reference to sixth-form education. Second, we examine higher education. While both sectors have expanded in the post-war period, further education has suffered from serious neglect in important respects, whereas higher education has secured the lion's share of new resources. As we shall argue below, this contrast of paucity and plenitude is highly significant from the standpoint of education inequality.

FURTHER EDUCATION

Further education is, and has been for a long time, fundamentally inadequate. It is inadequate not just in terms of international comparisons, but also when measured against reasonable expectations of what might have been done to develop this sector, especially in terms of providing for those who often have had the least by way of compulsory education and have entered employment with the most limited prospects. To argue that further education policy has failed in certain fundamental respects is not to import a utopian criterion by which to indict the education system. We do no more than judge the system by its own declared aspirations. The desirability of extending further education has long been realized, particularly in the form of compulsory part-time education.

In 1909 a Consultative Committee recommended a system of compulsory part-time education on the exercise of local option that (it was hoped) would spread to cover the whole country. The Fisher Act of 1918 provided a legislative framework for a national system of part-time education from 14 to 18. In the event, the prospect of day continuation schools was destroyed by the Geddes economy axe. Nevertheless, six LEAs, including London, embarked on the development of further education and by 1920 95,000 students were enrolled. The 1944 Education Act envisaged that LEAs would have a duty to establish and maintain county colleges for young persons who were not in full-time attendance at school or other educational institution. Attendance at a county college would be for one whole day or two half-days in each of forty-four weeks in every year. This provision was not implemented. In 1959 the Crowther Report on the education of 15- to 18-year-olds — which, as the first major Government-sponsored appraisal of the 1944 Act, was both important and authoritative — put the case again, albeit in different terms, for county colleges. Thus recognition of the case for developing further education is unequivocal. It is more than seventy years old and has been embodied in both major educational Acts of this century.

More is wrong with further education than the failure to legislate for compulsory part-time provision, though this is undeniably important. Both the scale and the distribution of voluntary provision can be criticized, although this is not to deny that there have been significant areas of growth in this sector during the past twenty years, as we shall show.

In 1958 60 per cent of all young people aged between 15 and 17 were receiving neither full-time nor part-time day education.[1] Twenty years later (1978), 62 per cent of 16- to 18-year-olds were in the same position.[2] Some aspects of further education contracted in the post-war period. In the period 1966-77 there was a 5.6 per cent drop in enrolments to part-time day courses and a 9.8 per cent decrease in evening-only enrolments.[3] In the period 1971-7 the number of young people on block and day release fell by 63,000 in absolute terms; enrolments as an estimated percentage of those not in full-time education fell from 19.8 per cent to 18.3 per cent, or, as the relevant DES document put it, 'remained fairly constant'.[4] However, these figures of contraction do not present the whole picture. Some aspects of further education have expanded in the post-war period. For example, between 1966 and 1977 there was a 93.6 per cent increase in the numbers enrolled in full-time sandwich courses.[5] The number of 16- to 18-year-olds engaged in full-time non-advanced further education (NAFE) increased from 93,000 to 204,000, as a percentage of the 16- to 18-year-old population from 4.3 per cent to 10.0 per cent.[6] Nevertheless, there are still important gaps in the provision for 16- to 19-year-olds, as is shown by the table on pp. 190—1, which was published in 1981.

A number of things should be noted about the table. The figures are only estimates. The 16- to 19-year-old group is a statistical fiction based on the assumption that all young people over 16 have two academic years in their life span in the period between their sixteenth and nineteenth birthdays. Nevertheless, at face value these figures suit our purpose, even though there may be other ways of categorizing these client groups. These DES figures demonstrate that the needs of some groups are being met to a greater extent than those of others. Provision for Group A is between only 2 per cent and 3 per cent of potential numbers. It would be misleading to suggest that this group is made up exclusively of working-class young persons of poor educational attainment and experience. For example, some white-collar employers have a poor record of releasing young employees for further education. Yet Group A is likely to contain a large proportion of severely educationally disadvantaged young people. So is Group G, of whom only 10 per cent are provided for. Contrast these groups with Group D (83 per cent provision) and Group B (56 per cent provision). Many in these groups could be described as educationally advantaged. Group C seems to be exceptional, in that there is a high level of provision for this disadvantaged group, namely, those without work or immediate prospects of work. This is commendable. However, it should be noted that the scheme has been criticized, especially by trade unions, which point to the high rates of continued unemployment among young people when they have completed their courses. In the first part of 1981 only 36 per cent of Youth Opportunity Programme (YOP) youngsters left the scheme to enter a job, or education, or training (the 1978 figure was 72 per cent) and a mere 2 per cent more after six months.[7]

Any extension of provision for this group of young people is to be welcomed. But what has been done so far should be kept in proportion. Work placements last generally only for six months, though sometimes for as long as twelve months. The figures of provision for Group C also include those that are on work-preparation schemes. These last for as short a time as between two and thirteen weeks, though most last between ten and thirteen weeks. No doubt, there are many laudable new developments. Perhaps the education/training of the YOP is exemplary for further

CLIENT GROUPS: ESTIMATES OF SIZE AND OF PRESENT PROVISION FOR 16- TO 19-YEAR-OLDS IN A SINGLE YEAR

	Client group	Potential numbers (000s)	Provision now made (000s)	Main types of provision
A	Those who enter employment without any structured part-time education or training	200-300	5	UVP pilot schemes
B	Those who enter employment and who have the opportunity for systematic education and/or training leading to an educational, vocational or professional qualification	500	280	Young operative courses: CGLI craft courses; TEC and BEC certificate courses; MSC/ITB courses; RSA courses; courses leading to professional qualifications or college awards
C	Those without work or immediate prospects of work	200-300	190	YOP schemes (not all with educational component)
D	Those staying on with a view to proceeding to higher education in due course	400	335	Full-time courses leading to A-Level

E	Those seeking an essentially vocational qualification to fit them for employment at some stage up to 18	200	140	CGLI craft courses, TEC and BEC diploma courses, OND courses; RSA courses; courses leading to professional qualifications or college awards
F	Those who do not wish to be committed to a specific vocational objective, but who wish to continue their general education, personal development and pre-employment preparation	200	135	A-Level, O-Level and CSE courses; pre-employment and foundation courses; BEC General Certificate; TEC Level 1 units
G	Those who require remedial education to enhance their employment and life prospects	50	5	Courses in literacy and numeracy; courses for the physically and mentally handicapped; English language courses

Note: The figures for potential numbers are estimates of the number of young people who might be provided for in a single year in the various ways shown. They are interdependent; the total size of groups A and C is put at some half million. The figures for provision now made show the number of young people actually receiving such education or training in a twelve-month period.

Source: Education for 16—19-year-olds, DES, January 1981. Reproduced by permission of the Controller of Her Majesty's Stationery Office.

education. But however excellent these courses are, little can be achieved in thirteen weeks, or even in six months (of part-time education), by way of compensating for educational disadvantage and laying the basis for subsequent education. A Manpower Services Commission (MSC) survey (1979) showed that only about a quarter of the respondents were receiving off-the-job training, over half in a college of further education. Only 13 per cent of respondents working on employers' premises received off-the-job training.[8] In sum, it is not unreasonable to argue that the educational provisions for Group C is markedly inferior to that of Group D. This need not remain the case. Indeed, the scale and the shape of the problem have been fully recognized in a recent MSC document *A New Training Initiative.* Summarising what has transpired, the document states: 'Taken together, these efforts are large in scale and their achievements substantial. The resources devoted to them by private and public sectors are considerable. But they are patchy and the plain fact is that the scale and nature of events is running ahead of the capability of institutions, private or public, to deal with them.'[9] Furthermore, there is a laudable universalistic tone to what the MSC envisages — witness: 'we must move towards a position where all young people under the age of 18 have the opportunity either of continuing in full-time education or of entering training or a form of planned work experience containing work-related training and education.'[10] The MSC document relates how present provision is likely to expand towards this end. The YOP scheme will expand to provide for 440,000 in 1981/82. By 1983/84 the Unified Vocational Programme (UVP) programme will cover 20,000 young people in employment.[11] This is described by the MSC as a sixfold increase, though it might be argued that a better yardstick by which to measure the scale of expansion is the size of the client group — between 200,000 and 300,000 — which will probably mean that less than one-tenth will be covered by the programme.

Part-time vocational education, the status of which is relatively low compared with that of other forms of post-school education, has often been regarded as the traditional route for working-class boys. However, Crowther's survey of national servicemen showed that 65 per cent of men from the homes of professional or managerial workers took a vocational part-time course within three years of leaving school, compared with 27 per cent of the men from the homes of unskilled workers.[12] A more recent study found that two-thirds of boys who sat GCE or CSE at school were taking a further education course within six to eight months of leaving school, whereas only 35 per cent of those who left school without sitting their examinations were doing so.[13]

Evidence of this kind gives a severely limited picture of the complex process of inflows and outflows relating to further education. A much more sophisticated picture of part-time further education has been presented by Halsey and others. The very sophistication of their analysis obstructs summary. According to Halsey, 'access to further education seems . . . to be fairly equal as between types of schools.'[14] Although 53 per cent of former grammar-school pupils in the sample have received part-time further education, compared with 40.9 per cent of former elementary and secondary-modern pupils,[15] in absolute terms part-time further education is dominated by the working-class. In terms of inflow analysis, 'part-time further education has recruited mainly from those with the lowest level of school success and not from the top of the academic hierarchy. In other words, those leaving school with no examination passes have been less likely than average to enter part-time courses, but they nonetheless constitute a majority.'[16] However, it is also the case that part-time further education 'is a frequently used educational alternative for poorly-qualified boys from the service class'.[17] The pattern of access to part-time further education has changed over time. Halsey argues that before the Second World War part-time further education was an extension of class-based educational opportunity. Since 1945 part-time further education has become more of an 'alternative' route, the effect of which has been to reduce educational inequality.

Other aspects of the character of post-school education should be noted. First, there are marked regional variations in the provision of further education, not only between regions but also within regions. In regional participation, rates of 16- to 18-year-olds in full-time NAFE ranged from 5 to 23 per cent.[18] As regards full-time participation in CSE or GCE courses in schools and further education by 16- to 18-year-olds, about 65 per cent of the variation between LEAs was explicable 'by a simple linear relationship with the socio-economic indicator'.[19] The indicator in question was the proportion of household heads in non-manual occupations. Of course, as the report points out, this variable might stand proxy for such things as parental income or education. Nevertheless, while the precise sigificance of the finding is unclear, what *is* clear is the middle-class basis of variation in participation rates for this form of post-compulsory education.

Second, there is gross variation between industries in terms of the extent to which they release people for further education. The vast majority of employees under 18 in such industries as gas, electricity, water, engineering and shipbuilding are released, whereas a minority of employees in industries like agriculture, distribution and retailing, banking and insurance enjoy day release.[20] Indeed, the pattern of day release is such that one observer has concluded that 'capitalist industry creates far fewer opportunities for further education among young workers than does the public sector.'[21] This fact should be borne in mind when evaluating policy proposals that are dependent, to some degree, on initiatives taken by the private sector.

Third, there are glaring disparities between the provision for men and women. Crowther's view that 'It is impossible to escape the conclusion that the country has hardly as yet made a beginning with the continuing education of girls after they leave school'[22] as well exemplified. Whereas 52.9 per cent of 15- to 17-year-old boys were receiving neither full-time nor part-time day education, the figure for girls was 69.3 per cent.[23] Part-time day release for girls had less than doubled since the Second World War, compared with a tenfold increase for boys.[24] As argued above, industries vary in their willingness to release young employees for further education. Girls tend to work in those industries that are poor in this respect, but even when girls work in industries that are generous in their day-release policy, they still do less well than boys — for example, in 1960 in the gas, electricity and water industries 82.3 per cent of boys did part-time courses, compared with 21.3 per cent of girls.[25] Figures for the electrical engineering industry show that in 1971 roughly equal numbers of boys and girls were taken on, yet 85 per cent of male entrants were sent on day release, compared with 7 per cent of girls.[26] In industries such as clothing, in which females predominate, it is the males who get apprenticeships and hence further education.

However, girls are not under-represented in all aspects of further education. Crowther showed that a higher percentage of 15- to 17-year-old girls than boys were in full-time further education.[27] Rates of evening enrolments were much the same for boys and girls in

1958.[28] In fact, a few years later Henniker Heaton found that of students following evening-only courses, girls were in a majority — 92,000 compared with 59,000 boys.[29] This is a particularly arduous educational route and may reflect the unwillingness of employers to offer girls day release. Still, the fact remains that in the period 1967-77 women made some advances in further education. In that period the number of women in full-time and sandwich NAFE rose by 126.7 per cent, whereas the number of men rose by only 67 per cent.[30] In terms of absolute numbers, by 1977 women exceeded men in full-time and sandwich further education enrolments by 150,000 to 136,000.[31] In the same period, the number of men in part-time NAFE fell by 18.7 per cent: that for women rose by 37.4 per cent, though in absolute numbers men still outnumbered women by 405,000 to 209,000 in 1977.[32] Throughout the ten-year period women continued to outnumber men in evening-only enrolments — in 1977 by 425,000 to 256,000.[33] Despite these gains, women are still in an inferior position with respect to further education. The key difference is their access to day release. In 1976 429,000 males, compared with 94,000 females, benefited from day release.[34]

This statistical litany of complaint presents a dismal picture of provision for 16- to 19-year-olds, but within this pattern of statistics lies another negative feature, namely, high wastage rates. Crowther showed that of students studying for National Certificate, only 26 per cent achieved Ordinary National Certificates (ONC) and 10 per cent Higher National Certificates (HNC). As to City and Guilds, 28 per cent achieved the Intermediate stage and 6 per cent the Final stage.[35] The traditionalist might argue that the drop-out rate was high because 'non-academic' students were asked to climb a ladder for which they lacked the necessary ability. Traditionalists invariably seek to explain the deficiencies of middle-class-controlled systems in terms of the personal deficiencies of the working-class. In this instance, the argument is not wholly convincing. Sixty-eight per cent of National Certificate students and 66 per cent of City and Guilds students had sufficient ability to complete the first year of study successfully, though four years later their numbers had declined to a level indicated by the above figures.[36]

Furthermore, students took a long time to complete their courses — this process Crowther called 'retardation'. Of the students who achieved HNC (normally a five-year course), 19 per cent had taken seven years or more.[37] The outcome was that 'only one student in eleven succeeds in climbing the National Certificate ladder from bottom to top, and only one in thirty does so in the time for which the course was designed.'[38] Recent evidence suggests that the situation has not improved a great deal. Eyken's study showed that a group of craft students were reduced by two-thirds after two years and technicians by about half.[39] Thus further education provides far from universal opportunity for working-class young people, and those fortunate enough to have access to it tread a path that appears to offer more obstacles than those confronted by other 16- to 19-year-olds following the sixth-form path of full-time education.

Crowther made a powerful case for developing provision for 16- to 19-year-olds, some aspects of which we have cited above. The major goal that Crowther wanted to attain was compulsory part-time provision for all young persons of 16 and 17 who were not in full-time education. One means of achieving this goal would have been to grant employees a statutory right to day release. Crowther rejected this, even though it was considered educationally desirable, in that those who exercised the right would be well motivated. It was argued that such a right would have been illusory in some respects. Employers might employ those who were prepared to forego their right to day release: some trade unions would have neither the will nor the means to prevent discrimination. Crowther also rejected compulsion at that stage. Instead, the Report recommended, the Government should declare that compulsory part-time education was to be introduced on a specific date. As a preliminary, Crowther advocated some compulsion in one or more geographical regions, commencing soon after RSLA. Possibly after five years, this compulsion should be extended to other regions over a further period of three to four years. In this way the organizational and financial costs of compulsory universal provision would be staggered and universality thus made more attractive both politically and administratively. This plan came to nothing. Crowther had advocated that RSLA should precede compulsory part-time education. The latter was thus cast into the limbo of 'waiting for RSLA'. Even had this not been the case, Crowther was naively optimistic in believing that 'the most appropriate incentive [for employers] was a declaration that compulsory part-time education [was] to be introduced at a certain date.'[40] More plausible incentives, like taxation changes, direct subsidies or levies, were held to be beyond the competence of the Committee, though the Committee did express enthusiasm for such instruments. Also, the principle of selective regional compulsion was unlikely to prove attractive to either central or local government. Reasonable criteria for regional selection are difficult to imagine, and arbitrary selection would have lacked consensual support, so important in our educational system for the advance of policy. As to employer initiative as the major dynamic of advance, competition between employers in the full exploitation of the cheap labour of young persons would have continued to discount day release until compulsion placed universal obligations on all employers.

That said, we would not wish to lose sight of the undoubted merit of the Crowther Report. The empirical data presented by the Report was of exceptional quality and was a compelling revelation of educational inequality. Despite elitist overtones, Crowther presented a powerful and committed case for extending opportunities to disadvantaged youth.

The 1964 Henniker Heaton Report on day release followed much the same lines as Crowther. The Report excluded as impracticable a right to claim day release. Instead a national target should be set, so it was argued, that would double the extent of day release by 1970. In explaining how this target was to be reached, Henniker Heaton argued: 'In our view the *spearhead* of voluntary development must be at a local level . . . We envisage a *sustained campaign* by each LEA with the active support of employers and trade unions directed at achieving local *targets*.'[41] The italicized terms in this quotation have a ring of purposive, even military endeavour. In plain truth it amounts to pomp of language without circumstance of policy. The Government was to ensure that necessary resources were made available, that accommodation and trained staff were in adequate supply. But all these were to derive from a reactive, not an indicative, governmental posture. The essential 'spearhead' of advance was continued reliance on voluntarism (aided by a 'whole range of public relations activities'),[42] blunt though this had proved to be in the past.

One of the twelve recommendations of the Report was that in the case of young people who, by attendance at evening-only vocational classes, demonstrated their eagerness for further education, 'A specific approach should be made to the employer to urge him to allow day release.'[43] The authors may have regarded this as one of the least significant of their proposals. However, it is hard to imagine that a somewhat limited proposal of this kind would be adequate in practice to ensure an extension of day release opportunities for the young people concerned.

Insofar as voluntarism seems to have become entrenched in government by the early 1960s, it is not unreasonable to view the cause of education for 16- to 18-year-olds as having suffered a reversal. The 1944 Act had spoken of compulsory provision. Some of those who would stop short of compelling student attendance would nevertheless advocate compelling employers to release young workers who requested part-time further education. Indeed, in 1960 Sir David Eccles, Conservative Minister for Education, speaking in a House of Commons debate, said that although Crowther had rejected compulsion as a method of giving young workers a right to claim day release, the Government of the day was of the view that there were strong arguments in favour of such a right. He was personally convinced that unless young workers were given this right, further education would never properly develop. The Government intended to 'explore seriously'[44] this prospect. The exploration soon ran into sand, as our account of the Henniker Report shows.

Indeed, the cause of further education seems not to have attracted much political attention during the late 1960s and early 1970s — though, of course, the system continued to develop. In 1964 a Conservative Government passed an Act that made for the creation of Industrial Training Boards (ITBs). Under this system employers either had to provide sufficient training for their own needs for young people or paid a levy to the ITB, which provided grants for others to undertake the provision of training (which, for the most part, meant apprenticeships). The most disadvantaged young people were unlikely to be embraced by the ITBs because they were in unskilled jobs providing little or no training. Labour regained office in 1964 and supported the ITB system, financed and controlled by industry. According to Glennerster, Labour expanded advanced courses in further education much faster than the previous Conservative Government or Robbins had envisaged.[45] However, it is in part-time, non-advanced day release and evening courses that working-class students predominate (though more full-time students at further education colleges are working-class than are students in the average sixth form), and this sector of further education expanded least in the 1960s. Whereas the numbers in sixth forms increased by nearly 50 per cent between 1963 and 1964, day release was almost static. This is further evidence of the unreasonable expectations that Crowther and Henniker Heaton had of a policy of voluntarism.

The Conservative Government virtually ignored provision for 16- to 18-year-olds in its major policy statement *Education: A Framework for Expansion* (1972). Further education merited little more than a mention in passing. At about the same time the Labour Party was making more positive, if ambiguous, commitments to further education. A so-called Opposition Green Paper, published in 1973, argued for compulsory release on the radical principle that 'all young people in the 16-18 age range must be considered as being primarily "in education" and subsequently day-released, block-released, etc., for employment.'[46] In the interim period, before this goal could be attained, the document argued that the Government should exert greater control over both young people at work and employers to ensure the fullest availability of day and block release. However, later the same year the Labour Party policy document published for the Annual Conference stepped back from the radical commitment of the Green Paper. Labour's objective was to offer, rather than to compel, further education. To this end legislation was promised that would give to all young people the right to continued education. In addition, this legislation would be designed to encourage continuing education, in that, for example, the employment of young people would be made impossible without the employer's providing for their education and training.[47] This commitment was strengthened in the Labour Party policy document *Into the Eighties* (1978), which promised to establish 'a universal scheme of education and training opportunities for *all* the 16-18 age group.'[48]

It was against this background that the Labour Government in 1979 published three consultative papers on provision for 16- to 18-year-olds. The document *Education and Training for 16-18-Year-Olds* made no precise commitments but reiterated the general case for expansion of further education. *Providing Educational Opportunities for 16—18-Year-Olds*, despite the breadth of the title, placed great emphasis on the problem confronting sixth forms. For demographic reasons, it predicted, the number of 16- to 18-year-olds would fall by 25 per cent in the period 1981—91. Sixth forms were expensive, it stated, since (in 1977) the ratio of pupils/teachers

averaged 10:1 — half that in secondary schools generally.
Interestingly, the paper presented a table that showed the number
of sixth forms of varying sizes. Later the Minister was quoted as
saying that a minimum of seventy, and preferably 100, pupils were
required for a viable sixth form.[49] If this yardstick of seventy is
applied to the table on sixth forms, then, excluding sixth-form
colleges and including the 516 sixth forms with no A-Level students,
48.7 per cent of sixth forms should close; with a minimum figure of
100, 64.9 per cent should close. Given the demographic factor cited
above, the position will deteriorate rapidly over the next ten years.
The extremity of the situation has not been lost on the DES,
although it has been slow to act, in view of the fact that the extent of
demographic decline has been known for some time. The consultative paper posed a series of questions which, though apparently
thrown into the arena for debate, have a telling common thread,
namely, they can be construed as questioning, in varying degrees,
traditional sixth-form education.[50] This specific concern with sixth
forms has been cloaked in the larger issue of education for all 16- to
18-year-olds, since direct confrontation of the closure of 64 per cent
of sixth forms would be politically impossible. Some rationalization
of sixth forms might be achieved within the larger remit of post-
compulsory education for young people. Yet how far this would
also entail the expansion of provision for disadvantaged 16- to 18-
year-olds is uncertain. There is an obvious policy tension between
expanding further education while contracting sixth forms — though
while from the standpoint of public expenditure retrenchment the
former may appear improbable, it might be facilitated by the latter.
In this document the issue of provision for 16- to 18-year-olds was
discussed primarily in terms of a desired contraction in the number
of sixth forms, concealed within the notion of rationalization and
willingness to talk about the 16-18 sector in general. It did not
entail a clear-cut commitment to the advancement of the interests of
disadvantaged 16- to 18-year-olds. Without change or centralization,
it is clear, however, that the cost per head of educating the minority
who stay in the sixth form will rise, thus widening the resource gap
between the privileged and the rest.

At about the same time *A Better Start to Working Life* was
published, not solely by the DES, as was the case with the previous
document, but jointly by the DES and the Department of
Employment and Department of Industry (as well as the Secretaries

of State for Wales and Scotland). This paper addressed the vitally important and potentially egalitarian issue of 'extending provision for those young people who enter jobs where little or no systematic training or further education is provided'.[51] These amounted to 200,000 young people. Yet the proposals in the paper have been described as no more than 'an essential step towards the *long term* aim of . . . a universal scheme'.[52] And the means by which this partial solution is to be secured is a continuation of a voluntary approach, despite the failure of voluntarism in the past. The paper asserts that 'vocational preparation should be based on experience at work, and the co-operation of employers and trade unions is vital to success. A sound system of vocational preparation is therefore best developed, initially at any rate, within a non-statutory framework.'[53] Why 'therefore'? How does the second sentence follow logically from the first? It could be as reasonably argued that since such co-operation is vital, and since it has not been forthcoming, a statutory framework is essential.

Admittedly, the 'new' voluntarism appears to be better orchestrated. Its aim initially was to achieve universal provision by the late 1980s. A minimum three-year development target was to be set of provision for one-third of young people in employment below craft level. If, after three years, there were a 'substantial' failure to achieve this target, the Government would reconsider legislation. However, some employers are poorly motivated to provide either education or training for young people below craft level. The measure of good augury that the paper saw in the UVP was not completely convincing. Launched in 1976, the UVP operated 200 schemes in 1979, though provided for a total of only 2000 young people in the three years. In fact, annex B to the consultative paper, which gives a more detailed account of the UVP, conveys a picture that prompts less optimistic expectations. Apparently, 'the main constraint on growth remains the difficulty of persuading employers to participate. Many remain unconvinced by the basic diagnosis and consider that there is no real problem to solve.'[54] Further, it reports, employers claimed that they could not maintain production if young people were released. Also, 'financial incentive does not appear to be a major consideration influencing decision to participate',[55] although, in the view of a Central Policy Review Staff (CPRS) report (1980), 'many employers' organizations are unenthusiastic about extending UVP courses because of the immediate costs.'[56]

More encouraging evidence about the UVP can be found in an NFER evaluation.[57] Of those employers who returned the NFER questionnaire, 77 per cent thought the scheme had been successful for both the company and the young trainees. 84 per cent expressed a willingness to participate in future schemes. However, the non-response rate to the questionnaire was about 50 per cent. Only 36 per cent of the trainees responded to the NFER questionnaire. Most felt they had benefited from the scheme in that they had acquired more confidence and were better able to communicate. However, the pilot scheme reached less than 16 per cent of the target group, which suggests a reluctance on the part of employers to bear the cost of releasing young workers, as the CPRS report and other evidence suggests. Another factor that constrains UVP is that colleges of further education and the Industrial Training Boards have hitherto in the main dealt with young persons of craft level and above. Nevertheless, despite these reservations, the consultative paper does talk of the ultimate expenditure of £30-50 million on the target group of those who, though in employment, currently receive neither training nor education. In 1981, as we have already described, the MSC envisaged a sixfold increase in the programme by 1983/84.

Such provision does nothing for the unemployed, and it is the fact of youth unemployment, not egalitarian reforming concern, that has kept provision for 16- to 18-year-olds on the political agenda since the Conservatives took office in 1979. Youth unemployment increased by 160 per cent between 1973 and 1977. By the summer of 1981 the youth unemployment figure was approaching half a million. Urban riots at that time were explained partly in terms of the consequences of youth unemployment. At the time of writing it was widely expected that these factors would lead to an expansion of the YOP beyond the figure of 440,000 envisaged by the MSC in May 1981. Thus resources are being allocated to the 16- to 18-year-old group, and new courses are developing in a way that must extend opportunities, in some sense, for all in this age bracket. The dearth of provision for young people has received public definition and political attention. The present pattern of development, resulting mainly from MSC initiative, does suggest that the most disadvantaged 16- to 18-year-olds are to be given priority in future provision and that the long-standing goal of universal part-time further education is a more real prospect than it has been before.

This goal seems likely to be pursued through the initial step of giving young people a statutory right to part-time further education. Whether this will be followed by the introduction of compulsory attendance in part-time education for all young people is much more uncertain. However, the most recent conspectus of provision in this field, *Education for 16—19-Year-Olds*, published by the DES in 1981, concentrates on other issues.

From our standpoint, the most important feature of the terms of reference of this report is the injunction to take account of 'geographically and socially disparate rates of participation in 16-plus education'.[58] From the standpoint of the MacFarlane Committee, this is clearly not centrally important, since there is virtually no detailed consideration of this issue. Instead, the problematic is defined in terms of rationalization and cost-effectiveness in the face of demographic and employment change.[59] The needs of the 200,000-300,000 who each year enter employment without opportunities for part-time education and training are described as 'urgent': but 'in the present financial climate we cannot hope for the massive new expenditure that universal provision for them would require.'[60] The report rests content to welcome the proposed extension of UVP as an important step towards necessary wider provision, though only about 3 per cent of this client group are now provided for. As we have already argued, there must be some doubt about employers' enthusiasm for extending UVP. For the 50,000 young people who require remedial education to enhance their employment and life prospects (Group G), the report has nothing to say beyond platitudes of concern.[61] By contrast, despite 'leaks' to the contrary, the report does not advocate the fundamental reorganization of sixth forms, despite the obvious pressure that they are under. There is an arguable case for directing resources away from the sixth-form elite and into compulsory universal part-time further education — that is, for redistribution from the advantaged to the disadvantaged. But there seems to be little prospect of this happening if ways cannot even be found to maintain current sixth-form sizes. Nevertheless, the pattern of provision for 16- to 19-year-olds is clearly changing. The dynamic for this change appears to be located within the MSC rather than the DES. This is understandable, given that a main aim of current policy is the politically expedient one of removing young people from the unemployment register. Without the YOP, youth employment in some areas would approach 50 per cent.[62] This has caused some commentators concern, particularly a group of academics at Birmingham University. They present the work of the MSC as strategic state intervention in the labour market at a time when capitalism is in crisis. MSC schemes provide work socialization and foster attitudes conducive to 'responsible autonomy' — 'the cheapest and most efficient mode of labour discipline'.[63] Such a radical critique seems to give insufficient recognition to the fact both that in the past provision for disadvantaged 16- to 19-year-olds has stagnated and that in the future it may advance considerably. Despite the expediency and deficiencies of current expansion, it provides a context of opportunity for egalitarian policy that is to be welcomed.

The dynamic of employment policy will not be the only factor to influence the development of further education. It is clear that in the future, as in the past, the provision of further education will be demand-led. No doubt, when a conjunction of employer, employee and trade union interests occurs, development will take place — as it has in the past. But this conjunction is unlikely to embrace those who enter unskilled employment after a meagre full-time education. In some respects, Government policy has moved little since the time of Crowther's counsel of despair — 'the presence or absence of students depends on employment and not educational policy.'[64] It is not difficult to see why this should be so. First, in the conflict over resources for 16- to 18-year-olds, sixth forms have powerful middle-class interests to defend their corner. The unskilled, ill-educated working-class youth does not even have a corner to defend. Extant provision carries more political weight than a gleam in the reformist's eye. Second, the DES is unlikely to take the initiative in further education. We have argued that in general DES policy is essentially that of facilitating 'trends'. But 'trends' in further education are linked to manpower needs, which are difficult to calculate and beyond even minor influence on the part of the DES. The DES is in a difficult position, standing as it does in differing relationships with the institutions involved in further education, and the overall character of these relationships is likely to be more complex, less amenable to negotiation, than the relationship between the newer employment agencies and their clients. Certainly, resources seem to be concentrated on employment rather than on educational needs. Though these two things are not and should not be exclusive, an emphasis on the former suggests that future policy is likely to continue to respond to the political imperative of employment policy, to the relative neglect of the educational needs of the unemployed and those in employment but without further education and with little educational experience.

In these circumstances the prevailing posture of voluntarism, tempered by political expediency in dealing with youth unemployment, might be a prescription for the perpetuation of unequal provision for 16- to 18-year-olds. The compulsory principle of the 1944 Act should be the goal of policy, otherwise it may be another sixty years before universal part-time further education is achieved. Further points in support of this case are best left until after a consideration of higher education, when the case for further education can be thrown into greater relief by the facts of higher education provision.

HIGHER EDUCATION

'We do not have a policy on the class balance of higher education':[65] Thus spoke Mark Carlisle in evidence to the House of Commons Select Committee on Education in June 1980. We take this admission as our starting point, since its bluntness highlights a fundamental lacuna in education policy. As in the previous section, we will demonstrate why this stance is inadequate, in terms not just of the social-class distribution of higher education but of regional and sex-based distribution as well. Then we will examine the extent to which the Robbins Report, the binary policy and recent statements of policy are concerned with greater equality.

Carlisle could have gone much further than he did in the above remark. His Government has scarcely framed *any* policy on higher education, unless a set of expedients amounts to a policy. Indeed, much the same could be said of all post-war Governments. A central outcome of this lack of policy has been the persistence of gross inequalities in access to higher education. Robbins — the seminal post-war statement on higher education — found that of children born in 1940—1, 45 per cent of the children of higher professional groups received higher education, compared with 4 per cent of the children of skilled manual workers. Ninety-eight per cent of the children of semi- and unskilled workers did not receive higher education — remarkable testimony of the efficiency of the middle-class education system in denying access to certain groups.[66] Such variations in access cannot be explained simply by ability. Holding ability constant, in terms of a measured IQ in excess of 130, Robbins found that twice as many children with non-manual parents followed a degree course than did children of manual workers.[67] Overall, the chances of a child of professional parents following a degree-level course was eight times those of a manual worker's child.[68] These differentials have changed little since Robbins. In 1976 the proportion of university students from working-class homes was 23 per cent, the same as for the period 1928-47.[69] As to higher education as a whole, in 1974 35 per cent were from working-class origins, a proportion that was *smaller* than at the time of the Robbins Report.[70] Halsey has argued that there is considerable wastage of ability among able working-class pupils who do not reach university. The proportion of working-class boys reaching university could comfortably be doubled without any lowering of standards — 'the working class was obtaining less than half the number of [university] places which, by service-class standards, it was entitled to.'[71]

Thus major post-war developments in compulsory schooling — such as RSLA and comprehensives — have not led to a significant change in working-class participation in higher education. In fact, it is conceivable that the working class could lose ground in future. The Universities Central Council on Admissions (UCCA) data shows that between 1974 and 1978 the number of children of clerical, skilled and unskilled workers declined, as a percentage of total university applicants, from 53 to 49, and from 51 to 46 in terms of successful candidates.[72] Too much should not be made of these figures, since the definition of parental occupation on UCCA forms is sometimes ambiguous. However, for demographic reasons it may be the case that the late 1980s will see an increase in middle-class dominance of universities. Between 1970 and 1975 the birth rate fell in social class 3 (non-manual) by 25 per cent, in class 3 (manual) by 29 per cent and in classes 4 and 5 by 33 per cent, whereas in social class 1 and 2 the fall was only 4 per cent.[73] Since a disproportionate number of university students are drawn from this social group, their dominance may be compounded at a time of cuts in higher education provision. Aside from demographic factors, teacher-training cuts have had a marked effect on opportunities for higher education for working-class students, especially women who have been attracted to colleges of education because of low aspirations and a sense of vocational.[74] Halsey has stressed how important, in the past, the level of provision was to social-class access. The cuts in university places announced by the Government in July 1981 are likely to have a disproportionate effect on working-class students.

Robbins found that there were massive variations between LEAs in the percentage of the relevant age group that entered full-time education. In 1961 the figure for the best county, Cardiganshire, was 24.9 per cent; for the lowest, Ely, it was 5.1 per cent. The best County Borough was Oxford, 17.9 per cent; the worst was West Ham, with 1.7 per cent.[75] Buried in a footnote in an Appendix to the Report was the pertinent conclusion that 'insofar as educational policy — rather than social variables — affects entry to higher education, some authorities are making more of their reserves of ability than others.'[76] Almost two decades later the House of Commons Select Committee could state that it was disturbed at regional variations in the age participation rate within the UK. For example, in evidence to the Committee NATFHE argued that northern areas such as Sunderland and South Shields had a higher education take-up rate half that of the regions like inner and outer London, and not much more than half the national average.[77]

Women have long been under-represented in higher education. In 1938/39 they comprised 23 per cent of full-time university students. By 1961/62 the figure was 25 per cent.[78] However, by 1980 it had risen to 40 per cent.[79] Robbins attributes this low level of female access to higher education to the fact that many girls with good O-Levels did not proceed to A-Level, even though nearly as many girls as boys obtained passes at O-Level.[80] Those who entered the sixth form in 1961 were significantly less likely than boys to attempt three A-Levels (60 per cent of girls compared with 82 per cent of boys) — even though the pass rate for girls who do attempt three A-Levels is as high as that for boys.

Since Robbins there have been important shifts in women's access to higher education. These changes are best expressed in terms of participation rates. The age participation rate (APR) is 'home' entrants as a percentage of the size of 18-year-old age group in the relevant year. The qualified participation rate (QPR) is an expression of the relationship between the young entrants to higher education and numbers with at least two A-Levels. Participation rates for women have shown an upward trend.[81] Nevertheless, it is still the case that for all higher education the participation rates for women are significantly less than those for men. In 1979, the APR for women was 10.6 per cent; that for men was 14.0 per cent. The corresponding QPRs were 75.3 per cent and 87.2 per cent.[82] Some of the less well-qualified girls, who previously got into colleges of education, have not necessarily been provided with alternatives to teacher-training courses. Between 1970 and 1977 the percentage of girls with one A-Level entering full-time higher and further education dropped by almost 25 per cent — boys suffered a 9 per cent fall, though from a markedly inferior position.[83] Bone argues, on the basis of several case studies, that taking advanced further education and teacher training together, although student numbers rose in absolute terms, the number and share of women were falling in the mid-1970s.[84]

Such evidence suggests that the future is uncertain. It cannot be assumed that some recent advances made by women will necessarily continue at an acceptable rate or that reverses are inconceivable. Throughout the last decade the female participation rate in the public sector of higher education has been higher than that of men — 8.1 per cent compared with 6.3 per cent in 1973. Since that year both APRs have declined, that for women most sharply.[85] Other portents are not so good. The Equal Opportunity Commission complained that the DES discussion document *Higher Education into the 1990s* almost totally neglected the position of women in higher education.[86] The continued application of the Robbins principle, namely, that opportunities should be provided for all young persons qualified by ability and attainment, was biased in favour of academically inclined male teenagers. The Commission went so far as to argue that higher education establishments should be designated under Section 47(3) of the Sex Discrimination Act, so that they could 'discriminate positively in favour of applicants who had been discharging domestic or family responsibilities to the exclusion of full-time employment'.[87]

While the Robbins Report did not ignore distributive issues of the kind we have described above, it cannot be said that the Report, or the massive subsequent investment of resources in higher education, was primarily or even significantly concerned with, or in fact achieved, the redress of unequal access to higher education. The expansion of higher education did not come about through egalitarian intent: it was a case of 'going where the arithmetic led' — the hallmark of conservative educational policy. The post-war 'bulge' meant that the number of 18-year-olds in the population increased rapidly in the early 1960s. The 'trend' was that a greater proportion of 18-year-olds were obtaining two A-Levels — was 6.9 per cent in 1961 and 10.9 per cent in 1967.[88] This meant increased competition for university places. Harold Wilson, in his speech to the Labour Party Conference in 1963, complained that in 1962 'a quarter of those who had the necessary A-Level qualifications could not get in [to university] because there were not enough places, and this year a much higher proportion than that will have been excluded.'[89] In 1956 the proportion of those with two or more A-Levels who entered university was 80 per cent. By 1962 it had fallen to 59 per cent.[90]

Pratt and Burgess claim that the Robbins Committee 'did not evolve a policy for the development of higher education. What they did was to accept historical trends and institutionalize them. In this they were not only conservative: they were reactionary.'[91] Indeed, it is generally accepted that the Robbins figures for expansion had been 'floated' within the DES for some time before the publication of the Report. Robbins's essential task was to legitimize these figures in a way that would overcome the universities' innate resistance to rapid change. The fundamental conservatism of Robbins lay in the promulgation of the principle of 'social demand', that is, expansion to provide places for all those suitably qualified who wished to enter higher education. But this is essentially middle-class demand, generated by a school system that is unequal as between social classes. 'Social demand' is therefore a prescription for the perpetuation of inequality in higher education, a device that transports inequality from one sector of education to another. This is inevitable in the absence of measures to foster increased working-class demand for higher education, which were not forthcoming from Robbins and have not been promoted by subsequent policy. Expansion, of itself, does not entail redistribution. In fact, even in terms of mere expansion Robbins was soon recognized to have had modest aspirations. Certainly, had Robbins started from the TUC's standpoint, the figures for expansion would have been much higher. In evidence to Robbins, the TUC argued that if children of manual workers were represented at university in the same ratio to the

numbers of such workers in the adult male population as were
children of non-manual workers — and why shouldn't they be? —
there would have been (in 1956) a need for 50,000, not 18,000
places.[92]

So the expansion of higher education was a policy that was
essentially a response to middle-class social pressures that provided
for mostly middle-class students. Because of it, massive resources
were directed towards the educationally and socially advantaged.
We should not lose sight of the scale of this. Robbins calculated that
the expansion would increase public expenditure on full-time higher
education from £206 million in 1963 to £506 in 1981 — as a
proportion of GNP, from 0.8 per cent to 1.9 per cent.[93] In 1972
recurrent spending on *all* schoolchildren, including those under 5,
was £1180 million. Spending on higher education, for a small
minority of young people, was a staggering £576 million, almost
half the former figure.[94] It was estimated that by 1981 capital
expenditure would drop by 35 per cent; that for higher education
would increase by 57 per cent — for demographic reasons (that is,
as a result of 'going where the arithmetic leads', which in our view,
in the face of major inequalities, is never the self-evidently justified
basis for distribution that it appears to be to the DES). Subsequent
expenditure, both recurrent and capital, was vitiated by retrenchment, but higher education's lion's share of resources has not been
fundamentally affected, though it has been reduced.

For example, recurrent expenditure on teacher training, as a
percentage of total recurrent expenditure, fell from 3.9 per cent to
0.9 between 1971 and 1978. University expenditure fell from 13.1
per cent to 11.2 per cent, whereas recurrent expenditure on primary
schools remained at about 24 per cent. Expenditure on secondary
schools rose from 27.6 per cent to 30.3, as did that on further and
adult education, from 14.8 per cent to 16.2 per cent.[95] In 1981 the
Government announced that it was to reduce expenditure on the
universities by about 17 per cent over three years, and that it was to
expand provision for 16- to 19-year-olds. Thus in crude terms the
pattern of the distribution of resources on post-school education is
changing. Nevertheless, university education is certain to remain
the most costly sector of education per capita, and one dominated
by the middle class.

Much of a general character has been written about the binary
policy since its formalization in 1966. Ours is a narrow concern. We

simply ask the question: to what extent can the binary policy be regarded, in intent and outcome, as action against inequality in higher education? Our brief answer is that while one aim of the binary policy was to improve working-class access to higher education, the policy was not successful.

In his Woolwich speech[96] Crosland concurred with Robbins's complaint that hitherto higher education had developed in a largely unco-ordinated way and that a 'system' should be imposed in future. Crosland's 'system', such as it was, could be summarized in a sentence. Higher education was, and would remain, divided into two parts: the autonomous sector, represented by the universities, and the public sector, represented by the technical colleges and colleges of education. None of the latter would change to the former. Crosland was convinced that the public sector could compensate for certain deficiencies in the autonomous sector. Four basic reasons were given for this conviction. Three covered much the same ground — vague expressions of a greater potential on the part of the public sector for responding to social and, most especially, economic needs. (How this potential was to be realized is by no means clear, and the precise significance of this potential for greater equality in higher education is indeterminate, speculative and unexplored.) The fourth reason was expressed in terms of unsubstantiated generalities on the collective psychology of public-sector institutions, especially the subjectivity of status awareness, in that it was claimed that colleges in the public sector were injured when others were elevated to the autonomous sector because the public sector was 'a permanent poor relation perpetually deprived of its brightest ornaments and with a permanently and openly inferior status'.[97] Reinforcement of the existing dual system rather than the development of a unitary system with ladders of 'academic drift' would prevent such injury. It marked a move away from 'our snobbish caste-ridden hierarchical obsession with university status'.[98] But it was not entirely clear how the 'hierarchy' and 'caste' of higher education was to alter. Unsurprisingly, status differentials remained both within and between the dual system. There was nothing to stop some colleges in the public sector from aping the universities by reducing part-time and sub-degree work. Some have argued that this aping did happen and that successive Governments did not use the instruments at their disposal to give some rigour to the nascent policy concealed in the Woolwich speech and other statements.[99] In other respects, it could be said that the binary policy, far from ridding higher education of 'caste', in fact ossified statification. There was no more parity of esteem between the public and autonomous sector than there had been between the secondary moderns and grammar schools. As to resources, it was possible by the late 1970s to argue with conviction that, certainly with regard to capital expenditure, Governments had given preferential treatment to the universities.[100] (However, the public sector does have a better staff/student ratio than the autonomous sector.) Neither is there any convincing evidence to suggest that the polytechnics have become the 'people's universities', with deep roots in working-class life, despite the fact that some have argued,[101] not unreasonably, that the expansion of the polytechnics offered new opportunities to the urban working-class.

The policy was, in part, an expression of the DES's wish to exert greater control over higher education. The DES felt able to exert more control over the public than over the autonomous sector; thus DES control over higher education would diminish if some regional colleges of technology became universities. The binary line prevented such migration and loss of control. In 1979 a DES policy document noted that while the universities had shown remarkable capacity for expansion, there was no evidence to show that they were in general more flexible. What was meant by 'flexible' was suggested by the cognate observation that 'the public sector has a long tradition of responding to changes in perceived demand, mounting *and discontinuing* courses at comparatively short notice.'[102] The document made it clear that the binary policy was to remain, though the DES had for some time been unhappy with the financial control of the public sector of higher education. The 1974-9 Labour Government set up a committee under Gordon Oakes, the Minister of State responsible for higher education, to examine ways of rationalizing the financing of public-sector higher education. The Government fell before its recommendations could be implemented. However, the new Conservative Government adopted and adapted a number of its most important proposals when it issued a Green Paper which, among other things, proposed a national body to co-ordinate the development of this sector.

This is a good example of the pursuit of managerial efficiency by the DES (see chapter 2). There is no necessary contradiction between this and the pursuit of greater equality. However, certain important issues, such as the need to promote greater working-class access to higher education, have been neglected. Carlisle, in evidence to the House of Commons Select Committee, acknowledged that working-class students were under-represented in higher education and expressed a desire to see this changed. But he gave little indication as to how this might be achieved, apart from the reasonable recognition that the development of continuing education might affect the class profile in higher education and the quite unreasonable expectation that the assisted places scheme and widening of access to direct-grant schools [sic] to all economic classes might have the same effect.[103] In Carlisle's view, 'unless you are saying that a Government ought to be able to intervene to effect the academic qualifications of entry to a university, I cannot see how, as such, you can have a direct class attitude towards entry into university.'[104] This seems somewhat defeatist. It is a prescription for inaction that leads to the bland recognition that somehow an answer to inequality in higher education must be found through the school system.[105]

What is to be done? There is no simple answer to this question, but there must surely be more scope for action than Carlisle implies. Given the evidence relating to social-class access that we have presented, Carlisle's view that the participation rate is what one would expect it to be 'unless it were artificially boosted or blown'[106] is both complacent and unjust. It precludes action to stimulate working-class demand for higher education as in some way unnatural, failing to recognize that the level and social character of the existing participation rate is 'artificially' middle-class, in that it could be other than it is were it not for certain social practices. For example, the structure of awards plays an important part in facilitating differential access to higher education as between social classes. Contrast the mandatory grants that underpin essentially middle-class access to universities with the paucity of discretionary awards for other courses. And few would dispute the present inadequacy of educational maintenance allowances (EMAs) that are intended to support those from low-income families who remain at school beyond the statutory school-leaving age, possibly with a view to entering higher education. It is indefensible that LEAs could spend nine times as much on fees for pupils attending independent and direct-grant schools than they spent on EMAs.[107] We need to construct and endow new working-class routes to higher education. Threshold courses are required to prepare working-class students for advanced study. Some courses could be rooted in trade union educational activity. Part-time study, with mandatory awards, both at pre-degree and at degree level, should be developed. Existing educational institutions should proselytize for working-class applicants. In broad terms, we should pose the question: how many more working-class students do we want in higher education? As one means of reaching the desired target, substantial financial incentives could be provided to encourage working-class applicants to come forward. But surely, the sceptic might ask, the DES view is that it is difficult in present circumstances to provide sufficient resources to meet current demand for higher education without stirring up further demand? The 1981 Budget brought the threat of university closures and staff redundancies. In our view, this is irrelevant. We are advocating the redistribution of existing resources. New opportunities for working-class students, both in higher education and in other sectors, could be financed by reduced expenditure on some aspects of university education.

For example, there is little to be said in favour of expenditure on halls of residence for university students. Students should be *required* to attend courses closer to home. It is said that living away from home enhances the emotional development of students. Perhaps it does. But there are more important needs to be met. Cheaper and (arguably) more effective means of enhancing the emotional development of largely middle-class youth could be deployed — for example, delayed entry to university, with the opportunity to participate in self-financing work-experience schemes on the factory floor, rather like those currently being massively developed to deal with unemployment among working-class youth. In 1971 about 40 per cent of university students in England and Wales were in halls of residence. Yet only 22 per cent of students in Scotland were similarly housed. Estimates put the figure for polytechnic students at 5 per cent.[108] Presumably, the emotional development of most Scottish students and virtually all polytechnic students was not seriously impaired. The House of Commons Expenditure Committee argued that the proportion of home-based students should be increased, voluntarily at first, under sanction if this measure failed.[109] Nothing happened. In evidence before the Committee the National Union of Students, with admirable strong-mindedness, complained of the 'luxuries' of some halls of residence. They were right to do so. University accommodation costs a great deal more than council flats — £4.72 per square foot (£945 per person), compared with £3 per square foot (£730 per person).[110]

Other changes could be made. The British universities have a favourable staff-student ratio — 1: 9.2 in 1979 (though it is expected to decline to 1:11, according to the 1981 Expenditure White Paper). France has a ratio of 1:20, and Italy 1:23.[111] If more working-class students were attracted to university education, there need not be an equivalent increase in staff; existing staff would have to do more teaching. Arguably, the social capital invested in the universities is under-utilized. In evidence to the House of Commons Select Committee, the Association of Principals of Colleges argued that building and equipment were used to the extent of only 11 per cent of their full potential use in universities and 17 per cent in polytechnics.[112] Even though it would be unwise to take these figures at face value, it is not unreasonable to argue the general case that the universities should make more extensive use of their resources in providing greater access to working-class students or should forego resources for use elsewhere.

None of this will happen without political directive. The prevailing climate of retrenchment is likely to make for conservatism rather than experiment on the part of both Government and universities. In a contracting system, without changes of the kind we have advocated above 'new' working-class students could be taken on only by displacing predominantly middle-class students, an unlikely reversal of their current domination of scarce and prestigious resources. Insofar as the universities are allowed by Government policy to solve the problem of declining numbers of 18-year-olds, they are likely to prefer lowering entrance standards for middle-class 18-year-olds to developing new access for (say) working-class mature students doing part-time degrees. Besides, the various models of future development put forward by the previous Labour Government, which did refer to increased participation by children of manual workers, seem to have been displaced by plain contraction.

In conclusion, it should be noted that there is no greater contrast in post-war educational provision than the contrast within post-compulsory education. Higher education for a substantially middle-class elite has been massively expanded. Further education has been sorely neglected, especially compulsory part-time education for young people which would greatly have benefited working-class

youth. It would have been preferable to give priority to further
education. Further education is cheaper to provide than higher
education. It does not entail the high costs of residence away from
home. Thus from any given sum more students would benefit. Part
of the costs of further education could be borne by employers,
especially if they envisaged an economic return. Indeed, in general
the economic utility of further education is likely to be greater than
that of higher education. Further education colleges are more
responsive to vocationalism than the universities, and working-
class further education students are more committed to vocational
study than are university students. Extended further education
would be a means to other desirable ends. It would afford some
protection to working-class youth from the rigours of low paid,
dead-end employment that can set a life pattern from which escape
is difficult. It might also facilitate greater working-class access to
higher education. It is impossible to make a comparable case for the
expansion of higher education. The denial of further education in
the face of university expansion was the grave price to be paid for
'tropism' — that is, the middle-class educational system responding
to middle-class pressures. Only an egalitarian political directive can
correct the neglect of further education, a conclusion compelled by
almost a century of evidence.

9

Conclusion

The post-war period has seen massive changes in, and expansion of, educational provision. First, in terms of actual cash expenditure the cost of education increased from £950 million in 1960/61 to £8340 million in 1977/78 — a ninefold increase. In real terms, expenditure doubled. In the same period educational expenditure increased as a proportion of the UK's gross national product from 3.6 per cent in 1975/76, though it had dropped to 5.7 per cent in 1977/78. The gross national product grew by 50 per cent in real terms; educational expenditure grew by 110 per cent.[1] This was a splendid achievement, especially in view of the economic difficulties of much of this period. Second, the structure of education has changed markedly since 1960. For example, the school-leaving age was raised to 16; the universities were greatly expanded and polytechnics were introduced; and the move to a comprehensive secondary system began. All these changes are to be welcomed and unquestionably represent an improvement in the education system, from which the disadvantaged will have benefited to some extent.

Expansion on this scale has presented a series of choices and opportunities to reduce inequality. The resources have been there. However, we have frequently failed to make the right choices. Instead we have allowed 'going with the arithmetic' (see chapter 2) to determine events, which to a large extent has meant acceding to middle-class pressures. Other aspects of the force of middle-class demand are evident in our case studies of higher education, nursery education and, to a lesser degree, the abolition of selection. Glennerster has calculated that between 1962 and 1968 increased educational expenditure, allocated by social class, benefited the professional/managerial class by an increase of 136 per cent and the unskilled by only 77 per cent.[2] Halsey has argued in relation to university expansion and educational expansion generally that 'though the fastest *rates* of growth almost always accrue to the

217

working class, the greatest absolute increments of opportunity go to
the service class.'³ The highly expensive expansion of sixth forms
and universities offered disproportionate benefits to the middle-
class. The Robbins principle of university expansion (that is, 'social
demand') was something of a misnomer; *middle-class* social demand
would be far more accurate.

Although the disadvantaged have secured some benefits from
change, there are a number of negative hallmarks to this change.
First, educational reform has been pitifully slow. Over long periods
successive, powerfully argued statements of support for educational
reform have come to nought, or little, against an apparent wall of
institutional inertia. In chapter 4, on nursery education, we argued
that the history of nursery education over the last *sixty years*
demonstrates clearly that it is one of the first items to suffer when
cuts are imposed. We listed five major post-war inquiries that have
called for an expansion of nursery education. We wrote of 'a
universal consensus about its need'. But we are still a long way
from even Plowden's modest level of desired provision. RSLA was
promised in 1944 and achieved in 1973. Comprehensivization
started in 1965, meandered forward for more than a decade without
the force of law and, in 1981, is still incomplete. The provision of
universal part-time further education was foreshadowed in 1918, in
1944 and, by Crowther, in 1959. It has yet to be attained. Eighteen
years ago Newsom called for an inter-departmental/inter-authority
working party to consider educational disadvantage. There seems
no prospect of this much needed, modest first step's being taken.
The lesson of all this is plain. The education system, while
responding to increased levels of demand — stemming from
demographic changes and secular shifts in client expectations (by
no means exclusively middle-class) — seems to find it much more
difficult to respond to attempts at social engineering. We stress the
reasonableness of these attempts. Crowther, Newsom, Plowden
and others in the pantheon of reform were not wild-eyed extremists.
They presented well argued, restrained, modest, pragmatic
programmes of reform. While many of the recommendations of
their reports were widely welcomed, in practice the response to
them was limited. It is an indictment of the education system that it
appears to be incapable of responding quickly and effectively to
non-partisan, non-utopian, appeals for change.

Second, when the education system *has* responded to demands for change, it has often been under the spur of political expediency. There were electioneering considerations associated with the timing of RSLA and the expansion of higher education; positive discrimination in the period 1968—70 embodied elements of the politics of race and the forthcoming election; the political management of youth unemployment and urban riots have played a part in the expansion of provision for 16- to 19-year-olds. Expediency can make for superficiality in policy that will not counter fundamental inequalities.

Third, we have deployed meagre resources in support of egalitarian policies. It has been a case of reform on the cheap. Positive discrimination is the best example of this, but the criticism applies equally to all the policy areas we have studied. In general, resources to support policies have been determined not by need as part of a properly worked-out strategy for change but by the 'Treasury factor'. Egalitarian policies have been made to take their place in the queue for 'new' resources and have not been accorded the priority they deserve. Redistribution as a means of facilitating such policies has rarely been given serious consideration.

Fourth, while egalitarian principles have entered policy deliberations, they have not been fully or consistently applied. Some post-Plowden nursery expansion was directed towards distressed areas. Arguably, *all* expansion should have been so directed. Plowden described positive discrimination as an 'absolute priority'. It was never this. When the principle did obtain, it was at the margins of resource programmes. Much desirable policy development has not been pursued to logical and desirable conclusions. Too little has been made of reforming opportunities. RSLA was not the catalyst for a reappraisal of the entire span of secondary education for the disadvantaged, as some had hoped; nor was the opportunity taken to develop more satisfactory bridges between school and work or further education; nor were other social policy issues sufficiently dealt with, such as questions of income maintenance for poor families. Specific educational reforms have been insufficiently closely related to other aspects of education or relevant areas of social welfare. Some reforming initiatives, having crossed an initial threshold of political acceptability, have suffered undesirable adaptation in application and/or have subsequently faded away. Both RSLA and positive discrimination demonstrated that reforming initiatives can become too much concerned with the moral reform of the working class and too little concerned with resource redistribution. In this way, the problematic of egalitarianism is distorted and, to a degree, reforming impetus neutralized. The sometimes temporary institutional response to educational disadvantage is also noteworthy. The Educational Disadvantage Unit and the Centre for Educational Disadvantage were set up to meet a need that was recognized by the DES. That need still obtains, but one has been dismantled and the other now appears to have a very low profile. The initial battle for recognition of disadvantage as an issue has to be fought all over again. Our educational system seems incapable of sustaining reforming initiatives within a sound institutional framework that would make for comprehensive, integrated, long-term change. Instead, reform has amounted to little more than an ad hoc series of disjointed, half-hearted, sometimes transient concessions that have marginally mitigated the effects of a fundamentally unequal education system.

Whether more *needs* to be done to create educational opportunity for the disadvantaged has been questioned by the political right. Whether more *can* be done to create educational opportunity for the disadvantaged has recently been questioned by the political left. In view of the ample evidence of insufficient educational provision, the doubt of both seems too defeatist. For example, Halsey has amply demonstrated that many more working-class students could attend university without any lowering of standards. Yet, as we have argued, those who call for more educational expenditure without saying where the resources are to be found indulge in a form of social irresponsibility. It is vitally important to identify the areas of high priority if we are to avoid ad hoc responses to the latest political pressure. In an article on public expenditure and education one of us has identified some possible priorities and has attempted to cost them.[4] They include the expansion of nursery education, the implementation of Warnock's proposals for the education of the handicapped and UVP. However, resource constraints dictate the need to consider possible savings in lower priority areas, out of which innovation can be funded at least in part. The cost could be secured by a 6 per cent reduction in unit costs in higher education, the removal of state subsidies for pupils in independent schools and a 10 per cent saving in the recurrent cost of primary and secondary education — which, given a 25 per cent decline in the school population, is not unreasonable. Doubtless, other shopping lists of this kind could be presented. There is, in fact, always something to be said for 'asking for more' by way of making reasoned demands for an extension of educational opportunity. Such demands foster higher levels of public expectation and political pressure for resources. The frustration of enhanced expectations may put political pressure on the prevailing distribution of resources or on the character of an economic system that is incapable of creating sufficient wealth. It is precisely for these reasons that those who manage public expenditure lay great stress on 'realism'.

Furthermore, there are positive features to benighted economic times. They sometimes make it easier to redistribute in favour of previously neglected groups. For example, high unemployment reduces the net extra cost of expanding educational opportunity for semi- and unskilled workers. Incurring some direct educational costs to allow the unemployed to study may mean that total expenditure on the unemployed gives better value for money, however unpalatable the concept of value for money may be in these circumstances. We should be alert to the possibility that shifts in relative costs could provide opportunities for advancing the interests of neglected client groups. It need not be the case, as the DES appears to believe, that in times of economic difficulties 'attention has to be concentrated on the short-term problem of distribution'[5] to the virtual exclusion of questions of long-term redistribution. Egalitarian policies could be advanced by trade-offs of the kind cited above. Arguably, the predominant style of policy-making should move from what we have called 'tropism' to indicative planning. For example, we should decide, on the basis of social justice, what level of nursery provision we want in disadvantaged areas or what proportion of working-class students in higher education. Then we need *actively to promote* working-class demand for, and access to, educational opportunity, financed, if need be, by the redistribution of resources.

One element of this promotion should be a clearly stated time scale for action. So often educational policy lacks a sense of urgency; action is suspended somewhere between the Keynesian certainty of long-run death and an unreasonable Civil Service sense of the fullness of time, perhaps best expressed by a complacent interpretation of a motto of the great civil servant of seventeenth-century France, Cardinal Mazarin: 'Time and I against the world.' In contemporary terms, this could be said to speak with a measure of disdain for an impatient world that appears to demand instant solutions to fundamental problems that are regulated by the rhythm of the political metronome of general elections. No doubt, those of 'the red hat' in contemporary Whitehall do not subscribe to another motto of seventeenth-century France, namely, that absolutism (bureaucratic absolutism?) is the only alternative to anarchy; but chapter 2 does suggest that the 'departmental view' may be lauded by policy-makers as a bulwark against 'precipitate' proposals that have only been around for sixty years or so. As we have shown, when political imperatives dictate, the system can respond with alacrity: Witness the expansion of higher education and the MSC. There is no reason why egalitarian policies should never have such imperatives or a sense of urgency.

A central reason why egalitarian policies have lacked dynamism in the past is that social control of the education system is concentrated in the hands of groups that, for the most part, enjoy varying degrees of educational advantage. Generally, these groups approve of, and maintain, the fundamental nature of the system. This elitist social control ranges from the centrally important influence of the DES to the peripheral influence of the 'great and good' who serve on public committees and the chairpersons of Parent-Teacher Associations. There is no *active* middle-class conspiracy to maintain an unequal system. There is no need for one. Middle-class people subscribe to much the same set of values, values that support privilege and class-based differential access to scarce educational resources, often as alleged just reward for successful educational 'competition'. Conformity is the basis of this reward. Change is non-conformity — or, as Machiavelli put it, the innovator incurs the enmity of those who prospered under the old order and only lukewarm support from those who would prosper under the new. Indeed, this support is sometimes not even lukewarm. Those who suffer from educational disadvantage are sometimes unaware of the scale of their deprivation, or are not politically mobilized, or do not see educational opportunity as a solution to their problems. Thus the social basis for reform often narrowly comprises progressive professionals, committed parents and political activists. It is therefore essential that those reforming impulses that do manage to emerge from our largely stagnant political system should be sustained.

Our case studies demonstrate that one reason why egalitarian policies have advanced too little, too slowly, has been because there is little or no central direction and authority at the implementation stage. Chapter 6, on the abolition of selection, argued that the Labour Government should have imposed its wishes on LEAs through legislation. Positive discrimination was for the most part abandoned to the good will of LEAs, which was not, in fact, forthcoming. Much the same has happened in the case of nursery education, and we argued in chapter 4 that officials at the DES were probably well aware of the fact that at a time of public expenditure constraints the good will of LEAs could not be relied upon. We stress that we do not wish to argue against LEA autonomy in general. There are good political and practical reasons why it should be preserved. Our political culture embodies a long-standing fear of centralized state power. Lord Alexander has described how in 1935 he received a letter from a German friend, a headmaster, revealing that teachers were dismissed on the spot if they refused to start the day by getting the children to say, 'To live we must eat; to eat we must fight. *Heil Hitler.*'[6] Alexander recognized the unlikelihood of indoctrination of this kind every happening in this country. But he wished to play safe: 'I believe fundamentally in the distribution of power in education as an essential condition of freedom in a democratic society.' Many of his generation, many key educational decision-makers with personal experience of a Europe oppressed by a barbarous totalitarianism, would have subscribed to similar views. A more common argument today is that it is difficult for central government to get right a wide range of complex and detailed issues and that centralism does not allow grass-roots initiative and innovation to flourish. In general, the political and pragmatic case against all-powerful centralism is convincing, but there is a *specific* case to be made against local autonomy with regard to the disadvantaged.

Nye Bevan once asked, 'How do Welsh sheep differ from those which graze in Westmoreland and Gloucestershire?' Admittedly, this was an unfortunate choice of metaphor, and local needs do vary. At present there is a considerable range in the level of educational provision between LEAs. For example, in 1981 ILEA came top of the table of estimated expenditure per secondary pupil (£1224). Manchester and Newcastle were in the top ten, with expenditures of £987 and £940 respectively. The bottom three places were occupied by Kirklees (£719), Wakefield (£689) and

Bradford (£657). These figures can hardly constitute a simple
reflection of variations in local needs. They are also difficult to
justify in terms of a desirable expression of local political choice and
autonomy. Such wide variation must embody real differences in the
quality of educational provision, partly rooted in the scarcity of
resources suffered by some areas. A radical Government might
seek to aid the disadvantaged by a policy of positive discrimination
both within and between LEAs. Were central government to embark
on such a course, it would be intolerable if local autonomy made for
serious 'discontinuities' between central policy and LEA action.
Some central direction of LEAs would then be justified. The 1981
consultative paper on higher education in the LEA-controlled
polytechnics considered the need for a central planning body to deal
with the 'national character . . . national assessment of priorities,
national planning and due degree of *central* control, which are
lacking under the present management structure'. The particular
challenge of the 1980s is to ensure that 'widely dispersed and
varied national provision is not haphazardly affected by decisions
taken in a local context'.[7] Arguably, the pursuit of greater educational
equality ought to have a national and centrally directed dimension.

Whatever form such a policy for the disadvantaged might take, it
can work in our kind of society only if it is based on a radical
consensus. We have signally failed to construct generally acceptable
radical policies. Recent attempts to make government more open
have met with little success. For example, an analysis of the impact
of the Croham directive, which sought to secure the greater
disclosure of official documents, showed that in the two-year period
July 1977 to May 1979 the DES released thirty-one items for public
scrutiny.[8] In our view, these reveal little about policy-making and
amount to much the same sort of material as that released before
Croham. Neither, as yet, has the House of Commons Select
Committee on Education had notable success in prevailing upon the
DES to be more open about its deliberations. In chapter 3 we cite
Shirley Williams, who has argued that more open government
might have advanced the cause of nursery education. In general,
chapter 2 sought to demonstrate that secret government serves the
interests of policy-makers, not the disadvantaged. In that chapter
we cited various ways by which more open government might be
achieved. Even if our recommendations were followed, it would be
naive to imagine that less secret government would of itself correct
disadvantage, but allied to further developments, such as community

schooling, open government might aid the politicization of educational disadvantage. Too much cannot be expected from the parents of the disadvantaged by way of political activity. In the short run middle-class opposition to change will be more vociferous, though we do not subscribe to negative views that attribute ineluctable political passivity to the working-class. Immediately there is a compelling case for taking more note of the views of the parents of the disadvantaged as consumers. Chapter 7, on RSLA, shows that the extra year has not provided the kind of vocationally oriented courses that both working-class pupils and parents want. This is a reasonable preference. On the other hand, as to parental influence in general, remember the parent in George Orwell's 'The Clergyman's Daughter', who wanted his child taught arithmetic, not decimals. There is a crucial problem associated with making education more attractive to certain sections of the working class. The well-known works of people like Bernstein and Midwinter are relevant here in highlighting the cultural irrelevance to working-class children of much of the curriculum.

In addition, change could be promoted by a national campaigning group devoted to the needs of the disadvantaged. Pressure-group activity at present lacks bite and clarity of focus. Chapter 3 shows that while a major pressure group like the NUT has consistently attended to the question of disadvantage, there is not much evidence of a major positive impact on policy-making. There is much to commend Kogan's stricture that those who wish to concern themselves with public policies must be political, evangelical as well as analytical. Yet a concluding note of self-criticism is appropriate. Most policies, especially egalitarian policies, are conceived with the aim of seeking to gain support by promising as much as possible. Inevitably, the fruits of social engineering are meagre, the gap between promise and performance disappointing. A long-term strategy designed to favour the disadvantaged must undergo constant renewal, fortified against short-term failure by moral conviction about the correctness of the ultimate goal of reduced inequality. This conviction can be expressed in what amounts to no more than an 'act of faith'. Secular transubstantiation makes sinners of us all. We hope we have demonstrated the need to cast stones.

Notes and References

Introduction

1 D. V. Glass (ed.), *Social Mobility in Britain* (London: Routledge & Kegan Paul, 1964).
2 R. H. Tawney, *Equality,* 4th edn. (London: Allen & Unwin, 1952).

1 The Historical Background

1 J. Stuart Maclure, *Educational Documents 1816-1967* London: (Methuen, 1956), p. 100.
2 ibid., p. 102.
3 N. Middleton and S. Weitzman, *A Place for Everyone* (London: Gollancz, 1976), p. 58.
4 B. Simon, *Studies in the History of Education 1780-1870* (London: Lawrence and Wishart, 1960), p. 357.
5 J. Hurt, *Education in Evolution* (London: Paladin, 1972), p. 20.
6 Simon, *Studies in the History of Education,* ch. 3.
7 ibid., p. 335.
8 Maclure, *Educational Documents,* p. 105.
9 ibid., p. 104.
10 ibid., p. 149.
11 ibid., p. 150.
12 O. Banks, *Parity and Prestige in Secondary Education* (London: Routledge & Kegan Paul, 1955), p. 29.
13 ibid., p. 18.
14 ibid., p. 2.
15 B. Simon, *Education and the Labour Movement 1870-1920,* (London: Lawrence and Wishart, 1965), p. 171.
16 W. Van Der Eyken, *Education, the Child and Society* (Harmondsworth: Penguin, 1973), p. 98.
17 ibid., p. 95.
18 ibid., p. 126.
19 ibid., p. 127.
20 ibid.
21 Maclure, *Educational Documents,* p. 154.

22 Van Der Eyken, *Education, the Child and Society,* p. 128.
23 E. J. T. Brennan, *Education for National Efficiency: The Contribution of Sidney and Beatrice Webb* (London: Athlone Press, 1975), p. 109.
24 ibid.
25 Simon, *Education and the Labour Movement 1870-1920,* p. 171.
26 Maclure, *Educational Documents,* p. 173.
27 Van der Eyken, *Education, the Child and Society,* p. 222.
28 Maclure, *Educational Documents,* p. 175.
29 ibid., p. 174 (our italics).
30 Van der Eyken, *Education, the Child and Society,* p. 222.
31 ibid., p. 232.
32 ibid., p. 232.
33 ibid., p. 237.
34 Maclure, *Educational Documents,* p. 174.
35 Van Der Eyken, *Education, the Child and Society,* p. 223.
36 Maclure, *Educational Documents,* p. 175.
37 For a detailed and definitive account of these events, see P. H. J. Gosden, *Education in the Second World War* (London: Methuen, 1976), p. 238.
38 ibid., p. 239.
39 ibid., p. 263.
40 ibid., p. 266.
41 The Green Book, 'Education After the War' (June 1941), is reprinted in full as an appendix in Middleton and Weitzman, *A Place for Everyone.* This quotation can be found on p. 391.
42 ibid. (italics added).
43 ibid., p. 393.
44 ibid.
45 ibid. (our italics).
46 ibid.
47 Middleton and Weitzman, p. 398.
48 *Educational Reconstruction,* Cmd. 6458, Board of Education, July 1943, para. 16.
49 ibid., para. 17.
50 ibid. para. 20.
51 ibid. para. 29
52 ibid., para. 25.
53 See, for example, R. Titmuss, 'War and Social Policy', in *Essays on the Welfare State* (London: Allen and Unwin, 1958).
54 *Educational Reconstruction,* para 1.
55 ibid. para. 27.
56 ibid., para. 23 (our italics).
57 ibid., table 1, p. 35.

58 R. A. Butler, *The Art of the Possible* (London: Hamish Hamilton, 1971), p. 117.
59 Gosden, *Education in the Second World War,* p. 285.
60 Butler, *The Art of the Possible,* p. 117.
61 ibid., p. 120.
62 Gosden, *Education in the Second World War,* ch. 14.
63 Butler, *The Art of the Possible,* p. 123.
64 See, for example, J. W. B. Douglas, *The Home and the School* (London: Panther, 1964).

2 *The Making of Educational Policy and Inequality*

1 See, for example, D. E. Regan, *Local Government and Education* (London: Allen & Unwin, 1977); R. Saran, *Policymaking in Secondary Education* (Oxford: Clarendon Press, 1973); M. Kogan, *Educational Policy-Making* (London: Allen & Unwin, 1975).
2 *Policy-Making in the Department of Education and Science,* Tenth Report from the Expenditure Committee (London: HMSO, 1976), p. 11 (hereafter referred to as *Policy-Making in the DES*).
3 ibid., para. 1548.
4 ibid., para. 1389.
5 M. Kogan, *The Politics of Education* (Harmondsworth: Penguin, 1971), p. 41.
6 *Policy-Making in the DES,* para. 901.
7 ibid., p. 4.
8 Kogan, *Educational Policy-Making,* p. 234.
9 *Policy-Making in the DES,* para. 252.
10 ibid., para. 191.
11 Kogan, *The Politics of Education,* p. 43.
12 OECD Report, *Times Higher Educational Supplement,* 9 May 1978.
13 ibid.
14 *Policy-Making in the DES,* para. 681.
15 Kogan, *The Politics of Education,* p. 138.
16 ibid., p. 41.
17 P. Kellner and Lord Crowther-Hunt, *The Civil Servants* (London: Raven Books, 1980), p. 218.
18 ibid., p. 219.
19 Kogan, *Educational Policy-Making,* p. 238.
20 *Policy-Making in the DES,* p. 192.
21 M. Kogan, *The Politics of Educational Change* (London: Fontana, 1978), p. 122.
22 Kogan, *The Politics of Education,* p. 169.

23 *Policy-Making in the DES,* p. 2.
24 'Portrait of Lord Hailsham', *New Statesman,* 15 August 1975.
25 *Policy-Making in the DES,* para. 30.
26 ibid., para. 50.
27 ibid., para. 81.
28 ibid., para. 98.
29 ibid., para. 99.
30 ibid., p. 70.
31 ibid., para. 241.
32 ibid., p. 130.
33 ibid.
34 ibid., para. 382.
35 ibid., para. 385.
36 OECD Report, *Times Higher Educational Supplement,* 9 May 1978, p. 9.
37 *Policy-Making in the DES,* para. 1619.
38 Kogan, *The Politics of Education,* p. 173.
39 T. Raison, *The Act and the Partnership* (London: Bedford Square Press, 1976), p. 48.
40 *Policy-Making in the DES,* para. 516.
41 Kellner and Crowther-Hunt, *The Civil Servants,* p. 223.
42 Kogan, *The Politics of Education,* p. 177.
43 *Policy-Making in the DES,* para. 446.
44 ibid., p. 50.
45 ibid., p. 31.
46 ibid., p. 54.
47 ibid., p. 53.
48 OECD Report, *Times Higher Educational Supplement,* 9 May 1978, p. 11.
49 *Policy-Making in the DES,* para. 350.
50 Kogan, *Educational Policy-Making,* p. 101.
51 M. Kogan, 'Damned planners', *Times Educational Supplement,* 9 May 1975, p. 5.
52 Kogan, *The Politics of Education,* p. 123.
53 *Policy-Making in the DES,* p. 49.
54 ibid., para. 191.
55 ibid., para. 197.
56 Shirley Williams, *Politics is for People* Harmondsworth: Penguin, 1981), p. 184.
57 M. Stewart, *Life and Labour* (London: Sidgwick & Jackson, 1980), p. 135.
58 Kogan, *The Politics of Education,* pp. 193-4.
59 ibid., p. 52.

60 ibid.
61 ibid., p. 177.
62 Kellner and Crowther-Hunt, *The Civil Servants,* p. 280.
63 Kogan, *The Politics of Education,* p. 177.
64 For example, Marcia Williams, *Inside Number 10* (London: New English Library, 1975), p. 274.
65 See T. Bottomore, *Elite and Society* (London: Penguin, 1964); W. C. Guttsman, *The British Political Elite* (London: MacGibbon and Kee 1963).
66 *The Civil Service,* vol. 3 (1) (London: HMSO, 1969), p. 19, table 2.3.
67 ibid., p. 25, table 2.7.
68 *Policy-Making in the DES,* para. 693.
69 ibid., p. 192.
70 ibid., para. 695.
71 *Educational Development Strategy in England and Wales* (Paris: OECD, 1975), p. 50.
72 OECD Report, *Times Higher Educational Supplement,* 9 May 1978, p. 10.
73 G. Fowler, *Central Government of Education 1: Decision-Making in British Education Systems, Unit 2* (Milton Keynes: Open University Press, 1974), p. 39.
74 Kogan, *The Politics of Education,* p. 75.
75 ibid., p. 89.
76 ibid., p. 102.
77 *Educational Development Strategy in England and Wales,* p. 54.
78 *Policy-Making in the DES,* para. 77.
79 ibid., para. 73.
80 *South Wales Echo,* 8 November 1978, p. 3.
81 ibid.
82 *Policy-Making in the DES,* p. 24 (italics added).
83 ibid., para. 381.
84 ibid., para. 417.
85 ibid., para. 339.
86 ibid., para. 471.
87 ibid., p. 5.
88 ibid.
89 P. Medlicott, 'The DES', *New Society,* 22 August 1974.
90 OECD Report, *Times Higher Educational Supplement,* 9 May 1978, p. 8.
91 *Policy-Making in the DES,* para. 1619.
92 ibid., para. 1248.
93 *Management Review of the Department of Education and Science,* DES and CDS, March 1979, para. 4.20.

94 ibid.
95 *Policy-Making in the DES,* p. 191.
96 Kogan, *The Politics of Educational Change,* p. 162.
97 *Policy-Making in the DES,* para. 93.
98 *Tenth Report from the Expenditure Committee: Policy-Making in the DES: Government Reply,* Cmnd 6678, 1976, para. 16.
99 *Policy-Making in the DES,* p. 136.
100 Kogan, *The Politics of Educational Change,* p. 161.
101 *Policy-Making in the DES,* para. 93.
102 Kogan, *The Politics of Education,* p. 185.
103 *Policy-Making in the DES,* para. 97.
104 ibid., p. 33.
105 Raison, *The Act and the Partnership,* p. 77.
106 *Policy-Making in the DES,* para. 100.
107 ibid., para. 87.
108 ibid., para. 99.
109 Kellner and Crowther-Hunt, *The Civil Servants,* p. 281.
110 M. Meacher, 'How the mandarins rule', *New Statesman,* 5 December 1980, p. 14.
111 P. Hennessy, 'How civil servants tame their masters', *The Times,* 5 December 1980, p. 4.
112 *Management Review of the Department of Education and Science,* para. 4.14.
113 ibid., para. 4.15.

3 *Unions and Pressure Groups*

1 *Policy-Making in the Department of Education and Science,* Tenth Report from the Expenditure Committee (London: HMSO, 1976).
2 Sir Ronald Gould, *The Teacher,* 19 April, 1963, p. 5.
3 Ronald A. Manzer, *Teachers & Politics,* (Manchester University Press, 1970).
4 ibid., p. 3.
5 R. D. Coates, *Teachers Union & Interest Group Politics* (Cambridge: Cambridge University Press, 1972), p. 12.
6 Manzer, *Teachers & Politics,* p. 19.
7 *First Things First,* memorandum submitted to CACE, under the chairmanship of Lady Plowden (London: NUT, 1964).
8 Shirley Williams, 'The Decision Makers', in *Policy and Practice: The Experience of Government* (London: Royal Institute of Public Administration, 1980).
9 *Nursery Assistants,* comments on DES Draft Administrative Memorandum, (NUT, mimeographed, 1972), p. 1.

10 ibid., p. 2.
11 *Nursery Education in Wales* (London: Welsh Committee of the NUT, 1972).
12 *The Provision of Pre-School Education in England and Wales* (London: NUT, 1974).
13 A. H. Halsey, *Educational Priority: EPA Problems and Policies* (London: HMSO, 1972).
14 *The Needs of the Under Fives* (London: NUT, 1977), p. 17.
15 ibid., p. 17.
16 *The Provision of Pre-School Education in England and Wales,* p. 15.
17 *The Needs of the Under Fives,* p. 29.
18 *The Provision of Pre-School Education in England and Wales,* p. 12.
19 Halsey *Educational Priority:* EPA Problems and Policies, Volume IV
20 *Education in Schools* (London: NUT, December 1977).
21 *Plowden: The Union's comments on some of the major issues of the Plowden Report* (London: NUT, 1969), p. 2.
22 ibid., p. 5.
23 ibid., p. 6.
24 Keith Banting, 'The case for revival', *Times Educational Supplement,* 13 June 1980.
25 *Section 11* (London: NUT, 1978).
26 *Replacing Section 11* (London: NUT, 1979).
27 *Educational Disadvantage and the Needs of Immigrants:* Observations on the Report of the Select Committee on Race Relations and Immigration, DES (London: HMSO, 1974).
28 Max Morris, quoted by Mary Castle, 'Second thoughts urged on 'arbitrary' closure of disadvantage centre', *Teacher,* 23 November 1979.
29 *First Things First,* p. 17.
30 ibid., p. 17.
31 See issue of 12 July 1965.
32 *Into the Seventies* (London: NUT, 1969), p. 4.
33 *The Union View of ROSLA* (London: NUT, 1971).
34 See A Certificate of General Secondary Education, (London: NUT, March 1970).
35 *Examining at 16-Plus: The Case for a Common System* (London: NUT, 1978), p. 5.
36 See issue of 30 September 1960.
37 *Manzer, Teachers and Politics,* p. 38.
38 ibid., p. 158.
39 Rogers, 'The case for revival'.
40 *Mixed-Ability Teaching in the Middle Age Range* (Oxford: CASE, 1979).
41 *Secondary Schools in Guildford* (Guildford: CASE, 1980).

42 *The Effects of Budgetary Cuts on Education in the St. Albans Division,* 1979-80 (St. Albans: Association for the Advancement of Learning, 1980).

43 Maurice Kogan, *Educational Policy-Making* (London: Allen & Unwin, 1975.

44 *Nursery Education* (Billericay: Home and School Council, 1973).

45 *Raising the School Leaving Age* (Billericay: Home and School Council, 1972).

46 *Young School Leavers* (London: HMSO, 1968).

47 Published by the Home and School Council in 1971.

48 *CASE Guidelines No. 5: Selection. Favoured Few or Selection for All?* (London: CASE, 1981), p. 3.

49 Rogers, 'The case for revival'.

50 Kogan, *Educational Policy-Making,* p. 23.

4 Nursery Education

1 Tessa Blackstone, *A Fair Start* (London: Allen Lane, 1971), ch. 2.

2 See, for example, R. Sharp and A. Green, *Social Control and Education* (London: Routledge & Kegan Paul, 1976).

3 Basil Bernstein, 'Education Cannot Compensate for Society', in D. Rubinstein and C. Stoneman (eds.), *Education for Democracy* (Harmondsworth: Penguin, 1970).

4 G. W. Brown et al., 'Social Class and Psychiatric Disturbance among Women in an Urban Population', *Sociology,* vol. 9 (1975), pp. 225-54.

5 For an earlier study of this phenomenon, see H. Gavron, *The Captive Wife* (London: Routledge & Kegan Paul, 1966).

6 Ministry of Education Circular 8, May 1960, p. 1.

7 ibid., p. 2.

8 *Children and their Primary Schools* (Plowden Report) (London: HMSO, 1967), Central Advisory Council on Education.

9 ibid., p. 117.

10 ibid., p. 118-19.

11 A. H. Halsey, Educational Priority, vol. 1 (London: HMSO, 1972).

12 *Education: a Framework for Expansion,* Cmnd 5174 (London: HMSO, 1972), p. 5.

13 ibid., p. 5.

14 Central Policy Review Staff, *Services for Young Children with Working Mothers* (London: HMSO, 1978), appendix 2.

15 *I Want to Work . . . but What About the Kids?* (Manchester: Equal Opportunities Commission, 1978).

16 *Children and their Primary Schools,* pp. 127-8.

17 See Tessa Blackstone, 'Early Childhood Education', *Trends in Education,* special European issue (1973), pp. 38-45, for a description of how the system works in some Western European countries.

18 Central Policy Review Staff, *Services for Young Children with Working Mothers.*

19 Tessa Blackstone, *First Schools of the Future,* Fabian Research Series no. 304 (London: Fabian Society, 1972).

20 *Low Cost Day Provision for the Under-Fives* (London: DHSS and DES, 1976).

21 Tessa Blackstone, *Education and Day Care for Young Children in Need: The American Experience* (London: Bedford Square Press, 1973).

22 J. Bruner, *Under Five in Britain* (London: Grant McIntyre, 1980).

23 Bridget Bryant, Miriam Harris and Dee Newton, *Children and Minders* (London: Grant McIntyre, 1980).

24 Bruner, *Under Five in Britain,* p. 180.

25 *Plowden* (London: NUT, 1969).

26 *Nursery Education in Wales* (London: Welsh Committee of the NUT, 1972); *The Provision of Preschool Education|in|England|and|Wales* (London: NUT, 1974); *The Needs of the Under Fives* (London: NUT, 1977).

27 *First Things First* (London: NUT, 1964).

28 *A Language for Life* (Bullock Report) (London: HMSO, 1975).

29 *The Educational and Other Needs of Handicapped Children and Young Persons* (Warnock Report) (London: HMSO, 1978).

30 *One Parent Families* (Finer Report) (London: HMSO, 1974).

31 *Fit for the Future* (Court Report), (London: HMSO, 1977).

32 B. Tizard et al., *Involving Parents in Nursery and Infant Schools* (London: Grant McIntyre, 1981).

33 See Blackstone, *A Fair Start.*

34 See Central Policy Review Staff, *Services for Young Children with Working Mothers,* appendix 2, for further information.

35 See J. H. Barnes and H. Lucas, Positive Discrimination in Education: Individuals, Groups and Institutions in *Educational Priority,* vol. 3 (London: HMSO, 1975).

36 See, for example, M. Bone, *Preschool Children and the Need for Day Care* (London: Office of Population Censuses and Surveys, 1977).

37 H. Glennerster, 'Inequality and Education' in N. Bosanquet and P. Townsend, *Labour and Inequality* (London: Fabian Society, 1972).

5 *Positive Discrimination in Education*

1 Our concern in this chapter is not to consider the technical difficulties in devising a policy to deal with educational disadvantage. This has

been done elsewhere. See, for example, A. Little and C. Mabey, 'An Index for the Designation of Educational Priority Areas', in A. Shonfield and S. Shaw (eds.), *Social Indicators and Social Policy* (London: Heineman, 1972). See also J. H. Barnes and H. Lucas, 'Positive Discrimination in Education: Individuals, Groups and Institutions', in *Sociological Theory and Survey Research* (London: SSRC 1976).

2 See Jo Mortimore and Tessa Blackstone, *Disadvantage and Education* (London: DHSS/SSRC, 1980).

3 *Half our Future* London: (HMSO 1963), para. 58.

4 ibid., para. 66.

5 ibid., para. 58.

6 ibid., para. 60.

7 ibid., para. 65.

8 ibid., para. 74.

9 ibid., page 273.

10 ibid., para. 68.

11 ibid., paras. 70 and 71.

12 *Children and their Primary Schools* (London: HMSO 1967), para. 1185.

13 ibid., para. 153.

14 ibid., para. 174 (italics added).

15 ibid., para. 151 (italics added).

16 ibid., para. 173 (italics added).

17 ibid.

18 ibid., para. 139.

19 ibid., para. 164.

20 See page 35.

21 *Children and their Primary Schools,* para. 158.

22 ibid., paras. 174-7.

23 ibid., para. 168.

24 K. Banting, *Poverty, Politics and Policy* (London: Macmillan, 1979), p. 128.

25 House of Commons, *Hansard,* vol. 743, col. 740. Boyle went on to say that Plowden showed the need for positive discrimination 'within the whole field of Government expenditure' and should give priority to growth, efficiency, and social need that cannot be met by any other agency. He quoted with approval Keynes's view that government should concentrate on those tasks which would not otherwise be carried out. It is not clear if Boyle would have included positive discrimination to meet social need in this category. If he did, he was ahead of his Party.

26 ibid., col. 755.

27 ibid., col. 756.

28 Circular 11/67, DES, para. 2.

29 Banting, *Poverty, Politics and Policy,* pp. 129-30.

30 House of Commons, *Hansard,* vol. 787, col. 874.
31 Banting, *Poverty, Politics and Policy,* p. 130.
32 ibid.
33 *A Study of School Building* (London: HMSO 1978).
34 *Educational Priority* vol. 2 (London: HMSO, 1974), p. 29.
35 ibid., p. 124.
36 ibid., p. 123.
37 *Educational Priority,* vol. 3 (London: HMSO, p. 4, table 3.
38 *Educational Priority,* vol. 1 (London: HMSO, 1972), p. 47.
39 ibid., pp. 145-8.
40 DES *Reports on Education,* No. 79, 1974, p. 1.
41 J. Gray, 'Positive Discrimination in Education', *Policy and Politics,* vol. 4, no. 2, (1975), p. 93.
42 Cited by M. Meacher, 'The Politics of Positive Discrimination', in H. Glennerster (ed.), *Positive Discrimination and Inequality* (London: Fabian Society, 1974), p. 3.
43 Circular 2/69, DES, para. 11.
44 ibid., p. 5.
45 *Hansard,* vol. 743, col. 755.
46 Circular 11/67, DES, para. 7.
47 ibid.
48 P. Townsend and N. Bosanquet (eds.), *Labour and Inequality* (London: Heinemann, 1980), p. 20.
49 For an account of this, see Mortimore and Blackstone, *Disadvantage and Education,* pp. 158-60.
50 House of Commons, *Hansard,* vol. 755, Col. 1652.
51 Policy-making in the *Department of Education and Science,* Tenth Report of the Expenditure Committee, (London: HMSO, 1976), para. 287 (italics added). (Hereafter referred to as *Policy-Making in the DES.*)
52 ibid., para. 528.
53 Meacher, 'The Politics of Positive Discrimination', p. 6.
54 House of Commons, *Hansard,* vol. 769, col. 40.
55 Circular 19/68, DES, para. 6.
56 Circular 2/69, DES, para. 11.
57 Circular 19/68, DES, para. 4.
58 Circular 11/67, DES, para. 11.
59 Circular 19/68, para. 3.
60 *Educational Disadvantage and the Educational Needs of Immigrants,* Cmnd 5720 (London: HMSO, 1974), p. 15.
61 *Policy-Making in the DES,* para. 528.
62 ibid., p. 133.
63 Mortimore and Blackstone, *Disadvantage and Education,* p. 165.

64 See, for example, *Preventive Social Work in Primary Schools*. Centre for Information and Advice on Educational Disadvantage, (London: undated) p. 5. The social worker reports that his work was valued by the teachers when he started to do 'something positive'; that is, advising parents on the suitability of a Special School place for two children and intervening in a dispute between school and parents, so that an assessment was made of a child and an appropriate place found at another school. In other words, the social worker was valued as an agent through whom problem children were removed from the school.

65 See A. Halsey, 'Whatever happened to positive discrimination?', *Times Educational Supplement,* 21 January 1977.

66 House of Commons, *Hansard,* vol. 769, col. 40.

67 *Educational Development Strategy in England and Wales,* (Paris: OECD, 1975), p. 61.

68 See, for example, J. Barnes, 'A Solution to Whose Problem?', in Glennerster, *Positive Discrimination and Inequality.* Barnes argues that most disadvantaged children are not in disadvantaged areas and most of the children in disadvantaged areas are not disadvantaged.

69 Banting, *Poverty, Politics and Policy,* p. 136.

70 Meacher, 'The Politics of Positive Discrimination', pp. 9-13.

71 Mortimore and Blalckstone, *Disadvantage and Education,* p. 164.

72 Banting, *Poverty, Politics and Policy,* p. 127.

73 ibid., p. 118.

74 ibid.

75 *Educational Priority,* vols. 1-5 (London: HMSO, 1972-5).

76 ibid., vol. 1, p. 6.

6 *The End of 11-Plus Selection*

1 House of Commons, *Hansard,* vol. 701, col. 1177.

2 House of Commons, *Hansard,* vol. 702, col. 1706.

3 ibid., col. 1781.

4 M. Stewart, *Life and Labour* (London: Sidgwick and Jackson, 1980), p. 131.

5 R. H. S. Crossman, *The Diaries of a Cabinet Minister,* vol. 1 (London: Hamish Hamilton and Jonathan Cape, 1975), p. 133.

6 ibid.

7 Stewart, *Life and Labour,* p. 134.

8 Crossman, *The Diaries of a Cabinet Minister,* vol. 1, p. 135.

9 House of Commons, *Hansard,* vol. 705, col. 444.

10 Crossman, *The Diaries of a Cabinet Minister,* vol. 1, p. 133.

11 M. Kogan, *The Politics of Education* (Harmondsworth: Penguin, 1971), p. 189.

12 S. Williams, *Politics is for People* (Harmondsworth: Penguin, 1981), p. 184.
13 Circular 10/65, DES, p. 2 (italics added).
14 ibid., p. 5.
15 A. Cicourel and J. Kitsuse, *Educational Decision-Makers* (New York: Bobbs-Merrill, 1963).
16 Circular 10/65, DES, p. 2.
17 ibid.
18 ibid., p. 13.
19 House of Commons, *Hansard,* vol. 702, col. 1793.
20 The Athenaeum is an exclusive London Club.
21 Circular 10/65, DES, p. 12.
22 ibid., p. 8.
23 ibid., p. 9.
24 Kogan, *The Politics of Education,* p. 50.
25 Circular 10/65, DES, p. 9.
26 House of Commons, *Hansard,* vol. 702, col. 1786.
27 Circular 10/65, DES, p. 6.
28 ibid.
29 House of Commons, *Hansard,* vol. 701, col. 1179.
30 Kogan, *The Politics of Education,* p. 78.
31 House of Commons, *Hansard,* vol. 702, col. 1785.
32 Circular 10/66, DES, para. 5.
33 ibid.
34 *Report on Education No. 87,* DES, 1977, p. 5, table A.
35 D. Marsden, 'Politicians, Equality and Comprehensives', in P. Townsend and N. Bosanquet (eds.), *Labour and Inequality* (London: Fabian Society, 1972), p. 124.
36 House of Commons, *Hansard,* vol. 795, col. 1468.
37 ibid., col. 1468.
38 ibid., col. 1470.
39 ibid., col. 1533.
40 ibid., col. 1577.
41 Circular 10/70, DES.
42 Circular 4/74, DES, para. 7.
43 D. Rubinstein and B. Simon, *The Evaluation of the Comprehensive School 1926-72* (London: Routledge & Kegan Paul, 1973), p. 117.
44 ibid., p. 118.
45 *Journal of Social Policy,* vol. 1 (4), p. 344.
46 *Journal of Social Policy,* vol. 3 (2), p. 152.
47 C. Benn and B. Simon, *Halfway There* (Harmondsworth: Penguin, 1972), p. 95.
48 *Report on Education No. 87.*
49 Circular 4/74, DES, para. 3.

50 ibid.
51 ibid., para. 7.
52 ibid., para. 10.
53 ibid.
54 ibid., para. 11.
55 ibid., para 13 (italics added).
56 ibid., para. 13.
57 ibid., para. 9.
58 *The Time.* Law Report, 12 July 1976.
59 *The Times* Law Report, 29 July 1976.
60 *The Times* Law Report, 21 October 1976.
61 J. A. G. Griffiths, *The Politics of the Judiciary* (London: Fontana, 1976), p. 129.
62 *1976 Education Act,* chapter 8, Clause 1.
63 Parliamentary Debates, House of Commons Official Report, *Standing Committee E,* 12 February 1976, col. 13.
64 *Report on Education No. 87,* p. 4.
65 *Standing Committee E,* 1st sitting, 12 February 1976, col. 49.
66 *Standing Committee E,* 6th sitting, 2 March 1976, col. 291.
67 Parliamentary Debates, House of Commons, Official Report, *Standing Committee A,* 13 March 1970 col. 140.
68 House of Commons, *Hansard,* vol. 947, col. 243.
69 *The Times,* 6 October 1978, p. 8.
70 *Standing Committee E,* 26th sitting, 27 April 1976, col. 1256.
71 *A Study of School Building* (London: HMSO, 1978).
72 *Journal of Social Policy,* vol. 7 (4), p. 474.
73 *Policy-Making in the Department of Education and Science,* Tenth Report of the Expenditure Committee (London: HMSO, 1976), para. 869.
74 *Guardian,* 26 August 1976, p. 4.
75 Kogan, *The Politics of Education,* p. 89.
76 M. Kogan, *Educational Policy-making* (London: Allen & Unwin, 1975), p. 219.
77 ibid., p. 220.
78 R. Batley *et al., Going Comprehensive* (London: Routledge & Kegan Paul, 1970), p. 40-2.
79 Kogan, *The Politics of Education,* p. 190.

7 *The Raising of the School-Leaving Age*

1 R. Bell (ed.), *Education in Great Britain and Ireland* (London: Routledge & Kegan Paul, 1973), p. 279.
2 *Parliamentary Debates, Official Report, 5th Series* 1959-60, vol. 620, col. 44.

3 ibid., col. 44.
4 ibid., col. 48.
5 ibid., col. 59.
6 ibid., col. 63.
7 ibid., col. 63.
8 House of Commons, *Hansard,* vol. 688, col. 62.
9 ibid., col. 40.
10 ibid., col. 59.
11 ibid., col. 40.
12 House of Commons, *Hansard,* vol. 756, col. 1586.
13 H. Wilson, *The Labour Government 1964-70* (Harmondsworth: Penguin 1974), p. 581.
14 R. H. S. Crossman, *The Diaries of a Cabinet Minister,* vol. 2 (London: Hamish Hamilton and Jonathan Cape, 1976), p. 636. Harold Wilson described George Brown as 'passionate in his previous defence of the decision about the school-leaving age' (see Wilson, *The Labour Government,* p. 609).
15 Crossman, *The Diaries of a Cabinet Minister,* vol. 2, p. 637.
16 ibid.
17 See chapter 4.
18 See speech by Harold Wilson, House of Commons, *Hansard,* vol. 756, col. 1980.
19 Schools Council, *Enquiry 1: Young School Leavers* (London: HMSO, 1968), p. 25.
20 *Guardian,* 27 May 1974.
21 *Times Educational Supplement,* 4 October 1974. Fifty per cent of university teachers were also against RSLA.
22 Schools Council, *Enquiry 1: Young School Leavers,* p. 88.
23 ibid., p. 86.
24 ibid., p. 113. Thus any failure in RSLA could be readily attributed to the inadequacies of pupils and parents rather than schools.
25 *Report on Education No. 73: Progress Report on RSLA,* DES, 1972, p. 2.
26 In 1974 48.9 per cent of staff in the education service were non-teachers. Clearly, most perform vital supportive roles, but the prolification of such roles (in 1954 the figure was 29.9 per cent) is nevertheless disturbing. For fuller details, see T. Raison, *The Act and the Partnership* (London: Bedford Square Press, 1976), p. 26.
27 *Statistics of Education 1970,* vol. 1: *Schools* (London: HMSO, 1971) p. 24.
28 J. W. Tibble, *The Extra Year* (London: Routledge & Kegan Paul, 1970), p. 21.
29 Central Advisory Council for Education (England) *Early Leaving* (London: HMSO, 1954), p. 5.

30 Schools Council, *Raising the School Leaving Age,* Working Paper No. 2 (London: HMSO, 1965), p. 1.

31 Central Advisory Council for Education (England), *15-18,* vol. 2 (London: HMSO, 1960), p. 127.

32 J. W. B. Douglas *et al., All Our Future* (London: Panther, 1971), p. 37.

33 ibid., p. 38.

34 Central Advisory Council for Education (England), *Early Leaving,* p. 34.

35 That is, measured ability at age 15.

36 Douglas, *All Our Future,* p. 216, table 4.

37 *Statistics of Education 1974,* vol. 1: *Schools* (London: HMSO, 1975), p. 26.

38 *Statistics of Education 1972,* vol. 1: *Schools* (London: HMSO, 1973), pp. 80 and 72.

39 *Statistics of Education 1974,* vol. 1: *Schools.*

40 ibid.

41 Of course, this is not to deny the continuation of other negotiations.

42 The national pattern of these differentials was complex, and the figures we have cited are meant to be illustrative not definitive.

43 House of Commons, *Hansard,* vol. 688, col. 59.

44 Central Advisory Council for Education (England), *Half Our Future* (London: HMSO, 1963), p. 7.

45 Central Advisory Council for Education (England), *15-18,* vol. 1 (London: HMSO, 1959), p. 60.

46 ibid., p. 60.

47 ibid., p. 118.

48 ibid., p. 132.

49 ibid., p. 118.

50 ibid., p. 123.

51 ibid., p. 124.

52 ibid., p. 124.

53 ibid., vol. 2, p. 127.

54 ibid., vol. 1, p. 118.

55 Central Advisory Council for Education (England), *Half Our Future,* p. 7.

56 Central Advisory Council for Education (England), *Early Leaving,* p. 32.

57 NUT, *Raising the School Leaving Age* (London: NUT, 1972), p. 1.

58 Central Advisory Council for Education (England), *Early Leaving,* p. 35.

59 Central Advisory Council for Education (England), *15-18,* vol. 1, p. 118.

60 Central Advisory Council for Education (England), *Early Leaving,* p. 18.

61 ibid., p. 88. However, more working-class than middle-class girls gave this as a reason for leaving.

62 Schools Council, *Enquiry 1: Young School Leavers,* p. 208.

63 ibid.

64 Central Advisory Council for Education (England), *15-18,* vol. 1, pp. 121, 124.

65 *Report on Education No. 73,* p. 1.

66 J. Stuart Maclure, *Educational Documents 1816-1967* (London: Methuen, 1968); p. 154 (italics added).

67 ibid., p. 157.

68 ibid., p. 202.

69 ibid., p. 201.

70 Central Advisory Council for Education (England), *Half Our Future,* p. 5 (italics added).

71 *Times Educational Supplement,* 23 February 1973, quoting Rhodes Boyson.

72 *Report on Education No. 83: The First Year after RSLA,* DES, 1975, p. 1.

73 Central Advisory Council for Education (England), *15-18,* vol. 1, p. 107.

74 Schools Council, *Society and the Young School Leaver,* Working Paper No. 11 (London: HMSO, 1967), foreword, para. 3.

75 Schools Council (Welsh Committee), *Another Year — to Endure or Enjoy?* (London: HMSO, 1967), p. 15.

76 Notwithstanding the discrimination the girls suffer in this respect by comparison with boys.

77 Schools Council (Welsh Committee), *Another Year — to Endure or Enjoy?,* p. 4.

78 Schools Council, *Raising the School Leaving Age,* p. 12.

79 ibid., p. 14.

80 Schools Council, *Society and the Young School Leaver,* p. 3.

81 Schools Council, *Enquiry 1: Young School Leavers,* p. 56.

82 ibid., p. 70.

83 W. R. Lotwick, 'Raising the School-Leaving Age — the Views of Pupils', *Collegiate Faculty of Education Journal,* University College, Swansea, 1965, p. 19.

84 Schools Council, *Enquiry 1: Young School Leavers,* p. 25.

85 ibid., p. 45.

86 Schools Council (Welsh Committee), *Another Year — to Endure or Enjoy?,* p. 20 (italics added).

87 Schools Council, *Raising the School Leaving Age,* p. 13 (italics added).

88 Central Advisory Council for Education (England), *15-18*, vol. 1, p. 125.

89 *Society and the Young School Leaver,* Working Paper No. 11. Cited in *Sorting Them Out: Two Essays in Social Differentiation,* (Bletchley: Open University Press, 1972), p. 123.

90 J. White, 'Instruction in obedience', *New Society,* 2 May 1968, p. 638.

91 ibid.

92 Schools Council (Welsh Committee), *Another Year — to Endure or Enjoy?,* p. 12.

93 Central Advisory Council for Education (England), *15-18*, vol. 1, p. 42.

94 Schools Council (Welsh Committee), *Another Year — to Endure or Enjoy?,* p. 8.

95 Conservative Party Manifesto, 1964, in Bell, *Education in Great Britain and Ireland,* p. 280.

96 House of Commons, *Hansard,* vol. 688, col. 60.

97 NUT, *Raising the School Leaving Age,* p. 3.

98 *Report on Education No. 73,* p. 1.

99 ibid., p. 3.

100 Schools Council, *Enquiry 1: Young School Leavers,* p. 89.

101 ibid., p. 246.

102 ibid., p. 94.

103 ibid., p. 95.

104 ibid., p. 245.

105 The report, *Half Our Future,* identified severe deficiencies in secondary modern schools — for example, 80 per cent of such schools in slum areas were deemed grossly deficient as buildings. Little had been done to remedy these deficiencies by the time of RSLA.

106 Circular 13/66, DES, para. 2.

107 House of Commons, *Hansard,* vol. 756, col. 1586.

108 *Report on Education No. 71,* DES, 1971, p. 1.

109 NUT, *Raising the School Leaving Age,* p. 3.

110 *Report on Education No. 73,* p. 1.

111 *Times Educational Supplement,* 4 May 1973, p. 9.

112 ibid.

113 NUT, *Raising the School Leaving Age,* p. 5.

114 Central Advisory Council for Education (England), *15-18*, vol. 1, p. 3.

115 M. Wynn, *Family Policy* (Harmondsworth: Penguin, 1972), p. 251. Direct cost includes teachers' salaries and school accommodation estimated for the original RSLA data of 1970.

116 House of Commons, *Hansard,* vol. 688, col. 64.

117 ibid., col. 67.

118 Committee on Higher Education, *Higher Education Report,* Cmnd 2154 (London: HMSO, 1963), p. 277.

119 E. M. Byrne, *Planning and Educational Inequality* (Slough: NFER, 1974).
120 Central Advisory Council for Education (England), *15-18,* vol. 1, p. 31.
121 ibid., vol. 2, p. 25, table 10.
122 ibid., p. 135, table 15a.
123 Central Advisory Council for Education (England), *Early Leaving,* p. 88, table 14.
124 Schools Council, *Enquiry 1: Young School Leavers,* p. 25, n. 19. Clearly, financial problems are an insufficient explanation of school-leaving age.
125 Wynn, *Family Policy,* p. 252.
126 *Report on Education No. 73,* p. 1.
127 *Absenteeism in the Schools of Wales,* Welsh Office, 1976, para. 7.1.
128 Statistical Bulletin 15/80, DES, 1980, p. 3, table 3.
129 ibid.
130 ibid.
131 ibid., p. 2, table 1.
132 Central Advisory Council for Education (England), *15-18,* vol. 1, p. 120.
133 R. Saran, *Policy-Making in Secondary Education* (Oxford: OUP, 1973), p. 31.
134 *Report on Education No. 83,* p. 4.
135 G. Orwell, *Collected Essays, Journalism and Letters,* vol. 2 (Harmondsworth: Penguin, 1970), p. 367.

8 Post-School Education

1 Central Advisory Council for Education (England), *15-18,* vol. 1 (London: HMSO, 1959), p. 164.
2 Statistical Bulletin 15/79, DES, 1979, p. 7.
3 *Report on Education No. 94,* DES, 1978, p. 4.
4 ibid., p. 5.
5 ibid., p. 4.
6 *Education and Training for 16 to 18 Year Olds,* DES, 1979, p. 58, table 2.
7 Robert Young, 'The delay of youth opportunity' *Observer,* 12 July 1981, p. 21.
8 Jo Mortimore and Tessa Blackstone, *Disadvantage and Education* (London: DHSS/SSRC, 1980), p. 234.
9 *A New Training Initiative* (London: MSC, 1981), para. 22.
10 ibid., para. 23 (2) (italics added).

11 ibid., paras. 52 and 54.
12 Central Advisory Council for Education (England), *15-18,* vol. 2 (London: HMSO, 1959), p. 141.
13 D. Rubinstein (ed.), *Education and Equality* (Harmondsworth: Penguin, 1979), p. 276.
14 A. Halsey *et al., Origins and Destinations* (Oxford: Clarendon Press, 1980), p. 178.
15 ibid., p. 178, table 10.1.
16 ibid., p. 190.
17 ibid., p. 191.
18 Statistical Bulletin 15/79, table 1.
19 ibid., para. 3.
20 Central Advisory Council for Education (England), *15-18*, vol. 1, p. 330.
21 Rubinstein, *Education and Equality,* p. 276.
22 Central Advisory Council for Education (England), *15-18*, vol. 1, p. 340.
23 ibid., p. 164.
24 ibid., p. 167.
25 *Day Release,* DES, 1964, appendix B, p. 39.
26 Central Policy Review Staff, *Education, Training and Industrial Performance* (London: HMSO, 1980), p. 20.
27 Central Advisory Council for Education (England), *15-18,* vol. 1, p. 321.
28 ibid., p. 167.
29 *Day Release,* para. 138.
30 *Report on Education No. 94,* table 4.
31 ibid.
32 ibid.
33 ibid.
34 Central Policy Review Staff, *Education, Training and Industrial Performance,* p. 20.
35 Central Advisory Council for Education (England), *15-18,* vol. 1, para. 517, table 66.
36 ibid., para. 517.
37 ibid., para. 518.
38 ibid., para. 527.
39 Rubinstein, *Education and Equality,* p. 276.
40 Central Advisory Council for Education (England), *15-18,* vol. 1, p. 283.
41 *Day Release,* paras. 114/5 (italics added).
42 ibid., para. 119.
43 ibid., para. 141.
44 House of Commons, *Hansard,* vol. 620, col. 81.

45 H. Glennerster, 'Education and Inequality', in P. Townsend and N. Bosanquet (eds.), *Labour and Inequality* (London: Fabian Society, 1972), p. 95.

46 Labour Party, *Higher and Further Education* (London, 1973), p. 27.

47 Labour Party, *Labour's Programme 1973* (London, 1973), p. 76.

48 Labour Party, *Into the Eighties* (London, 1978).

49 *Providing Educational Opportunities for the 16-18 Year Olds,* para. 29.

50 ibid., para. 16.

51 *A Better Start in Working Life,* DES, foreword.

52 ibid., para. 2 (italics added).

53 ibid., para. 5.

54 *A Better Start in Working Life,* annex B, para. 13.

55 ibid., para. 13.

56 Central Policy Review Staff, *Education, Training and Industrial Performance,* para. 24.

57 J. M. Wray, C. Moor and S. Hill, *Unified Vocational Preparation: An Evaluation of the Pilot Programme* (Slough: NFER, 1980). For an account of this work, see Jo Mortimore and Tessa Blackstone, *Disadvantage and Education* (London: DHSS/SSRC, 1980) pp. 231-2.

58 *Education for 16-19 year olds,* DES, 1981, p. 49.

59 ibid., p. 1.

60 ibid., para. 32.

61 ibid., paras. 40 and 41.

62 *Arcade,* no. 5, 9 January 1981.

63 Education Group, *Unpopular Education* (London: Hutchinson, 1981) p. 238.

64 Central Advisory Council for Education (England), *15-18,* vol. 1, para. 508.

65 *The Funding and Organisation of Courses in Higher Education* Fifth Report from the Education, Science and Arts Committee Session 1979-80, vol. 2 (London: HMSO, 1980), para. 1270.

66 *Higher Education Report,* CMND 2154 (London: HMSO, 1963), para. 139.

67 ibid., Appendix 1, p. 43.

68 ibid., p. 38.

69 *The Funding and Organisation of Courses in Higher Education,* vol. 2, p. 261.

70 Peter Scott, *What Future for Higher Education?,* Fabian Tract 465 (London: Fabian Society, 1979) p. 15.

71 Halsey et al., *Origins and Destinations,* p. 201.

72 Communist Party of Great Britain, *Higher Education: a New Perspective,* (London, undated), p. 9.

73 *The Funding and Organisation of Courses in Higher Education,* vol. 2, p. 102.

74 Anne Bone, *The Effect on Women's Opportunities of Teacher Training Cuts,* (Manchester: Equal Opportunities Commission, 1980), p. 9.

75 *Higher Education Report,* Appendix 1, p. 66.

76 ibid., p. 68.

77 *Higher Education Report,* vol. 2, para. 503.

78 *Higher Education Report,* Appendix 2 (A), pp. 24-5, tables 9 and 10.

79 Statistical Bulletin 3/81, DES, 1981, table 3.

80 *Higher Education Report* Appendix 1, para. 8.

81 Statistical Bulletin 12/80, DES, 1980, para. 10.

82 ibid., para. 10.

83 Bone, *The Effect on Women's Opportunities of Teacher Training Cuts,* p. 60.

84 ibid., p. 70.

85 *Funding and Organisation of Courses in Higher Education,* vol. 3, p. 534.

86 *Higher Education into the 1990s: Response of the EOC* (undated) paras. 1-2.

87 ibid., para. 4.8.

88 R. Layard (ed.), *The Impact of Robbins* (Harmondsworth: Penguin, 1969), p. 15.

89 R. Bell (ed.), *Education in Great Britain and Ireland* (London: Routledge & Kegan Paul, 1973), p. 192.

90 Layard, *The Impact of Robbins,* p. 24.

91 J. Pratt and T. Burgess, *Polytechnics: A Report* (London: Pitman, 1974), p. 36.

92 *Higher Education Report* vol. E, p. 1440.

93 *Higher Education Report,* para. 632.

94 *Education: A Framework for Expansion,* Cmnd 5174 (London: HMSO, 1972), p. 48, table 2.

95 T. Blackstone and A. Crispin, 'Education', in D. Blake and P. Ormerod (eds.), *The Economics of Prosperity* (London: Grant McIntyre, 1980).

96 See Pratt and Burgess, *Polytechnics,* pp. 203-7 for full text of speech.

97 ibid., p. 204.

98 ibid., p. 204.

99 ibid., ch. 5.

100 Scott, *What Future for Higher Education?,* p. 7.

101 Bone, *The Effect on Women's Opportunities of Teacher Training Cuts,* p. 73.

102 *Future Trends in Higher Education,* DES, 1979, para. 14 (5) (italics added).

103 *The Funding and Organisation of Courses in Higher Education,* vol. 2, para. 1271.

104 ibid.

105 ibid., para. 1278.

106 ibid., vol. 1, para. 17.

107 *Educational Maintenance Allowances in the 16-18 Year Age Group,* Third Report from the Expenditure Committee, (London: HMSO, 1974), p. 84.

108 *Further and Higher Education,* Report of the Expenditure Committee 1972-3, vol. 1 (London: HMSO, 1974), para. 87.

109 ibid., p. xxxv.

110 *Higher Education Report,* Appendix 2(A), p. 208.

111 *The Funding and Organisation of Courses in Higher Education,* vol. 2, p. 266.

112 ibid., p. 105, para. 3.11.

9 Conclusion

1 T. Blackstone and A. Crispin, 'Education', in D. Blake and P. Ormerod (eds.), *The Economics of Prosperity* (London: 1980), p. 147.

2 H. Glennerster, 'Education and Inequality', in P. Townsend and N. Bosanquet (eds.), *Labour and Inequality* (London: Fabian Society, 1972), p. 96.

3 A. H. Halsey *et al., Origins and Destinations* (Oxford: Clarendon Press, 1980), p. 188.

4 Blackstone and Crispin, 'Education', p. 170.

5 *Policy-Making in the Department of Education and Science,* Tenth Report from the Expenditure Committee (London: HMSO, 1976), p. 5.

6 ibid., para. 854.

7 DES Press Notice, 'Higher Education in England outside the Universities', July 1981.

8 Outer Circle Policy Unit, *A Consumer's Guide to Open Government* (London, 1980), p. 26.

Select Bibliography

Association for the Advancement of Learning, *The Effects of Budgetary Cuts on Education in the St Albans Division, 1979-80* (St Albans: AAL, 1980).

Banks, O., *Parity and Prestige in Secondary Education* (London: Routledge & Kegan Paul, 1955).

Banting, K., *Poverty, Politics and Policy* (London: Macmillan, 1979).

Barnes, J., 'A Solution to Whose Problem?', in H. Glennerster (ed.), *Positive Discrimination and Inequality* (London: Fabian Society, 1974).

Barnes, J., and Lucas, H., 'Positive Discrimination in Education: Individuals, Groups and Institutions', in *Sociological Theory and Survey Research* (London: SSRC, 1976).

Batley, R., *et al., Going Comprehensive* (London: Routledge & Kegan Paul, 1970).

Bell, R. (ed.), *Education in Great Britain and Ireland* (London: Routledge & Kegan Paul, 1973).

Benn, C., and Simon, B., *Halfway There* (Harmondsworth: Penguin, 1972).

Bernstein, B., 'Education Cannot Compensate For Society', in D. Rubinstein and C. Stoneman (eds.), *Education for Democracy* (Harmondsworth: Penguin, 1970).

Blackstone, T., *A Fair Start* (London: Allen Lane, 1971).

Blackstone, T., *First Schools of the Future* (London: Fabian Society, 1972).

Blackstone, T., 'Early Childhood Education', *Trends in Education,* special European issue, 1973.

Blackstone, T., *Education and Day Care for Young Children in Need: The American Experience* (London: Bedford Square Press, 1973).

Blackstone, T., and Crispin, A., 'Education', in D. Blake and P. Ormerod (eds.), *The Economics of Prosperity* (London: Grant McIntyre, 1980).

Blake, D., and Ormerod, P. (eds.), *The Economics of Prosperity* (London: Grant McIntyre, 1980).

Bone, A., *The Effect on Women's Opportunities of Teacher Training Cuts* (Manchester: Equal Opportunities Commission, 1980).

Brennan, E. J. T., *Education for National Efficiency: The Contribution* of Sidney and Beatrice Webb (London: Athlone Press, 1975).

Brown, G., *et al.,* 'Social Class and Psychiatric Disturbance among Women in an Urban Population', *Sociology,* vol. 9 (1978), pp.

Bruner, J., *Under Five in Britain* (London: Grant MacIntyre, 1980).

Butler, R. A., *The Art of the Possible* (London: Hamish Hamilton, 1971).

Byrne, E. M., *Planning and Educational Inequality* (Slough: NFER, 1974).

CASE, *Mixed-Ability Teaching in the Middle Age Range* (Oxford: CASE, 1979).

CASE, *Secondary Schools in Guildford* (Guildford: CASE, 1980).

Central Advisory Council for Education (England), *Early Leaving* (London: HMSO, 1954).

Central Advisory Council for Education (England), *15-18* (London: HMSO, 1960).

Central Advisory Council for Education (England), *Half Our Future* (London: HMSO, 1963).

Central Policy Review Staff, *Services for Young Children with Working Mothers* (London: HMSO, 1978).

Central Policy Review Staff, *Education, Training and Industrial Performance* (London: HMSO, 1980).

Children and their Primary Schools (the Plowden Report) (London: HMSO, 1967).

The Civil Service (London: HMSO, 1969).

Coates, R. D., *Teachers' Unions and Interest Group Politics* (Cambridge: C.U.P., 1972).

Committee on Higher Education, *Higher Education Report,* Cmnd 2154 (London: HMSO, 1963).

Crossman, R., *The Diaries of a Cabinet Minister* (London: Hamish Hamilton and Jonahan Cape, 1975).

Douglas, J. W. B., *The Home and the School* (London: Panther, 1964).

Douglas, J. W. B., *et al., All Our Future* (London: Panther, 1971).

Education: A Framework for Expansion, Cmnd 5174 (London: HMSO, 1972).

Education Group, *Unpopular Education* (London: Hutchinson, 1981).

Educational Development Strategy in England and Wales (Paris: OECD, 1975).

Educational Disadvantage and the Educational Needs of Immigrants, Cmnd 5720 (London: HMSO, 1974).

Educational Priority, vols. 1-5 (London: HMSO, 1972-5).

Equal Opportunities Commission, *I Want to Work . . . but What About the Kids?* (Manchester: EOC, 1978).

Fowler, G., *Central Government of Education 1: Decision-Making in British Education Systems,* Unit 2 (Milton Keynes: Open University Press, 1974).

The Funding and Organisation of Courses in Higher Education, Fifth Report from the Education, Science and Arts Committee (London: HMSO, 1980).

Glennerster, H., 'Education and Inequality', in P. Townsend and N. Bosanquet (eds.), *Labour and Inequality* (London: Fabian Society, 1972).

Glennerster, H. (ed.), *Positive Discrimination and Inequality* (London: Fabian Society, 1974).

Gosden, P. H. J., *Education in the Second World War* (London: Methuen, 1976).

Gray, J., 'Positive Discrimination in Education', *Policy and Politics,* vol. 4, no. 2 (1975), pp. 85-111.

Halsey, A. H., *EPA Problems and Policies* (London: HMSO, 1972).

Halsey, A. H., 'Whatever happened to positive discrimination?', *Times Educational Supplement,* 21 January 1977.

Halsey, A. H., *et al., Origins and Destinations* (Oxford: Clarendon Press, 1980).

Hennessy, P., 'How civil servants tame their masters', *The Times,* 5 December 1980.

Hurt, J., *Education in Evolution* (London: Paladin, 1972).

Kellner, P., and Lord Crowther-Hunt, *The Civil Servants* (London: Raven Books, 1980).

Kogan, M., *The Politics of Education* (Harmondsworth: Penguin, 1971).

Kogan, M., 'Damned planners', *Times Educational Supplement, 9 May* 1975.

Kogan, M., *Educational Policy-Making* (London: Allen & Unwin, 1975).

Kogan, M., *The Politics of Educational Change* (London: Fontana, 1978).

Layard, R. (ed.), *The Impact of Robbins* (Harmondsworth: Penguin, 1969).

Little, A., and Mabey, C., 'An Index for the Designation of Educational Priority Areas', in A. Schonfield and S. Shaw (eds.), *Social Indicators and Social Policy* (London: Heinemann, 1972).

Low Cost Day Provision for the Under-Fives (London: DHSS/DES, 1976).

Maclure, J. Stuart, *Educational Documents 1816-1967* (London: Methuen, 1956, 1968).

Manzer, R. A., *Teachers and Politics* (Manchester: M.U.P., 1970).

Marsden, D., 'Politicians, Equality and Comprehensives', in P. Townsend and N. Bosanquet (eds.), *Labour and Inequality* (London: Fabian Society, 1972).

Meacher, M., 'The Politics of Positive Discrimination', in H. Glennerster (ed.), *Positive Discrimination and Inequality* (London: Fabian Society, 1974).

Meacher, M., 'How the mandarins rule', *New Statesman,* 5 December 1980.

Medlicott, P., 'The DES', *New Society,* 22 August 1974.

Middleton, N., and Weitzman, S., *A Place for Everyone* (London: Gollancz, 1976).

Mortimore, J., and Blackstone, T., *Disadvantage and Education* (London: DHSS/SSRC, 1980).

NUT, *First Things First* (London: NUT, 1964).

NUT, *Into the Seventies* (London: NUT, 1969).

NUT, *Plowden* (London: NUT, 1969).

NUT, *Raising the School-Leaving Age* (London: NUT, 1971).

NUT, *Nursery Education in Wales* (London: NUT, 1972).

NUT, *The Provision of Pre-School Education in England and Wales* (London: NUT, 1974).

NUT, *The Needs of the Under Fives* (London: NUT, 1977).

NUT, *Examining at 16-Plus: The Case for a Common System* (London: NUT, 1978).

NUT, *Replacing Section 11* (London: NUT, 1979).

Policy-Making in the Department of Education and Science, Tenth Report from the Expenditure Committee (London: HMSO, 1976).

Pratt, J., and Burgess, T., *Polytechnics: A Report* (London: Pitman, 1974).

Raison, T., *The Act and the Partnership* (London: Bedford Square Press, 1976).

Regan, D. E., *Local Government and Education* (London: Allen & Unwin, 1977).

Rubinstein, D. (ed.), *Education and Equality* (Harmondsworth: Penguin, 1979).

Rubinstein, D., and Simon, B., *The Evaluation of the Comprehensive School 1926-72* (London: Routledge & Kegan Paul, 1973).

Rubinstein, D., and Stoneman, C. (eds.), *Education for Democracy* (Harmondsworth: Penguin, 1970).

Saran, R., *Policymaking in Secondary Education* (Oxford: Clarendon Press, 1973).

Schools Council, *Raising the School Leaving Age* (London: HMSO, 1965).

Schools Council (Welsh Committee), *Another Year — to Endure or Enjoy?* (London: HMSO, 1967).

Schools Council, *Society and the Young School Leaver* (London: HMSO, 1967).

Schools Council, *Enquiry 1: Young School Leavers* (London: HMSO, 1968).

Scott, P., *What Future for Higher Education?* (London: Fabian Society, 1979).

Simon, B., *Studies in the History of Education 1780-1870* (London: Lawrence & Wishart, 1960).

Simon, B., *Education and the Labour Movement 1870-1920* (London: Lawrence & Wishart, 1965).

Tawney, R. H., *Equality,* 4th edn. (London: Allen & Unwin, 1952).

Tibble, J. W., *The Extra Year* (London: Routledge & Kegan Paul, 1970).

Tizard, B., *et al., Involving Parents in Nursery and Infant Schools* (London: Grant MacIntyre, 1981).

Townsend, P., and Bosanquet, N. (eds.), *Labour and Equality* (London: Heinemann, 1980).

Van Der Eyken, W., *Education, the Child and Society* (Harmondsworth: Penguin, 1973).

White, J., 'Instruction in obedience', *New Society,* 2 May 1968, p. 638.

Williams, M., *Inside Number 10* (London: New English Library, 1975).

Williams, S., 'The Decision Makers', in *Policy and Practice: The Experience of Government* (London: Royal Institute of Public Administration, 1980).

Wilson, H., *The Labour Government 1964-70* (Harmondsworth: Penguin, 1974).

Wray, J. M., *et al., Unified Vocational Preparation: An Evaluation of the Pilot Programme* (Slough: NFER, 1980).

Young, R., 'The delay of youth opportunity', *Observer,* 12 July 1981.

Index

254